Research Methods
IN
Social Work

Nelson-Hall Series in Social Welfare
Consulting Editor: Charles Zastrow
University of Wisconsin—Whitewater

Research Methods
IN
Social Work

David Royse
UNIVERSITY OF KENTUCKY

Nelson-Hall Publishers
Chicago

Library of Congress Cataloging-in-Publication Data

Royse, David D. (David Daniel)
    Research methods in social work / David Royse.
      p.   cm.
    Includes bibliographical references and index.
    ISBN 0-8304-1210-7
    1. Social service—Research—Methodology.   I. Title.
HV11.R69   1991
361.3′2′072—dc20   90-38779
                                    CIP

Manufactured in the United States of America

10 9 8 7 6 5 4 3 2 1

Contents

Appendices   271

Index   283

Preface

From my experience in teaching and from talking with my colleagues, it is apparent that most social work students are less than thrilled about the requirement of a research methods course. But certainly not all students feel this way. Some are excited about acquiring research skills, because they want to conduct meaningful research, evaluate their practice, or better comprehend research that already has been published. Unfortunately, these students do not represent the majority—although students may be more receptive to research now than at any time in the past.

This text is written to be "user friendly." That is, I want to present the essential topics and techniques with a minimum amount of dry prose. My goal is not to lose readers with technical details, but to demystify research and to infuse readers with a sense of "Hey, research is understandable!" Further, I want readers to see how research is actually used by social workers. This text draws heavily upon examples and illustrations from social work journals.

I have tried to write for both undergraduate and graduate audiences. Those students who wish to have more information are encouraged to make use of the extensive references at the end of each chapter. By reading these books and journal articles, students can obtain more details than I can include in an introductory text.

Several colleagues were gracious enough to use a draft of this text in their classes before it was published. The comments of Ken Wellons, Vernon Wiehe, Surjit Dhooper, and Beth Rompf were especially helpful and supportive. My thanks to other colleagues who read portions of the text and made helpful suggestions. I also appreciated the kind comments and useful contributions of the reviewers, notably Dick DuBord and Al Roberts.

Finally, thanks to all the students who suffered through reading the spiral-bound, photocopied manuscript and who took the time to point out areas where the text needed work. I owe a special note of appreciation to all of the students whose questions, life experiences, and involvement with research (even if only through assignments) provided examples that will benefit other students.

One

Why Study Research?

Social work is an exciting career choice. Students select this profession because they like people and want to help families where there has been abuse, mental illness, or alcoholism and to assist such special populations as the aged and the homeless. As a consequence, social work students are often eager to soak up instruction that will assist them in becoming better counselors or practitioners. They approach practice-oriented courses with enthusiasm and vigor. All goes well until they learn that they must take a research course (sometimes two courses) as part of the requirements for a degree. Immediately they are resentful. "Research!" they say, "Why do I have to take research?" "I don't want to do research. I want to work with the severely mentally ill." Variations of this are: "I want to work with children" and "I want to work with adolescents who have eating disorders."

Why, then, must social work students study research? Consider a few examples that will demonstrate its usefulness to practitioners of social work.

1. You are asked to direct an adolescent AIDS prevention program. The goal of the program is to supply adolescents with information about how to avoid contracting the AIDS virus. You are convinced that the adolescents in your program are more knowledgeable after participation in the program. How would you convince others of the success of your intervention?

2. You are hired by an agency that provides counseling to families in which children have been sexually assaulted by a family member. Counseling seems to go well with your first several clients. It is now time for the perpetrators to return to their families. How would you go about providing evidence that your in-

tervention was effective—that it was safe to reunite the family members?

3. What is the relationship between adult illiteracy and unemployment? Can welfare dependency be reduced by making basic education more accessible to adults? How would you go about intelligently investigating this problem for concerned policymakers?

In each of these three examples, some research skills are required—skills that can be used with other problems and concerns. However, before these skills can be taught, oftentimes it is necessary to address and "neutralize" negative attitudes about research so that there is the greatest opportunity for learning to occur.

Social Work Students and Research

Few students come into their first research methods class understanding the necessity for the course. In fact, Epstein (1987) has observed that "no other part of the social work curriculum has been so consistently received by students with as much groaning, moaning, eye-rolling, bad-mouthing, hyperventilation, and waiver-strategizing as the research course" (p.71). Epstein has cited other studies that document social work students' disinterest in research—what he calls the "resistance phenomenon" (Rosenblatt, 1968; Kirk and Fisher, 1976; Dane and Epstein, 1985). Also, Bogal and Singer (1981), in a study of faculty who taught research in undergraduate social work programs, obtained data showing that students enter research classes with apprehension and negative attitudes. However, the majority of the faculty believed that students left their courses with a heightened appreciation of research.

We can understand why students may not want to study research. Oftentimes students misunderstand both the value of research and the research process. Briar (1980) has noted that there is a widespread belief among social workers that the same person cannot be both a good researcher and a good practitioner. He continues:

> The personal qualities believed to make a good researcher are seen as handicaps for a practitioner, and the reverse also has been said to be true. The stereotypes are familiar. Researchers are supposedly intellectual, rational, unfeeling creatures who lack the sensitivity to understand the subtle nuances that are of primary concern to practitioners. Practitioners are purported to be intuitive, sensitive, creative persons more akin to artists than scien-

2

tists; they emphasize the importance of seeing clients as whole persons who should not be subjected to the categorization and atomization that research allegedly requires. It is easy, of course, to show that these stereotypes are invalid, but such beliefs, although less prevalent than they once were, continue to influence the relationship between practice and research in social work. (P.31).

As many research instructors have found out, most students in social work do not want to take a research methods course. What explains this? Do some students choose social work as a major because it was perceived to have less of a quantitative emphasis than such disciplines as sociology, psychology, or medicine? Other disciplines are better known for their research emphasis. The research tradition in clinical psychology, for instance, dates back to its roots in experimental psychology; precise methods and procedures were developed for studying such phenomena as sensation and perception. Later, Alfred Binet's work with intelligence tests led to psychologists becoming interested in the quantitative problems associated with testing and test construction. This interest in the quantification of phenomena generalized to other areas. Shortly after World War II clinical psychology programs adopted an integrated *Scientist-Professional Training Model* that has become their pre-eminent approach (Hersen and Bellack, 1984).

The dual emphasis on research and practice has been absent in social work programs. As a result, social workers seem to have little identity as researchers and may be ill prepared or uncomfortable in conducting it. Some evidence of this can be seen in Glisson's study (1983), which reviewed all articles published over a six-year period in five major social work journals. He found that less than half of the articles in these journals reported or summarized the results of empirical research. Other studies have reported even lower percentages of articles with empirical research (Jayaratne, 1979; Simpson, 1978; Weinberger and Tripodi, 1969). This compares with a research content of over 90 percent in the articles published during 1986 in five American Psychological Association journals and 90 percent of the articles published in four American Sociological Association journals (Glisson and Fischer, 1987).

While social workers' identity as researchers may not be quite as strong as psychologists' and sociologists', this is not to say that it is nonexistent. Howe (1974) proposed use of the term "caseworker-researcher" for the clinician engaged in research. While some students may have a difficult time conceiving of a social worker engaged in research and practice simultaneously, Briar (1979, 1980) has discussed a *Practitioner-Scientist Training Model*. He says that an empirically based model of practice was inconceivable only a few years ago because the research tools were not available to permit small-scale but rigorous research.

It is possible that students who choose to major in social work may not want to learn anything about how to conduct research. They may think of research as something that consultants or bureaucrats do. As for themselves, they want to roll up their sleeves and "help" people. Gockel (1966) found over twenty years ago in a study of career preferences that social work students tended to be more strongly attracted by the opportunity to work with people than to other occupational values.

Social workers may believe that research is less interesting than "people work" because they do not immediately see how research can have a practical application for them or their clients. Students may have an image of researchers as academics who contemplate social problems from a distance. They may not understand that social work research also involves interviewing and talking with clients, and that it aims to improve the lives of clients through a better understanding of factors involved in their problems and through evaluating the relative effectiveness of interventions.

As long as we are speculating, or hypothesizing, we might consider the possibility that social work students *fear* research. And perhaps this fear is grounded in reality. Maybe they have always done poorly in math—even in elementary school. It is not uncommon for students, given a choice, to avoid those courses that they perceive to be too difficult for them to master. Students may not be interested in taking a research course because they perceive it to be laden with statistics and mathematical computations for which they see absolutely no utility. They anticipate that the course will be boring and a waste of their time, so they don't attend class or apply themselves. At the end of the term they find themselves in a position where they have not understood what was going on and are even more angry because they were *required* to take a research course for which they did not get a good grade. However, learning research methodology does not require performing mathematical computations. If you skim quickly through these pages, you'll find no statistical formulas of any kind!

Human nature is complex. It is likely that no one explanation but rather several interrelated factors together best explain why social work students don't always look forward to their research courses. For instance, a multi-variable explanation could be as follows: (1) a student has a beginning attitude that research has no practical application, (2) as a consequence, not enough time is spent in mastering the subject, (3) which leads to poor performance, and (4) all of this results in a self-perception that the subject is too difficult or that the student doesn't have an aptitude for research. What other variables do you think might be involved?

Why Research Is Required

There are several reasons why you, as a social work student, should take at least one research course. First of all, both as a student and as a social worker you will be reading journal articles and technical articles in which research results are presented. You need to have a basic knowledge of how research is conducted, or could be conducted, to help you evaluate the strengths and weaknesses of the published research. As an informed consumer, you ought to be able to know if too few subjects were interviewed, if the methodology was flawed, or if the author generalized well beyond his or her findings. Research studies can be biased or flawed for a lot of different reasons, and you might not be able to detect these reasons without a basic understanding of research methodology. To make effective use of research that you encounter, whether in journals or unpublished reports produced in your agency, you need to know something about how proper research is conducted.

Second, social workers are accountable for their interventions. As a professional, you must be able to determine whether the intervention you are using with a client is making any difference. Could you demonstrate that the client is improving? Or, at the very least, could you show that your intervention has not harmed the client? Even if you are not interested in conducting research on a large scale, you owe it to your clients and yourself to be able to evaluate your practice with them. A research approach discussed in this book, the single system design, will help you evaluate your practice with individual clients.

Accountability is important on another level. Social service agencies vary enormously in size and may employ several to many hundreds of social workers (e.g., in large state departments of human resources). Taxpayers, governmental agencies, and funding sources, such as United Way organizations, often expect social service agencies to conduct or provide evaluation research on such issues as client utilization of the agency's services and the effects or outcomes of the services provided. Agencies must show that they are meeting the needs of their target populations, that their clientele feel satisfied with services, and that the agency's operation is productive and efficient. Even as a new social worker, fresh from the university, you might be asked to conduct research to meet some reporting or accreditation requirement. Occasionally, students tell me how surprised they were on their first jobs when they were assigned a research project—especially when it was not even discussed during the job interview. Would you be more interested in learning how to conduct research if you knew you would be responsible for conducting research sometime in the near future?

Suppose you become a program director or manager in a social service organization, and the executive director wants you to begin a new program. The director insists that the program have a good evaluation system built into it. Would you know how to go about evaluating a social service program? Would you know a poor evaluation if you saw one? Programs are sometimes funded with the provision that they can demonstrate some impact on the problem. This usually means that research in some form or fashion is required. Faced as we are with major social problems and fairly limited amounts of monies that can be applied to these problems, it is incumbent upon us social workers to strive for implementation of programs that have the best success rates. Frequently, it is not an outside consultant who is brought in to plan or conduct the research, but someone within the agency. A little knowledge of research could provide you with a stepping stone to involvement in administrative or policy issues. Graduates of social work programs are often surprised by how rapidly they become involved in middle management even though they always thought of themselves as caseworkers.

As a profession, social work must have individuals who can conduct research on social policies at the state and national levels. While it may seem unlikely that you would ever be involved in such research, consider for a moment the extent to which most social workers are affected by state and national policies. Some of these policies are good, and some could use modification. Consider, for example, how you might go about convincing legislators and government officials that cutting funds to social services will have an adverse effect upon your client population. Can you see the value of having "hard data" to show skeptics how many people depend upon a certain social service and how their lives might be affected if funds were cut? The profession needs researchers who can show that cuts in social service programs ultimately result in greater tax burdens. I am convinced that greater funding for social services will come as social workers are better able to demonstrate that adequate levels of social services are cost-effective for reducing or eliminating some of the major social problems facing us today.

Another reason for studying research as an undergraduate is that it will provide the necessary foundation for other research courses in graduate school. It's very likely you will be required to take at least one research course (and probably more) in a masters' program in social work. Should you work on a doctorate, you will be required to complete more research courses and may conduct original research for a dissertation. By that time you may be taking elective courses in research and statistics because you see their usefulness!

One more good reason for studying research methods is that this is required by the Council on Social Work Education (CSWE). CSWE is a national, nongovernmental organization, recognized by the U.S. Department of Education, which has the responsibility for accreditation and other standard-setting activities. The council sets curriculum policy for baccalaureate and master's degree social work programs. Research is one of the five professional foundation content areas required by CSWE. Each institution that grants degrees in social work must periodically submit documentation that it conforms with curriculum policy in order for the institution's program to be accredited by CSWE.

The Council on Social Work Education's curriculum policy would have social work students (at both the BSW and MSW levels) understand that a "spirit of inquiry" and "informed criticism" are the bases of scientific thinking and lead to the acquisition of knowledge and the application of that knowledge in practice. Further, research content should familiarize the student with the methods and skills needed both to build knowledge for practice and to evaluate his or her own practice. The goal is to move social work students beyond passive consumption of research to a position where they are able to evaluate their own practice and are capable of generating practice knowledge for the profession (Council on Social Work Education, 1982).

Without basic research competencies, social workers cannot advance practice theories. New practice principles ought to come from practitioners who are able to objectively test and demonstrate their usefulness. To the extent that social workers do not have research skills, new practice theories and principles will come from researchers in other disciplines and not from social workers. Unlike some academic research endeavors, social work research has the goal of advancing theory (Polansky, 1986). However, in social work there has been a tendency for practice to outdistance its knowledge base. Unlike medicine, for example, where practice follows research, social work practice has often been the source of innovation, and research has followed (Reid, 1987).

How Research Benefits Social Workers

Much of our knowledge about the specific problems experienced by our clients comes to us as a result of research. Consider the case of John, a veteran and an alcoholic, who is facing the loss of his job and family because he refuses to admit to himself that he has a drinking problem. We can predict that John is on a downward spiral and that further problems are in store for him, because as an alcoholic John is similar to other alcoholics. If we were interested in doing so, we could find a body of literature on alcoholism, and we might even find some specialized literature on young male alcoholics who are veterans. This body of knowledge exists because practitioners and researchers saw beyond the individual client and conceptualized a group of persons having similar characteristics and problems. Some of these practitioners and researchers gathered data and conducted studies that have become part of our literature. All alcoholics might not look like John; their age and marital status may vary. But they will have some identifiable characteristics in common. This body of knowledge will assist us in knowing how best to treat this special population. The more John is like other alcoholics discussed in the professional literature, the more confident we will be with our predictions and interventive approaches. Research can help us to know more about our clients and our interventions. (We could use a research instrument to help us assess the extent of John's alcoholism and later to determine if treatment was effective.)

The illustration of John is used here to show not only that research has some benefits to social workers, but also that you can start thinking about research even if you have an individual client focus. Research is composed of individual cases, but often goes beyond a single case. Research is a systematic process that examines problems or questions in an orderly and logical way. Just like good therapy, good research does not proceed without a plan or design. It states its intentions early, defines what will be examined, follows a specific methodology, and examines the results. These findings can expand our knowledge base and are often of direct benefit to practitioners.

Like it or not, we are all consumers of research. We hear the results of studies or polls on the television and radio, and we read about studies that are reported in newspapers, magazines, and journals. Some of this information may be clearly applicable for social workers. However, how do you know if these studies are any good? Could you identify a poorly designed study? What criteria would you use? One recent bestseller that used thousands of questionnaires to support its conclusions has been called the "functional equivalent of

8

malpractice for surveys" (Butterfield, 1987). Just because something finds its way into print does not mean that it is based on good research or scholarship. Learn to be a skeptical reader. Ask questions of what you read. Do the findings seem consistent with what you know about the subject. Even a little knowledge of research will help you to become a more informed consumer of the information you routinely encounter.

Being an informed consumer will lead you to evaluate the reported research and enable you to make more substantial contributions when you are called upon to disseminate knowledge in your everyday practice. Social workers are often required to prepare reports, conduct inservice training, or make workshop presentations. Information is shared not only with fellow professionals but also with clients and the community. As you make greater use of professional journals, you will find that you need an understanding of research in order to fully comprehend what is being reported.

As a professional you may wish to report on the effectiveness of some treatment approach or exciting innovation that you have devised. You believe that your approach works; you have demonstrated it repeatedly and convinced a lot of your skeptical colleagues. Do you know enough about research to know what and how to report and whether your research methodology was rigorous enough for a professional journal or conference paper? There may be times when even the most thoroughly convinced "I'll-always-want-to-be-a-clinician" wishes that he or she understood a little more about research.

Finally, social work research is important because, as Fanshel (1980) has noted:

> a sustained and creditable program of research is also essential to a profession's self-respect and to its ability to maintain the positive regard of outsiders whose opinions help support and legitimize the profession's endeavors. No profession can afford any equivocation on the importance of research. (P.3)

Social science research is exciting because it studies a lively topic—people. As we learn more about people and their problems, we become better practitioners. Research is conducted by social workers in the field and in universities who are adventurers extending the frontiers of their field of knowledge. Much about human nature is yet to be discovered. Our clients supply a seemingly endless list of problems about which we need more information. One of the characteristics of social work research is that it is oriented towards solving problems. Social work research is intentional; it seeks knowledge that will be put to use on behalf of those needing the services of social workers (Lewis, 1980). Forget your notions that research is so theoretical that it will be of no use to you. The research skills that you can acquire, described in this text, can make you a more competent practitioner!

Desired Outcome

Every social work educator wants his or her students to be skilled, competent practitioners. Research can play an instrumental role in making you the best practitioner possible. Siegel (1984) has described the social worker who engages in empirically based practice as one who can use research as a tool. Her description of such a social worker is one that I hope you become as a result of using this text to learn research methods. Siegel identifies the characteristics of a social worker who engages in empirically based practice as one who:

1. makes maximum use of research findings;
2. collects data systematically to monitor the intervention;
3. demonstrates empirically whether or not interventions are effective;
4. specifies problems, interventions, and outcomes in terms that are concrete, observable, and measurable;
5. uses research ways of thinking and research methods in defining clients' problems, formulating questions for practice, collecting assessment data, evaluating the effectiveness of interventions, and using evidence.
6. views research and practice as part of the same problem-solving process; and
7. views research as a tool to be used in practice. (P.329)

The best way to approach research methodology is to think of a question or a problem that you have encountered at work with your clients or that suggests itself from your life experiences or reading. This should be a question that interests you—one that piques your curiosity. Keep this question in the back of your mind as each new chapter is presented. As you review each chapter, think about how that information could be used to assist you in answering your question.

Research begins when people like you develop questions from real-life situations or become concerned about problems that have not been satisfactorily answered. Questions arise from observations of human nature and social problems. We wonder whether an old theory can explain some new phenomenon or whether a new theory can explain a recurrent problem. In some instances, a thorough search of resources in the library will provide answers to these questions, but not always. If the question cannot be adequately answered after a careful search, we may have identified a gap in our field's knowledge base, one that is in desperate need of research. Finding gaps in the literature (or areas where more is unknown than known) is exciting to those with an inquiring mind. There is no shortage of problems needing additional investigation; many opportunities exist for social work researchers to make important contributions to our knowledge base. If you had the time and the funding to explore one question, what would it be?

QUESTIONS FOR CLASS DISCUSSION

1. What are your fears about taking a research class?
2. What do you hope to learn from this research class?
3. What experiences have you had that might help you in this research class? Describe any research-related experiences you may have had.
4. What are the problems that might develop when a profession's knowledge base and research lags behind its forms of practice?
5. As a class, make a list of problems and questions that you think would make interesting research.
6. Have you ever come across a piece of research that you thought was worthless? Why did you have this opinion?
7. What stereotypes do you have about researchers?
8. In what ways could research be used to affect a local, state, or national policy that you think needs to be changed?
9. Discuss ways you might go about investigating the problems in the three examples at the beginning of this chapter.
10. Make a list of reasons why it is important for social workers to engage in empirically based practice.

MINI-PROJECTS FOR EXPERIENCING RESEARCH FIRSTHAND

1. Informally survey your class to find out the most popular explanation for why social work students do not want to study research methods. What is the second most common explanation?
2. Using the following questions, and others you want to develop, compare a group of social work students with another

group of students (e.g., engineering, premed). Decide upon the kind of response choices to use. Choose either a "yes"-"no" format or a "strongly agree, agree, undecided, disagree, strongly disagree" format.

a. I have always hated math courses.

b. I found my high school algebra courses enjoyable.

c. I dread speaking before a large group of people more than taking a research course.

Did you find differences among the groups of students?

3. Think of a social problem that you have recently read about (e.g., homelessness). Do we need more research on this problem? What additional research should be conducted? What is it that we don't know about the problem? List what you feel to be gaps in our knowledge of this problem.

RESOURCES AND REFERENCES

Bogal, R.B. and Singer, M.J. (1981). Research coursework in the baccalaureate social work curriculum: A Study. *Journal of Education for Social Work*, 17 (2), 45–50.

Briar, S. (1979). Incorporating research into education for clinical practice in social work: Toward a clinical science in social work. In Allen Rubin and Aaron Rosenblatt (Eds), *Sourcebook on Research Utilization*. New York: Council on Social Work Education.

Briar, S. (1980). Toward the integration of practice and research. In David Fanshel (Ed.), *Future of Social Work Research*. Washington, DC: National Association of Social Workers.

Butterfield, F. (1987). Hite's new book is under rising attack. *New York Times* (Nov. 13), B4.

Council on Social Work Education. (1982). Curriculum policy for the master's degree and baccalaureate degree programs in social work education. New York.

Dane E. and Epstein, I. (1985). A dark horse in continued education programming at the post-master's level: Monitoring and evaluation skills for social workers in middle management. *Journal of Continuing Social Work Education*, 3(2), 3–8.

Epstein, I. (1987). Pedagogy of the perturbed: Teaching research to the reluctants. *Journal of Teaching in Social Work* 1(1), 71–89.

Fanshel, D. (1980). The future of social work research: Strategies for the coming years. In David Fanshel (Ed.), *Future of Social Work Research*. Washington, DC: National Association of Social Workers.

Glisson, C. (1983). Trends in social work research. Presented to the annual meeting of the Group for the Advancement of Doctoral Education at the University of Alabama, Tuscaloosa.

Glisson, C. and Fisher, J. (1987). Statistical training for social workers. *Journal of Social Work Education* 23(3), 50–58.

Gockel, G.L. (1966). Social work as a career choice. In E.E. Schwartz (Ed.), *Manpower in social welfare: Research perspectives.* Washington, DC: National Association of Social Workers.

Hersen, M. and Bellack, A. (1984). Research in clinical psychology. In A.S. Bellack and M. Hersen (Eds.), *Research Methods in Clinical Psychology.* New York: Pergamon.

Howe, M. (1974). Casework self-evaluation: A single-subject approach. *Social Service Review*, 48, 1–24.

Jayaratne, S. (1979). Analysis of selected social work research journals and productivity rankings among schools of social work. *Journal of Education for Social Work*, 15 (3), 72–80.

Kirk, S. and Fisher, J. (1976). Do social workers understand research? *Journal of Education for Social Work*, 2(1), 63–71.

Lewis, H. (1980). Toward a planned approach in social work research. In D. Fanshel (Ed.), *Future of Social Work Research.* Washington, DC: National Association of Social Workers.

Polansky, N.A. (1986). There is nothing so practical as a good theory. *Child Welfare*, 65(1), 3–15.

Reid, W.J. (1987). Research in social work. In Anne Minahan (Ed.), *Encyclopedia of Social Work.* Silver Spring, MD: National Association of Social Workers.

Rosenblatt, A. (1968). The practitioners' use and evaluation of research. *Social Work*, 13(1), 53–59.

Siegel, D.H. (1984). Defining empirically based practice. *Social Work*, 29(4), 325–331.

Simpson, R.L. (1978). Is research utilization for social workers? *Journal of Social Service Research*, 2 (2), 143–158.

Specht, H. (1972) The deprofessionalization of social work. *Social Work*, 17 (March), 3–15.

Weinberger, R. and Tripodi, T. (1969). Trends in types of research reported in selected social work journals. *Social Service Review*, 43(4), 439–447.

Two

Basic Research Terms and Concepts

William James once remarked, "The difference between the first and second best thing in art absolutely seems to escape verbal definition—it is a matter of a hair, a shade, an inward quiver of some kind." Unlike a subjective reaction to art, acquiring social work research skills requires more than "an inward quiver." Verbal definitions of research terms are essential. A unique set of terms or vocabulary is often found in research studies and is needed for discussing these studies. Arkava and Lane (1983) have acknowledged this in discussing the "language of research," and True (1989) has also talked about the "special language" used in research.

This chapter specifies some of the basic terms required to understand research methodology. Learning these terms will give you tools needed to communicate about research when you encounter it in the literature and when you use it in an empirically based practice. For the sake of clarity, fairly concise definitions are provided. With some of the terms, you'll find that their use in subsequent chapters provides additional clarification.

Concepts

A **concept** is a mental idea or representation of a class of events or group of objects. For instance, most of us have a concept or commonly held notion of what constitutes a "good student." We may talk to one another about Susan possessing the quality or having the characteristic of being a good student. Seldom would our friends ask us what we mean when we say that Susan is a good student. We might also talk about Susan's self-esteem, and we all tend to know what that means. Self-esteem is another example of a hypothetical construct, or concept. Concepts allow us to express complex notions or abstract ideas succinctly. Depression, school phobia, and borderline personal-

15

ity are other examples of concepts developed from observations and generalizations. Because concepts are "invented" or constructed, they are sometimes called constructs. Do not be confused if some authors use the term constructs instead of concepts; they have the same meaning. For example, constructs have been called the "rich theoretical concepts . . . like social status, power, intelligence and gender roles" (Kidder and Judd, 1986, p. 40).

Operational Definitions

In everyday conversation we easily accept concepts that are somewhat vague because we think we understand what they mean. However, researchers must be precise about the concepts employed in their studies; this is called developing **operational definitions.** For instance, in most conversations we all understand the terms "heavy," "frequent," and "problem drinker" to mean the same thing. However, the way one researcher defines problem drinking for the purposes of a study may be quite different from the way another investigator defines the concept. Robertson's (1989) article on the development of a tool to assess adolescents' involvement with alcohol is a good illustration. From this article we learn that one research team defined problem drinker as a person who was drunk five or more times in the past year or had experienced two or more negative consequences from drinking. Another research team defined the same concept (only they called it "heavy drinker") as a person who drank several times a week. Obviously, operational definitions have considerable impact on who is included or excluded from studies.

As a researcher, you may use the operational definitions employed by other researchers or you may revise and improve upon them. Whatever the case, it is important to state your operational definitions so that others can understand the characteristics of persons who were a part of (or excluded from) your study. Operational definitions facilitate the replication (or reproduction) of your research by allowing others to locate persons having the same characteristics or severity of problem as those in your study.

Theories

A **theory** is a set of interrelated concepts that guide actions and conceptualizations (Nugent, 1987). Theories provide clues or suggestions for intervention and help to explain things that we don't understand very well. Theories result from weaving together what is known with what is conjecture. Theories help us to organize facts or what is known about a given phenomenon for the purpose of explaining or predicting. The three main functions of a theory are to organize, explain, and predict (Munson, 1983).

Theories vary considerably in their complexity, their perspective or orientation, and the amount of evidence that can be mustered to support them. A good example of how various theories from different disciplines might be used to explain a social phenomenon is found in *Incest as Child Abuse: Research and Applications* (Vander Mey and Neff, 1986). Chapter three in their book reviews anthropological, psychological, sociological, ecological, and feminist theories—each attempting to explain incest using somewhat different mechanisms or theories.

The research you do, or at least the way you go about it, is strongly influenced by your theoretical orientation. If you assume that "deviant socialization" or cultural explanations largely explain the occurrence of incest, then the types of questions you ask will be different than questions you would ask if you assume "mental illness" will explain most cases of incest. Your theoretical orientation directs your attention to events that are assumed to be important and allows you to ignore those that are expected to be irrelevant.

Theories, for the social work researcher, lead to predictions about the world in which we operate. A theory might be likened to a mental map in that it can suggest avenues or directions. A good theory can be built upon and provides a foundation for further research. Theories are equally valuable to both the practitioner and the researcher. Practitioners employ theories in their interventions, and these theories provide guidelines or suggest techniques as well as offer explanations of observed phenomena. Even social workers who think of themselves as eclectic have some theoretical orientations, which they use in making decisions about what is best for a client. The usefulness of theory is well illustrated in an article of Polansky (1986), who identifies numerous functions of theory and provides practical examples of its use for social workers. I recommend this article for those who are somewhat skeptical about the value of theory.

Hypotheses

A **hypothesis** is an assumption that is expressed as a statement. It is a premise that can be used as a basis for investigation. Babbie (1986) defines hypothesis as "an expectation about the way things ought to be in the world if the theoretical expectations are correct" (p. 31). Hypotheses may be thought of as formal versions of hunches, notions, or speculations. Researchers test hypotheses as part of the research process. Hypotheses can predict a direction or express an assumed relationship between variables.

As an example, suppose you are interested in the concept of impulsivity. Because of your work with young people, you observe that some are much more impulsive than others. Several hypotheses might be suggested from your observations. For instance:

1. Adolescent males are more impulsive than adolescent females.
2. Teens who have been arrested for shoplifting are more impulsive than teens who have never been arrested.

After you gather the necessary data to statistically test one or both of these hypotheses, your results either support (confirm) or fail to support your hypothesis.

Occasionally hypotheses are stated neutrally (e.g., there is no relationship between high school grade point averages and college grade point averages); these are known as **null hypotheses**. A null hypothesis states that there is no difference between the groups being compared (e.g., adolescent males are no more impulsive than adolescent females). Researchers sometimes hope to find sufficient evidence to allow for rejection of the null hypothesis. The researcher does not have to believe that there is no difference or no relationship in order to state a null hypothesis.

Variables

A **variable** is a concept that can be measured (e.g., age, weight, or height). The term implies that persons from whom we are collecting data vary along numerous dimensions. Variables may also be thought of as rules for classifying people or their attitudes or behaviors into different categories (Kidder and Judd, 1986). Think about your research methods class; in how many ways can you classify the students? In how many ways do your classmates differ? The more ways you can think of to differentiate among your classmates, the more variables you have identified. Variables are sometimes also referred to as factors.

Variables can be **discrete** or **continuous**. Discrete variables present either/or choices. That is, a person is either a male or a female. Social workers sometimes place people into one of two categories—as when we divide our clients into those who are adults and those who are minors. Examples of continuous variables are age, weight, and scores on a given test. These are continuous in terms of their variation within a range of possibilities. For instance, on a cer-

18

tain test it may not be possible to score higher than 100 points, and individual scores may vary between 63 and 97. The wide range in these test scores is an example of measurement with a continuous variable. Classifying students in terms of whether they pass or fail is an example of measurement with a discrete variable.

Attributes

Attributes are the component parts of a variable. For instance, the attributes of the variable "gender" are male and female. There are no other possibilities. The attributes of the variable "political affiliation" might be Democrat, Republican, and Independent. You could add more categories if you wished to capture information on those who might be affiliated with other political groups. If you are collecting data on marital status, you may need no more information than whether the respondent is single or married. A need for greater precision might lead you to ask whether the respondent had ever been married or is currently married, separated, divorced, or widowed. Most often, you as the researcher will decide how these attributes will be defined.

Independent Variables

Independent variables are variables that are suspected to influence, affect, or cause the event or situation that you are studying. For example, prior hospitalizations for mental illness or alcoholism might be important independent variables to use to help explain or predict the problem of homelessness. Also, you might want to include such independent (or socio-demographic) variables as age, education, and job skills. What other variables may be associated with and might explain homelessness?

In experimental settings, independent variables are those which the researcher can manipulate or control. For example, in studying the effect of positive reinforcement upon the retention of research terminology, the researcher might decide to examine the usefulness of words of praise as a reinforcement as compared to a reward of candy for each new vocabulary term learned. The amount, type, and timing of the receipt of the candy are controlled by the researcher and could be considered independent variables; which words of praise are actually used, how they are uttered, and when they are spoken would also be independent variables.

Dependent Variables

Dependent variables are what you are trying to explain or predict—the topic of your investigation. Suppose you were studying weight gain among anorexic adolescents. You want to know whether anorexic adolescents put on just as much weight (the dependent variable) when participating in group psychotherapy as when they receive individual counseling or no therapy at all. Your hypothesis is that individual counseling is more effective than group counseling for this particular problem. You believe that the gain or loss of weight (the dependent variable) by those in your study will depend largely upon the therapeutic approach (the presumed causative factor or independent variable) utilized with them. It may be helpful to think of the dependent variable as depending upon the presumed causative factor (the independent variable). Sometimes these dependent variables are thought of as the outcome measures (Arkava and Lane, 1983).

Dependent variables in one study may be used as independent variables in another study. For instance, you could start off your research career by studying the level of self-esteem in ninth grade boys. In a subsequent study, you may wish to use those self-esteem scores to predict juvenile delinquency (which is now the dependent variable).

Data

Information that is obtained during a study and that has not been analyzed constitutes the **data** (sometimes called the raw data). For instance, if a test is administered to a group of thirty students, their test scores are the data used for analysis. (Note that the term data is always plural: The data *are* ready to be entered into the computer). From examining data, we attempt to find patterns to help us understand the social problem or phenomenon under investigation. Sometimes data are reported in tabular form, as in table 2.1. What patterns do you find in this table?

Measurement

One of the keys to understanding social science research is the notion that if a thing can be defined, then it can be measured. If we can precisely define concepts such as depression or anxiety, for example, then we can measure how much less a client is depressed or anxious after intervention. Since problems brought to social workers are sometimes indefinite or ambiguous, it is helpful to collect data in or-

Table 2.1   Foster Care and Educational Attainment in a Random Sample of Adults

		Less than High School Graduate	High School Graduate	College	Row Totals
Persons in foster care as children	n =	11	6	9	26
		(42%)	(23%)	(35%)	(3.5%)
Never in foster care	n =	170	301	247	718
		(24%)	(42%)	(34%)	(96.5%)

Source: Reported in Royse and Wiehe (1989).

der to determine the intensity or severity of these problems. Just how anxious is the client? How severe is the depression? Social workers sometimes design or use instruments to measure the extent of such problems. These instruments provide a way to have quantifiable (numerical) values for problems like depression so that we can discuss relative levels of depression and talk more precisely about those who are very depressed and those who are somewhat less depressed. Simply stated, **measurement** is the process of quantifying states, traits, attitudes, behaviors, and theoretical concepts (e.g., hyperactivity).

The importance of measurement is revealed in two axioms of treatment formulated by Walter Hudson (1978): "The first states: 'If you cannot measure the client's problem, it does not exist.' The second, a corollary of the first, states: 'If you cannot measure the client's problem, you cannot treat it' " (p. 65). While some may feel that these axioms are overstated, they have a direct applicability to research. Clinicians and researchers alike must be able to precisely assess (measure) clients' problems. Without precise measurement, it may be impossible to show that clients have improved as a result of intervention. The importance of having quantifiable data (as opposed to subjective labels) to represent concepts will become more apparent.

Subjects

Subjects are the persons or individuals who participate in a study. They may complete questionnaires, be interviewed in person or over the phone, or be observed. Subjects provide the data that are examined or analyzed. Respondents (those who consent to be interviewed or who return your questionnaires) are also subjects. In this text the terms client, subject, and respondent will be used interchangeably.

Correlations

A **correlation coefficient** (sometimes expressed as **r**) is a statistic which helps us to understand relationships between two variables. This relationship is summarized as a numerical value that ranges between − 1.00 and + 1.00. For example, test grades in this research course may have a strong positive relationship (.50 or higher) to the amount of time students spend studying. With this correlation coefficient, we would predict that as students' studying time increased, so would their test grades. If a negative correlation (− .80) had been obtained, this would indicate the ludicrous situation where test grades deteriorate the more students study.

Just because two variables are correlated, this does not mean that one variable caused the other. Not long ago I read about a study which found that nearsightedness was correlated with high intelligence (Rosner and Belkin, 1987). This study found that persons who do well on intelligence tests tend to be nearsighted. This does not mean, however, that all nearsighted persons are intelligent or that one could improve one's I.Q. by becoming nearsighted.

Scales

A **scale** is a cluster or group of statements or questions (items) that are designed to measure a single concept. Social scientists constantly work on and develop new scales to measure more accurately concepts of interest to them. It is not unusual for scales to be revised over time. Also, you will find that different investigators approach the measurement of even the same concept in different ways, so scales measuring the same general concept may vary in length, in the type item used, and the response categories available to the subject. For example, it is possible to find a ten-item self-esteem inventory (Rosenberg, 1965) and a twenty-five-item one, which Hudson (1982) calls the Index of Self-Esteem.

Hudson has developed several scales of interest to social work practitioners. Others are the Index of Marital Satisfaction, the Index of Sexual Satisfaction, the Index of Parental Attitudes, the Child's Attitude toward Father, the Index of Family Relations, and the Index of Peer Relations (Hudson, 1982). Scales can be developed to measure many different kinds of problems or concepts.

Corcoran and Fischer (1987) have collected over one hundred twenty-five brief scales, which they refer to as "rapid assessment instruments," for social workers to use with problems commonly encountered in clinical practice. Complete scales as well as information on the scales' availability, primary reference, scoring, and other essential information is found in their reference book, which contains many interesting and useful scales to use for research projects and for evaluating one's practice.

It is likely that sometime in your life you have been asked to complete a questionnaire that used a *Likert* scale (sometimes referred to as a five-point scale). In this usage of the term, the scale is the standard set of response choices: (1) strongly agree, (2) agree, (3) undecided, (4) disagree, and (5) strongly disagree; these are used to record the degree of agreement or disagreement with the statement. While Likert-type response choices are commonly used, there are variations. Hudson (1982) uses the following five-point response set to measure the variation in frequency or intensity associated with items composing such scales as the Index of Marital Satisfaction: (1) rarely or none of the time; (2) a little of the time; (3) some of the time; (4) a good part of the time; and (5) most or all of the time. Each of the response choices has a certain numeric value attached to it that is used to compute a client's score on that scale. Each of Hudson's scales is designed to have a score ranging from 0 to 100. A low score indicates the absence of the concept or trait being measured, while a high score indicates the presence of the concept. High scores, then, indicate to the practitioner the possibility of a severe problem in this area.

Scales vary enormously in how well they measure the concept they were designed to measure and in how dependable they are. The terms that researchers use to describe the worth or value of scales are *reliability* and *validity*. While these topics will be discussed below, it is worth noting that scales may contain many items (which improves their reliability), or they may be composed of a single item. The reliability of single-item scales cannot be computed.

The following is an example of a single item scale:

Rate how useful you think your research course will be to you:

Not very useful				Some use				Very useful	
1	2	3	4	5	6	7	8	9	10

Instruments

An **instrument** is a questionnaire or test that is usually completed by the respondents. When completed by a subject, the instrument is often referred to as a self-report or a self-inventory (meaning that persons can complete the instrument on their own with minimal supervision). The instrument provides data for the study. An instrument might, for instance, measure a person's potential for abusing children (Milner, 1986) or could be used to determine the amount of psychopathology present (Derogatis, 1983). Numerical values obtained with instruments allow one to monitor the amount of improvement or change in a client and to make comparisons with other clients.

An instrument is often a scale or, more precisely, composed of several scales, in addition to items which seek socio-demographic information (e.g., age, sex, race). For instance, Milner's Child Abuse Potential Inventory contains an abuse scale as well as scales to measure distress, rigidity, unhappiness, problems with child and self, problems with family, and problems caused by others. Derogatis's Symptom Checklist 90-R contains scales to measure phobic anxiety, paranoid ideation, depression, anxiety, hostility, psychoticism, and interpersonal sensitivity (among others). Attitudes about Research Courses and the Drug Attitude Questionnaire, instruments with several scales, are provided for your review in the appendix.

Instruments should not be understood as having only a clinical application. Social scientists have developed instruments (1) to measure anti-semitism and authoritarianism; (2) to study values, and (3) to measure such concepts as faith in people, social responsibility, radicalism-conservatism, and hundreds (if not thousands) more. There are instruments already available and ready for use no matter what your research interest. A good place to begin to review some of these instruments is in collections that have applications for research and program evaluations in a variety of social service settings, such as Corcoran and Fischer (1987), McDowell and Newell (1987), Brodsky and Smitherman (1983), and Robinson and Shaver (1973).

Reliability

Reliability is an easy term to understand because its usage by researchers is very close to its use in the everyday world. When a watch keeps time accurately, it is said to be reliable. If, on the other hand, your watch in one week gained a half hour, lost seventeen minutes the second week, and gained three hours at the end of the third week, you would suspect that something is wrong with it—that it is not reliable. Similarly, a scale or instrument that consistently measures some phenomenon with accuracy is said to be **reliable**. The instrument is dependable and has a certain amount of predictability associated with it. If an instrument is reliable, then administering it to similar groups under comparable conditions should yield similar results. This is one of the principles upon which standardized tests (such as I.Q. tests) are developed.

Most standardized instruments report their reliability. Generally this is reported in a way that resembles a correlation coefficient; it is a numeric value between 0 and 1. Nunnally (1978) says that in the early stages of research one can work with instruments having modest reliability, by which he means .70 or higher; that .80 can be used for basic research; and a reliability of .90 is the minimum where important decisions are going to be made with respect to specific test scores. Professional journal articles often carry information on the reliability of scales that were used in the study reported. If there is no reliability information given, and the scale is not well-known, it should be treated as suspect. Reliability cannot be assumed.

To determine reliability, researchers will often administer a scale to the same group on more than one occasion (**test-retest reliability**) to see how closely the results correspond or correlate. If, for example, you are interested in determining whether junior high students have a positive attitude toward street drugs, those attitudes should remain fairly consistent over a short span of time. If the instrument you use is reliable, it is logical to assume that those attitudes should not vary greatly within a four to five week period. If the attitudes vary quite a bit with a reliable instrument, you would look for the occurrence of some intervention or other event that influenced those attitudes.

A second approach to measuring reliability is to devise a *parallel or alternate form* of the instrument and administer both forms (to different subjects). Then compare the results. A third approach is to divide the scale on the basis of odd or even items and see how well the two halves correlate with each other (*split-half technique*). With both of these approaches, the higher the correlation coefficient, the better the reliability.

If you devise a scale and have your data on a university's mainframe computer, you can get an idea of how well a group of items hang together as a scale by running the Reliability procedure available through the *Statistical Package for the Social Sciences* (SPSS-X). This computer program will provide you with a rough estimate of the internal consistency of your scale. The program will indicate items that do not correlate well with the rest; dropping these items would improve the scale's reliability coefficient. Unless you are planning to market a scale or to prepare a paper for publication, you will not need to know a great deal more about the computation of reliability.

Validity

An instrument is said to be **valid** when it measures what it was designed to measure. An intelligence test should measure intelligence. An instrument designed to measure anxiety should provide an accurate assessment of anxiety but probably would not be valid for measuring such concepts as social responsibility, dogmatism, and paranoia. Validity research demonstrates what an attitudinal or psychological measure can and cannot do—its limitations as well as its advantages. No test or scale is applicable in all circumstances. The purpose of validity research is to identify situations in which the instrument is valid.

There are numerous ways to go about establishing the validity of an instrument. Research texts generally discuss the types of validity efforts in terms of the following categories:

1. Content validity
2. Criterion validity
   a. Concurrent approaches
   b. Predictive approaches
3. Construct validity

In order to have **content validity**, an instrument needs to sample from the entire range of the concept that it was designed to measure. For instance, it could be difficult for a scale measuring anger in children under the age of eight to be valid if the scale did not consider pouting, hitting, or temper tantrums as manifestations of anger. Likewise, a scale measuring anxiety in adolescents might not have content validity if it did not include such behavior as nail-biting, crying, stomachaches, and sleeplessness. To the extent that an instrument contains a representative sampling of the universe of behaviors, attitudes, or characteristics that are believed to be associated with the concept, then it is said to have content validity. Content validity is established when a panel of experts examines the scale and agrees that the items selected are representative of the range of items associated with the concept to be measured. However, there are no standardized procedures for assessing content validity.

While the terms "content" and "face validity" are sometimes used interchangeably, they do not have the same meaning, even though a similar process is used to establish both. An instrument is said to have **face validity** when several experts on the topic being investigated agree that the instrument measures what it was intended to measure. This process might be formal (as when a percent of agreement among the experts is computed) or informal (as when colleagues are asked to examine an instrument and express their opinions about whether the proposed instrument has face validity). While it is necessary to insure that a new instrument has face validity, this term refers to what the instrument "appears" to measure and therefore is not technically a form of validation (Bostwick and Kyte, 1988). Both face validity and content validity are necessary for acceptance of the scale by others; however, they are not sufficient for establishing that the scale will allow generalizability, a test for "true" validity (Sechrest, 1984).

Once content validity is established, the instrument is ready to be put to use. One begins to establish **criterion validity** when positive correlations are obtained between the test or scale values and some external criteria that are assumed to be indicators of the concept. Criterion validity, the second major category of validity research activities, is based upon the scale's ability to correspond with other test results that are thought to be indicative of the attitude, trait, or behavior being measured. There are several ways to establish criterion validity. We will quickly discuss two approaches.

Concurrent validity is demonstrated by administering your scale simultaneously along with another scale that has documented validity to the same subjects. If the two scales correlate well in the direction expected, then your scale has demonstrated one form of concurrent validity. As an example, suppose you had developed a scale (the Drug Attitude Questionnaire) to measure junior high students' attitudes about drug abuse. One way to demonstrate concurrent validity would be to administer your new scale along with another "proven" instrument that also measures drug attitudes. The data from these two tests are correlated to see if high values from one test correspond (correlate) with high values on the other test and vice versa (those who scored low on one test should also score low on the second test). If high correlations are obtained, then concurrent validity has been shown.

Predictive validity is the second form of criterion validity and is demonstrated when scores on a test or scale predict future behavior or attitudes. Your Drug Attitude Questionnaire has predictive validity if three years later you find that within your study group of junior high students, those who had pro-drug attitudes were suspended from school or arrested for drug possession, while those with anti-drug attitudes were not suspended or arrested for drug possession.

The third major category in validity research is **construct valid-**

ity. Evidence for construct validity comes from how well the scale differentiates along expected lines. For instance, you might have some evidence that your Drug Attitude Questionnaire had construct validity if it showed that students attending religious schools tended to have antidrug attitudes and also that known drug abusers (ordered by the court to attend a drug treatment program) tended to have pro-drug attitudes. That is, these results showed that the instrument could discriminate between those who had positive or negative attitudes about drugs. This makes the instrument useful. (What good would the instrument be if it couldn't discriminate between these two basic orientations?) The ability to do this is a demonstration of construct validity—the instrument did what it was constructed to do. Establishing construct validity is an on-going confirmatory process that builds upon other criterion-oriented validity efforts.

For the purpose of instruction, reliability and validity are usually presented as separate concepts. However, these two concepts are interrelated in a complex fashion. On one hand, when we can empirically demonstrate that an instrument is valid, it can generally be assumed to have adequate reliability. On the other hand, a reliable instrument may not be valid. That is, an instrument may provide dependable measurements but of some concept unrelated to what we thought we were measuring. Both reliability and validity ought to be demonstrated as evidence that an instrument is psychometrically strong.

As you come across various instruments in practice or in your reading, it is important to realize that if you know nothing about the reliability and validity of a scale, then any results that are obtained from its use may have very little meaning. The scale may not provide consistent results (poor reliability) or it may measure something quite different from what was intended (poor validity). The importance of knowing a scale's reliability and validity cannot be emphasized enough.

Bias

Researchers strive to eliminate **bias** from their studies. Bias is an outside influence or prejudice that tends to produce some distortion from what is actually occurring or present. This results in inaccuracy. Bias can be conscious or unconscious, glaring or subtle, and may creep in and affect the research process at various points. For instance, in developing a questionnaire you might inadvertently use all masculine pronouns and offend female readers. Offended respondents, if they are angry, may not respond to the questionnaire as you had intended. Complex instructions (which might be confusing to persons with less than a high school education) can also result in biased data. While we all have values and biases of our own, researchers should strive to keep their studies as free from bias as possible. A biased questionnaire can give information that does not produce a true picture or representation of the attitudes or behaviors you are investigating.

Bias can also result from the way we select interviewees or respondents. This commonly happens when not enough thought has been given to the sampling design. For example, suppose you are interested in getting social work majors to evaluate their undergraduate program. You decide, because it is convenient for you, to go to a nearby men's dormitory and interview all of the social work majors you can find. Obviously, if you base your study on just the interviews from that one dorm, you would have ignored all female social work majors. Your study, then, would be very biased as female social work students may have different experiences and evaluations of the social work program. Bias is generally minimized as survey samples approach **representativeness**—that is, as samples more closely resemble the larger population being studied. Remember that there can be many sources of bias, but in the conduct of research, objectivity is the proper and necessary stance.

Generalizability

Generalizability means how well the findings from a specific study fit another situation. Let's say that I think that my spaghetti sauce is the greatest in the world. I invite my aunt Bessie over to try it. She agrees that it is the best she has ever tasted. My wife also agrees. Even the kids like it. I then decide that I am ready to sell it across the country. Is it reasonable to assume from a small sample of family members that enough of the American public would buy my spaghetti sauce to justify spending all my savings to market it? In this instance I would have been guilty of overgeneralization. In other words, I assumed too much. I went beyond what my data would support.

Suppose that you are interested in predicting an upcoming presidential election. You ask all the social work majors in your college or university how they will vote. In this instance, a much larger sample is involved, but will your findings indicate which candidate will win the national election? The answer is probably not. Why? Because social work majors do not adequately represent a cross-sampling of

American voters. For one thing, social work majors probably tend to be more liberal and younger than the average voter. Social work majors at any one school may or may not represent the opinions of other students attending the same school. Similarly, you probably could not predict a national election based upon interviews of all the residents of several retirement centers located in South Carolina. However, depending upon the size of your sample and how the retirement centers were selected, you might be able to discover the candidate most preferred by older adults living in retirement centers in South Carolina.

As a rule, you can generalize only to the specific universe of people from whom you selected your subjects. If you draw an unbiased national sample, then you can speak to the attitudes or preferences of the nation. If you draw an unbiased sample from all the adults in a given state, then you can speak about the knowledge or attitudes of adults residing in that particular state. An unbiased sample from a large city will allow you to speak about the citizens of that city only. It would not be responsible, for instance, if you had data from a sample of adults living in Las Vegas, Nevada, concerning their attitudes towards prostitution to assume that the data were representative of attitudes in other American cities. That would be a case of overgeneralizing.

Journals

Unlike magazines that are written largely for public entertainment, **journals** are publications reporting studies for students, professionals, and scholars. Journals usually lack vivid graphics and multi-color advertisements. New knowledge in a field is often first introduced or reported in that field's journals. *Newsweek, Time, Family Circle,* and *U.S. News & World Report,* for example, may be useful in providing current information in some areas, but do not mistake these for journals. Many instructors will not count magazine articles when students are given the assignment of preparing a bibliography on a special topic.

A number of social work journals are listed below to help you become familiar with some of the important journals in our profession. This is by no means a comprehensive listing. There are many more journals than could conveniently be listed here, and the number of new journals has increased in recent years. Also, there are many specialized journals (e.g., *Crime and Delinquency, Gerontologist, Evaluation Review*) that are not listed but may be of interest to some students.

EXAMPLES OF MAJOR SOCIAL WORK JOURNALS

Administration in Social Work

Areté

Child Welfare

Clinical Social Work

Health and Social Work

Human Services in the Rural Environment

Journal of Applied Social Sciences

Journal of Education for Social Work

Journal of Independent Social Work

Journal of Social Service Research

Journal of Social Welfare

Journal of Sociology and Social Welfare

Public Welfare

Social Casework

Smith College Studies in Social Work

Social Service Review

Social Work

Social Work with Groups

Social Work in Health Care

Social Work Research & Abstracts

Such journals as these and other very specialized journals allow for in-depth reporting and discussion of a topic because they are written for a specific audience. Typically, a journal article starts with a literature review or a historical overview of the problem and then explains the current study. At the end, the findings are discussed in terms of implications for professionals. An article may also identify areas where future research should be directed. Contrast this with the coverage of a report in a newspaper article or a magazine; often these accounts do not explain the investigator's approach (the methodology), the sample size, and how the data were analyzed, or address implications of the findings. You should get all of this information in a journal article. At the end, you should be able to make a conclusion about the worth of a study. What other major differences do you notice between journals and magazines?

QUESTIONS FOR CLASS DISCUSSION

1. Look around the classroom. In how many different ways do your classmates vary? Make a list of as many different independent variables as may be represented by the diversity of characteristics found among your classmates.
2. Identify as many concepts used by social work practitioners as you can. If you have problems identifying any, think of specific theories (e.g., psychoanalytical theory). What concepts are basic to that theory?
3. As social workers, we use theories every day. What theory or theories have you found most useful to you as a social work student?

4. Consider the concept of "bad marriage." To what extent does your class agree upon the definitions of this concept? Operationally define a bad marriage for the purpose of conducting research on homes with domestic violence.
5. What independent variables might you want to include in a study examining whether individual or group counseling techniques produce the largest weight gain in a group of anorexics?
6. You are interested in obtaining information about whether a group of women have served in this country's armed forces. Give this variable a name and then list the attributes of this variable.
7. What would be the attributes of the variables identified in question 1 above?
8. Develop a hypothesis using the concept of elder abuse.
9. From the hypothesis developed in question 8, state the dependent variable and an independent variable.
10. Bring in examples of scales for the class to examine. Break into small groups and examine them. How are they scored? What information can be found about their reliability and validity?
11. Makeup examples showing how bias could affect a study.
12. Consider the operational definitions suggested for problem drinking. Who is included and who is excluded in these definitions? How could you improve them?
13. In how many different ways do you think social work students differ from the "average American voter"?
14. How many of the journals listed in this chapter are in your library? How many are familiar to you?
15. What is wrong with each of the following operational definitions?
    a. A good television program is one that meets the needs of the viewer.
    b. A good television program is one that has a plot or theme.
    c. A good television program is one that is educational in some way and also enjoyable.
16. How would you operationalize the concept of "a good television program"?
17. Brainstorm in class how to go about demonstrating that the questionnaire "Attitudes about Research Courses" (found in the appendix) has predictive validity.
18. What is the difference between a concept and a theory?

MINI-PROJECTS FOR EXPERIENCING RESEARCH FIRSTHAND

1. Sue Fictitious is a manager of an intake unit in a state agency responsible for investigating complaints of child abuse and neglect. She also is a part-time MSW student. One day, while in the library, she came across an article in a professional journal describing the Child Abuse Potential Inventory. She began to think of applications—ways in which her office might use the instrument to identify adults who are potential abusers.
   a. What hypothesis would interest you if you were Sue?
   b. Who would be your subjects?
   c. What personal or independent variables would you like to include?
   d. What would make you confident that the instrument was a good one?
   e. What potential dependent variables do you find?

2. Look at the questionnaire "Attitudes about Research Courses" in the Appendix. Imagine it being used in a research effort that you are planning. Answer the following questions:
   a. What independent variables will be employed?
   b. What are the attributes of those variables?
   c. Give one hypothesis that you could explore using this questionnaire.
   d. What other hypotheses might be explored using this instrument?
   e. What dependent variable might be used?
   f. What scales seem to be contained within the instrument? Do they seem to have face validity?
   g. Does the questionnaire appear to be biased in any way?

3. Refer to Corcoran and Fischer's (1987) *Measures for Clinical Practice*, Robinson and Shaver's (1973) *Measure of Social Psychological Attitudes*, or McDowell and Newell's (1987) *Measuring Health: A Guide to Rating Scales and Questionnaires*. Try to find a scale that you could use in planning some future research. As you look at the instrument you have chosen, make a list of the questions that occur to you when you think about employing such an instrument for research or evaluation purposes. Write a brief description of the population that would be the subjects of your study. What hypothesis will you test? What will the instrument tell you?

4. In a journal of your choosing, skim several articles until you find one in which the author used a scale and reported the reli-

ability and validity. After you've read the available information on the scale, list what you know about the scale and discuss what more you would like to know about it. Can you conclude that it is a "good" scale?

5. Go to the library and select a journal with which you are not familiar. Skim the back issues for the last year. What is the major focus of the journal? What kinds of articles does it tend to carry? What topics are not found in the journal? Is it written on a technical or academic level or for the practitioner? What do you like best about the journal? What do you like least?

RESOURCES AND REFERENCES

Arkava, M. I. and Lane, T. A. (1983). *Beginning Social Work Research.* Boston, MA: Allyn and Bacon.

Barratt, E. S. (1985). Impulsiveness defined within a systems model of personality. In C. D. Spielberger and J. N. Butcher (Eds.), *Advances in personality assessment.* Vol. 5. Hillsdale, NJ: Erlbaum.

Babbie, E. (1986). *The Practice of Social Research.* Belmont, CA: Wadsworth.

Bostwick, G. J. and Kyte, N. S. (1988). Validity and reliability. In Richard M. Grinnell, Jr. (Ed.) *Social Work Research and Evaluation.* Itasca, IL: Peacock.

Brodsky, S.L. and Smitherman, H. O. (1983). *Handbook of Scales for Research in Crime and Delinquency.* New York: Plenum Press.

Corcoran, K. and Fischer, J. (1987). *Measures for Clinical Practice.* New York: Free Press.

Derogatis, L. R. (1983). *SCL-90-R: Administration, Scoring and Procedures Manual: II. For the Revised Version.* Towson, MD: Clinical Psychometric Research.

Hudson, W. W. (1978). Notes for practice: First axioms of treatment. *Social Work,* 23(1), 65–66.

Hudson, W. A. (1982). *The Clinical Measurement Package.* Homewood, IL: Dorsey.

Kidder, L. H. and Judd, C. M. (1986). *Research Methods in Social Relations.* New York: Holt, Rinehart and Winston.

McDowell, I. and Newell, C. (1987). *Measuring Health: A Guide to Rating Scales and Questionnaires.* London: Oxford University Press.

Milner, J. S. (1986). *The Child Abuse Potential Inventory: Manual.* Webster, NC: Psytec Corp.

Munson, C. (1983). *An Introduction to Clinical Social Work Supervision.* New York: Haworth Press.

Nugent, W. R. (1987). Use and evaluation of theories. *Social Work Research and Abstracts,* 23(1), 14–19.

Nunnally, J. C. (1978). *Psychometric Theory.* New York: McGraw-Hill.

Polansky, N. A. (1986). There is nothing so practical as a good theory. *Child Welfare*, 3–15.

Robertson, J. F. (1989). A tool for assessing alcohol misuse in adolescence. *Social Work*, 34(1), 39–44.

Robinson, J. P. and Shaver, P. R. (1973). *Measures of Social Psychological Attitudes*. Institute for Social Research. University of Michigan, Ann Arbor.

Rosenberg, M. (1965). *Society and the Adolescent Self-Image*. Princeton, NJ: Princeton University Press.

Rosner, M. and Belkin, M. (1987). Intelligence, education, and myopia in males. *Archives of Ophthalmology*, 105 (11), 1508–1511.

Royse, D. and Wiehe, V. R. (1989). Assessing effects of foster care on adults raised as foster children: A methodological issue. *Psychological Reports*, 64, 677–678.

Sechrest, L. (1984). Reliability and validity. In A. S. Bellack and M. Hersen (Eds.), *Research Methods in Clinical Psychology*. New York: Pergamon.

True, J. A. (1989). *Finding Out: Conducting and Evaluating Social Research*. Belmont, CA: Wadsworth.

Vander Mey, B. J. and Neff, R. L. (1986). *Incest As Child Abuse: Research and Applications*. New York: Praeger.

Three

The Way Research Proceeds

Research in the social sciences usually results from a real problem or a problematic situation. The process is logical and similar to the problem-solving model so familiar to social workers. You may be surprised to find that the research process is not much different from the way that you normally go about solving problems. This chapter will provide an overview of the various steps.

The research process (sometimes called the scientific method) is based on the assumptions that the natural world is essentially orderly and that observed phenomena have some stimulus or cause. If the laws of nature are not haphazard in their operation, then it follows that laws that govern the phenomena can be learned. Our knowledge about the world is obtained through the use of a logical sequence of steps. It is only when we don't know very much about a phenomenon that there seem to be no discernible laws. The more we know about something, the better we can see certain laws or principles in action. Let's take an example of a problematic situation suggested by Leedy (1974) that illustrates a research-like process.

You leave your home to go to class. You are running a little bit late, and you are in a hurry. You put the key in your car's ignition and turn it. Nothing happens. At first you don't believe your bad luck. You turn the key again and again. Nothing happens. You pull the key from the ignition and look at it to make sure that it's the right key. You try again. Nothing. At this point you have a problematic situation and almost immediately you pose questions to yourself. Did I leave the lights on? Is there enough gas? You select a logical explanation and begin the "research" process. Suppose you have a notion (or hypothesis) that you left the car lights on all night. You can test the hypothesis of weak battery by turning on the car's radio or the car's headlights. If they work, then you can assume that the car's battery still has a charge, and you can move on to another hypothesis. You remember telling your brother to put gas in the car, and you wonder whether or not he did. You look at the fuel indicator and see that it registers "Full." Does the gauge work properly? Assuming it does, you move on to the next hypothesis: perhaps your ten-year-old car is in need of spark plugs, or the distributor got wet from last night's rain. Those of you who have had the experience of owning an old car could probably proceed with such hypotheses longer than anyone else would be interested. The point is that a series of questions needing investigation flows from the problematic situation. As this example reveals, research involves an orderly thought process that moves from what is known to what is not known. Numerous and varied hypotheses may be tested. Information gained leads to the consideration of other questions or hypotheses.

The Research Process

The research process is composed of a few relatively simple steps or stages. These are presented below as being sequential. However, sometimes these stages are not always so discrete. Various steps of the process might be undertaken simultaneously or out of order. Also, it should be noted that these steps may be described differently in various texts.

Step 1: Posing a Question or Stating a Problem

Before you can begin conducting research you must necessarily limit yourself to one question (or at least to a small set of related questions) or one problem to be solved. Ideas may emerge from observations of clients, personal experiences, discussions with colleagues, or reading the literature pertinent to a certain problem.

Research questions may come about as a result of **deduction** (where knowledge of a theory or general principle allows you to make a prediction or application to a single specific case) or from **induction** (where your observations about a case or cases seem to suggest a theory or set of principles). For instance, your learning of a two-year-old child in a housing project who has been eating plaster may result in your developing a theory that this problem is widespread. Induction goes from the specific to the general. Unlike research questions in other disciplines, those in social work generally stem from problems that actually need to be solved. We tend as a profession to be inductive rather than deductive thinkers. Our research tends to have more of an applied focus.

Once a question has been roughly posed or drafted, it will need to be restated as a researchable question. There is a definite knack to developing a good question. If too few words are used, the question tends to be too large to investigate. "What causes child abuse?" is an example of a research question that is too expansive. Such a question needs to be narrowed down. There is nothing wrong with wanting to provide answers to such questions, but practically speaking, the research needed to answer them would be well beyond the resources of most undergraduate or graduate students. As you read about child abuse, you will discover that the role of certain factors has already been demonstrated. It is usually better to ask questions that allow you to examine a specific theory or perhaps a small part of the problem. Better questions might be, "Were child abusers abused themselves as children?" or "Do perpetrators of child abuse tend to be chemically dependent?"

Questions that are asked in research studies are often very specific. This specificity is reflected in the titles of journal articles. Browse through an issue of *Social Work Research & Abstracts* and read the titles of the abstracts. Then look up some of the abstracts listed in the Index under "Child abuse." The abstracts will demonstrate how specific research questions are.

It should be noted that there are philosophical and theological questions that cannot be addressed using methods commonly used by social scientists. And there are questions that are not appropriate for investigation. Clearly, research that does not respect individuals or is in conflict with the commonly accepted social work values should not be conducted. (More about this topic when we discuss ethics and research methods in chapter 12.) A good researchable question also should not be trivial but have some significance for the social work profession.

The research process starts with *either* a question to be answered *or* with a hypothesis to be tested. Most students find it easier to understand the research process in terms of asking questions rather than testing hypotheses. However, both are legitimate starting points for the research process. Either one can be converted into the other; the following question and hypothesis deal with the same research.

Example of a research question: What is the level of empathy among fathers who have sexually abused their children?

Example of a hypothesis: Fathers who have sexually abused their children will have less empathy than nonabusing fathers.

Hypotheses are essential in explanatory studies because they suggest an explanation to be tested. Elaborate studies may have several major hypotheses as well as a number of minor or subhypotheses. Some investigators like to use null hypotheses, statements that specify the object of the study without specifying an expected direction. Null hypotheses are rejected when major differences are found between the variables being compared. You don't actually have to be convinced that there is no difference between groups in order to use a null hypothesis.

Example of a null hypothesis: There is no difference in the empathy level of fathers who have sexually abused their children and nonabusing fathers.

Hypotheses, like research questions, may be suggested from theories, the literature, or interactions with colleagues or clients. Hypotheses need not always be stated but may be the driving force behind exploratory or descriptive studies. After studies have been completed and more data are available, hypotheses can be tested in a more formal manner.

Step 2: Reviewing the Literature

Once you have a question roughly drafted, review the professional literature in order to relate your problem or hypothesis to existing theory. In the process of reviewing the literature, you learn what others have written about the topic. You might find that others have already investigated your topic and that there is abundant information on it. An example of a topic that has too much literature is schizophrenia. This subject is so vast that it would take years to read all the relevant journal articles on it. Once again we can see the utility of having a research question that is relatively narrow in its focus. An abundance of literature means that an idea that you thought novel is not new. You would have to do a lot of reading to find a gap in what is known about the problem. As a result, you may decide to pursue another question.

There are several ways to begin a literature search; you might use only one approach or many, depending upon your success in finding relevant articles of interest. If you love to browse in libraries, check the subject index to find where the books on your topic are located. Then review the books on those shelves. As you review the books, you may find references to other books or journals. The more you read, the more you have "reviewed the literature."

The approach I sometimes use is to get specific journals that I know publish articles on the subject of my literature review. For instance, *Child Abuse and Neglect: An International Journal* would be a logical place to start if one wanted to find journal articles on child abuse. You might also look at *Child Welfare* or *Social Work,* and skim the table of contents in issues of the last two years. If you find several articles of interest, they almost always direct you to additional journal articles or studies that you can use to further explore what is known about your question.

A third approach is to use the various abstracting services in the reference section of your library. *Psychological Abstracts* will provide you with a comprehensive subject index that will guide you to articles about your topic in a large number of professional journals. An abstracting service called *Sociological Abstracts* will direct you to articles that have appeared in sociological journals. If your topic borders upon the medical realm (e.g., the treatment of hyperactivity), you could consult *Index Medicus,* one of the more comprehensive abstracting services that includes relevant social work and psychology articles as well as those from the field of medicine. *Social Work Research and Abstracts* is the resource that will be most helpful on issues of interest primarily to social workers.

For instance, a listing under child abuse in the subject index of *Social Work Research and Abstracts* (1986), 22(3) will direct you to abstract 1093 on page 31. There you will find that Deborah Ann Daro has completed a doctoral dissertation that has drawn together "the major findings and practice implications of over 20 years of research on and demonstration efforts concerning child maltreatment." Even if you aren't so fortunate as to find such a comprehensive review of the literature, you will find articles directly relevant to your interest. If, for example, you were interested in permanency planning and its effects on foster children, you might come across an article by Seltzer and Bloksberg (1987) that summarizes the quantitative outcome research on this topic. As you review the literature, you will discover that some articles report the results of studies that have been done, others discuss the problem from the practitioner's perspective, and still other articles may be concerned with specifics that may not interest you at all.

To search through volume after volume of these abstracts is a time-consuming chore. A fourth approach makes use of a computer to search the abstracts. Typically, you work with the reference librarian to identify a topic and then to specify more narrowly the type of articles you want. Let's say you are still interested in child abuse articles. Since there may be several hundred articles on child abuse, the librarian may ask you what aspect of child abuse should be used in the search. You narrow the topic by indicating that the treatment of adults who are child abusers is your primary interest. The librarian then searches for articles containing the key words "treatment" and "child abuse" in the titles of the articles in the data base. Or, you might be interested in legislation that has been developed around the emotional abuse of children. The key words in this instance might be "legislation" and "emotional abuse."

Computerized data bases abound. A partial listing includes: Social Work Abstracts, Sociological Abstracts, Psychological Abstracts, Ageline, Druginfo, Social Planning/Policy and Development Abstracts, Family Resources, and Social Sciences Citation Index. Most of these data bases can be accessed from your home if you have a personal computer and a modem. However, if you have never conducted a computer search of bibliographic data bases, do several with a librarian to learn the procedures.

The librarian is also likely to know of other specialized data bases (for instance, there is one that contains only child abuse and neglect information). Once the data base and key words have been selected and the librarian "logs on" to the computer network, it takes only a few seconds to learn how many references on your topic were found in the data base. You may then be able to have these printed out while you wait on an adjacent printer (online printing), or at a cheaper rate offline (meaning you get them in one to three days).

The computer search approach has much to recommend it. It is fast, provides a large number of references, covers many more journals than you could reasonably browse through, and is flexible in the sense that several terms or related topics can often be combined in one search. On the other hand, there may be a charge for conducting literature searches. A simple search could cost as little as $8 but could range up to $35 or more. The charge is based on the amount of time you are connected to the mainframe computer. The more difficult the search (articles on your topic may be relatively rare or hard to find), the more expensive it will be. However, most librarians are capable of providing you with rough estimates on how much the search will cost and are usually able to tell you how much more it might cost to go after additional references or to search additional data bases. Since references can be provided to you chronologically with the most recent ones first, you can sometimes pare down the expense on a large data base by taking only the most recent references.

As you become more familiar with the literature relevant to your research problem, you will be able to refine your question. You may even decide to significantly change or modify it. You may discover that some researchers have indicated areas where additional or new research is needed. Even if it is not so directly stated, you may find gaps in the literature or gaps in knowledge relating to your special interest.

The necessity for immersing yourself in the literature cannot be emphasized strongly enough. There are many good reasons for learning as much as possible about your topic before beginning to conduct a study. A thorough review of the literature can save you a lot of unnecessary work and prevent you from working on a question only to discover that five other people have already investigated the question and obtained similar findings. Just as important, a thorough review of the literature will help you to ground your question within a theoretical framework. You can learn of other's efforts and approaches that have already been tried. Authors may suggest innovative instruments and ways to design the research or to think about and interpret the data. Practically speaking, your research should build upon the efforts of others.

If you are unfamiliar with the library and would like to learn more about such things as how to find public documents, federal publications, and other references or handbooks relevant to your interest, *A Guide to Information Sources for Social Work and the Human Services* by Henry Mendelsohn (1987) is strongly recommended. You may also want to examine *Where to Find What: A Handbook to Reference Service* by James Hillard (1984) or *How To Use a Reference Library* by David Beasley (1988).

Step 3: Developing a Research Design

A research design or methodology is something like a blueprint. It outlines the approach to be used to collect the data. It describes the conditions under which the data will be collected, how the subjects or respondents will be selected, what instrument will be used, and generally provides information about the who, what, when, where, and how of the research project.

The research design should be carefully thought out to insure that the information that you obtain will be the information you need to support or reject your hypothesis. In developing a research design, ask yourself, "What do I need to know?" and then "How will I go about getting it?" The answers to these two questions will guide the development of a research design.

Several types of research designs exist and there are variations within these major types. Further information about specific designs and their use is provided later in this text. For now, research designs can be broadly categorized as having one of three prime purposes:

1. Exploration
2. Description
3. Explanation

Exploratory research designs are used with topics about which very little information is available. For example, the first studies on the psychosocial impact of AIDS on the lives of gay men were important even if they involved only a relatively small number of respondents. Because these exploratory studies are responsive to new concerns or to areas that have not been subjected to research, they tend to be more tentative and small scale. Their value derives from the new insights they provide or the unanswered questions they generate for future research. The data they produce may not be conclusive, and, as a consumer of a report of some exploratory data, you may come away wishing that they had included a larger number of respondents. Exploratory studies generally do not have stated hypotheses. An example of an exploratory study is Donovan, Jaffe, and Pirie's (1987) "Unemployment among Low-Income Women: An Exploratory Study."

Descriptive studies tend to build upon exploratory efforts, but these studies are generally surveys on a large scale that adequately represent the population being studied. Descriptive studies can provide precise information on the characteristics of a group of respondents. For example, the characteristics and service needs of black homeless persons are described in First, Roth and Arewa's (1988) article, "Homelessness: Understanding the Dimension of the Problem for Minorities." Descriptive studies tend to be concerned with sample size, representativeness, and generalizability.

Explanatory studies test hypotheses and attempt to explain a phenomenon. These studies may involve comparison groups or social experiments. (See, for example, Kohn and Smart's 1984 study, "The Impact of Television Advertising on Alcohol Consumption: An Experiment"). Explanatory studies tend to be elaborate and focus on the way one or more variables affect another (dependent) variable. For instance, Wiehe (1987) found support for his hypothesis that abusive mothers have lower levels of empathy than nonabusing mothers. This study suggests that at least some part of the problem of child abuse may be explained by an insufficient level of empathy. Knowing this, then, social workers can develop treatment approaches that stress empathy development in abusive parents.

Step 4: Operationalizing

Before you can begin to collect data, an important part of the research process is to define the concepts or phenomena that are to be recognized or counted in your study. We want to operationally define variables so precisely that no one would have any problem understanding exactly what was measured or observed. For instance, to conduct research on the topic of child abuse, you must be specific as to what manifestations of child abuse you will be studying. Will the study be concerned only with physical abuse to a child? Will it include or exclude sexual abuse and emotional abuse? Is neglect to be considered along with physical abuse or is neglect seen as having a different set of dynamics?

Variables must have an operational definition in order to reduce the role of subjectivity. During the course of your study, variables will be defined specifically. The goal is to define your terms and variables so well that others have enough information to be able to repeat (replicate) your study should they desire to do so.

Since developing operational definitions is a little difficult initially, here is another example. Let's say that you want to study self-esteem in persons who have recently been divorced. Do you think that you could come up with a single indicator of good or poor self-esteem that everyone in your class would agree with? The review of the literature assists with this problem; you can learn how others have defined the concept of self-esteem. If they have used standardized instruments to measure self-esteem, you may want to define self-esteem within the parameters of the instrument. Individuals would have good self-esteem if their scores on the scale were high and poor self-esteem if their scores on the instrument were low.

The importance of operationalizing variables might be better understood with the following example. Suppose a friend is going to fix you up with a date. Your friend knows a lot of people and asks you what you are looking for. You indicate that you appreciate people who have a nice smile. "Well," your friend says, "that's no problem. What else?" You think a bit more and reply that you would prefer someone tall to someone short. Again, your friend knows several individuals who fit into that category. Your friend asks, "Is that all you are looking for?" Now you become concerned, because you realize that actually you would prefer a date who is somewhat athletic and who has values and interests about the same as yours. You end up giving your friend a list of five more essential characteristics. Now you have operationalized what you want in the way of a date. Similarly, researchers must define rather precisely what is to be measured in their studies and who is qualified to be a subject.

You may find that sometimes the variables that you intend to use have already been defined in a specific way because of the policies or the clientele served by the agency that collected the data. Agencies might be limited in that they may serve clients only through the age of twelve or until their eighteenth birthday. If you had previously operationally defined your variables to include thirteen-year-olds or had wanted to look at youths up to the age of nineteen, you have two choices: you can revise your operational definition to be consistent with that of the agency providing the source data, or you can reject that data base and attempt to find another that collects data on youths more in accordance with your definition.

Step 5: Collecting Data

This step is sometimes referred to as "implementation of the study." Depending upon your research design, you interview people, mail out questionnaires, or go to the library to obtain data that have already been published (such as suicide rates, marriages, divorces, or births by county and year).

This phase of the research process is obviously important. Without data you will have nothing to analyze or report. If your choice of methodology was well-considered, it will not allow for unconscious influence (bias) upon the responses you hope to obtain. Even though you may hope to find a specific outcome, you don't want to gather your data in such a way that the respondents tell you what they think you want to hear. You want your data to be as free from bias as possible.

The way, the time of day, and the place you collect your data can have major effects upon the outcome of your study. Suppose you go to a neighborhood supermarket to conduct a survey on attitudes about abortion. You choose to do your interviewing on Mondays, Wednesdays, and Fridays for two weeks during the hours between 9:00 A.M. and 4:00 P.M. However, a friend tells you that a better day to go is Saturday because everyone is more talkative. When should you collect your data?

Had you chosen to interview solely on Mondays, Wednesdays, and Fridays until 4:00 P.M., you may discover that your study underrepresented those persons who generally are at work during those hours. By interviewing persons who buy their groceries only on Saturday, you may collect a group of respondents who are employed Monday through Friday. The older, retired, or unemployed persons could be underrepresented. One approach would give respondents who would likely be older and possibly more conservative, while the other could result in younger, potentially more liberal respondents. If you choose to do your interviewing on Sunday mornings between 10:00 A.M. and 12:00 noon, what segment of the population would be underrepresented?

Some research questions or populations of interest determine how the data will be collected. Because homeless persons do not have telephones and may not have an address to which mail could be sent, it would be ludicrous to attempt a mail or telephone data collection procedure with this population. Pragmatic considerations such as the amount of time available to conduct the study, the amount of money that can be spent, the availability of subjects, and the ease of locating them all have a direct bearing on the way researchers go about collecting their data and the research design chosen.

Step 6: Analyzing and Interpreting the Data

Once you have finished interviewing or have obtained the information that you sought, you are ready to analyze your data. One of the purposes of analysis is to express the data in a way that is "mentally digestible." It may be easy to present detailed responses from three or four individuals, but when you have more than five responses, full descriptions become very cumbersome. Further, it is awkward, if not impossible, to display information from a large number of persons (e.g., fifty or more) without summarizing the data in some fashion. Your research design should suggest ways that you can summarize, categorize, or organize your data. For instance, if your hypothesis is that women voters are more supportive than men of tax levies that directly benefit persons with low income, your data naturally suggest two divisions: male and female voters. In your analysis, you will compare and contrast the voting behavior of males and females on specific social service election issues.

Analysis is a logical process that begins with looking at the raw data. For example, you will first want to determine how many persons of each sex, race, or age grouping completed your questionnaires. More than likely, you will then order or arrange your data in some fashion. If you looked at several elections in different years, you might array the data by year of the election. You may begin to notice a trend, for example, of men being more supportive of social service issues up until five years ago, and then women became more supportive.

As you categorize your data, you may identify patterns or directions that have been suggested in the literature. However, this is not always the case. Sometimes the data are hard to interpret, and the findings are not intuitively obvious.

Interpreting the data is made easier by comparing your findings with those of other studies. Perhaps your respondents are more conservative or less knowledgable than those in a study that you found during the literature search. Often it is helpful to brainstorm with others as to what could account for the findings that you obtained. Then, look for evidence to support these findings.

Occasionally, research findings can be portrayed in the form of pie or bar charts. Sometimes maps can be shaded to indicate high or low densities of one variable or another. These visual presentations are useful for helping others to understand the results of your study. However, statistical methods may also be needed to determine if there is a statistically significant difference between two or more groups. Statistics aid in the interpretation of data. With the advent of computer technology, the computation of statistical tests has become relatively easy. (Chapter 9 deals with statistics and analyzing data.)

Step 7: Writing the Report

Once the data have been collected and analyzed, the final step is preparing your findings in such a way that they can be made available to others. There may be times when a memorandum to your supervisor or director summarizing the results of your study will be adequate. However, it is much more likely that you will be required to make a full report.

The first part of a research report puts the research question or hypothesis in context (a description of the extent or severity of the problem, the length of time it has been a problem, what is generally known or believed about the problem), and reviews the important studies found in the literature.

Next is an explanation of the research methodology—how the data were collected, which variables were included and how they were operationalized, and who the subjects were, their characteristics, and how they were recruited. Enough information should be presented so that others can follow what you did and replicate the study.

The third section of the research report presents what was actually learned from the study. Tables and graphs may be employed to visually demonstrate differences and to help with comparisons. Statistical tests may be used. The final section contains suggestions for additional research in this area, how future research could be improved, and the limitations of the existing study.

It almost goes without saying that many fine research reports are filed away or relegated to dusty shelves because the social work investigators did not exert a little extra effort and prepare the report for publication in a journal or as a paper for a professional symposium. In order to rectify this situation, the last chapter of this text will focus on writing the research report.

Social Work Research and Practice

While it is often convenient to think of social work practice and research as completely separate and sharply contrasting with each other, they both share a logical problem-solving process. A number of social work educators have discussed the similarities between the two (Fischer, 1983; Karger, 1983; Rosen and Proctor, 1978). Both Grinnell (1985) and Powers, Meenaghan, and Toomey (1985) have thoroughly discussed the commonalties in the problem-solving processes used by researchers and practitioners in their research texts. Powers et al. (1985, p. 50) have correctly noted:

> Much of what the practitioner does, or ought to do, in the process of solving problems in practice is essentially the same as what the researcher does, or ought to do, in the process of solving problems in science—frame questions for practice, collect and/or access data, posit possible meaning, and test effects of intervention.

We can briefly summarize the similarities between the research process and the task-centered or problem-solving process used by social workers as follows:

RESEARCH PROCESS	TASK-CENTERED PROCESS
Starts with a problem, question, or hypothesis	Starts with a client's problem
Review of the literature	History-taking, identification of resources, strengths, networks
Development of research design and operationalization of variables	Negotiate a contract
Data collection	Begin intervention
Data analysis	Evaluation of intervention
Final report	Termination

Look for the areas of overlap between research and practice, and use these to further your understanding and competencies in both. The similarities in the problem-solving process used in social work research and practice make it one generic process (Fischer, 1981).

49

The research process is no more complicated than a good problem-solving model that is used every day by most social workers in practice. The research process is not an artificial contrivance to make life difficult for you; it is an orderly and logical process that is familiar to all social workers.

QUESTIONS FOR CLASS DISCUSSION

1. Share with the class examples of ways you have informally used the research process.
2. In what ways is the research process like the problem-solving process described by Reid (1978), Epstein (1980), and others? List as many similarities and differences as possible.
3. Practice operationally defining the following:

   a. alcoholism
   b. effective psychotherapy
   c. fear of open spaces
   d. depression
   e. good students
   f. social drinkers
   g. racist attitudes
   h. heavy cigarette smokers

4. Develop a hypothesis or research question for each of the concepts in question 3.
5. Discuss why the following is not a good research question: "Why is there suffering in the world?"
6. Besides those suggestions given in the text, list ways to narrow down the topic of child abuse so that the amount of literature to be read will not be overwhelming.
7. Identify the dependent variables in the following studies:

   a. Relapse in Alcoholism: New Perspectives
   b. Predictors of Repeat Pregnancies among Low-Income Adolescents
   c. Long-term Effects of Parent's Death or Divorce on College Students' Concepts of the Family.
   d. Impact of Social Work Education upon Networking among Community Agencies

8. What is the importance of having a research design?

MINI-PROJECTS FOR EXPERIENCING RESEARCH FIRSTHAND

1. Select a social problem and state it clearly.

   a. How do social workers encounter this problem? What do they do about it? What additional information would assist them in combating this social problem?

b. Frame either a research question or a hypothesis suggested from what you know or would like to know about the social problem.

c. What is the dependent variable?

d. What data would you need to collect in order to test your hypothesis? Who would be your subjects? Where would your instrument come from?

e. What independent variables would help you to analyze and understand your findings? List them.

f. Operationally define your dependent variables.

2. Select a social problem and locate ten relevant abstracts on the same subject using *Social Work Research & Abstracts, Psychological Abstracts*, or one of the other abstracting services.

3. Using the scale "Drug Attitude Questionnaire," plan a mini-survey of twenty to thirty students who might be conveniently interviewed.

a. What hypotheses could be developed and tested with this questionnaire?

b. What additional independent variables might you need?

c. How would you score the responses so as to detect those who have prodrug or antidrug attitudes?

d. What did you learn from this study?

4. In small groups of three or four students attempt to devise a self-esteem scale. Compare your finished project with those of others in the class. Do others agree that your items have face validity? Compare your items with existing self-esteem scales in the literature. (See, for example, Corcoran and Fischer's *Measures for Clinical Practice*, 1987). How many items are similar? How many are completely different?

RESOURCES AND REFERENCES

Beasley, D. (1988). *How to Use a Research Library*. New York: Oxford University Press.

Corcoran, K. and Fischer, J. (1987). *Measures for Clinical Practice: A Sourcebook*. New York: Free Press.

Daro, D. A. (1985). Confronting the crisis of abused children: Theory, policy and practice. Doctoral dissertation, University of California, Berkeley.

Donovan, R., Jaffe, N., and Pirie, V. M. (1987). Unemployment among low-income women: An exploratory study. *Social Work*, 32 (4), 301–305.

Epstein, L. (1980). *Helping People: The Task-Centered Approach*. St. Louis, MO: Mosby.

First, R. J. Roth, D. and Arewa, B. D. (1988). Homelessness: Understanding the dimensions of the problem for minorities. *Social Work*, 33 (2), 120–124.

Fischer, J. (1981). New and emerging methods of direct practice: The revolution in social work. In N. Gilbert and H. Specht (Eds.), *Handbook of the social services*. Englewood Cliffs, NJ: Prentice-Hall.

Fischer, J. (1983). Evaluations of social work effectiveness: Is positive evidence always good evidence? *Social Work*, 28, 74–77.

Grinnell, R. M. (1985). *Social Work Research and Evaluation.* Itasca, IL: Peacock.

Hillard, J. M. (1984). *Where to Find What: A Handbook to Reference Service.* Metuchen, NJ: Scarecrow Press.

Karger, H. J. (1983). Science, research and social work: Who controls the profession? *Social Work*, 28, 200–205.

Kohn, P. M. and Smart, R. G. (1984). The impact of television advertising on alcohol consumption: An experiment. *Journal of Studies on Alcohol,* 45 (4), 295–301.

Leedy, P. D. (1974). *Practical Research: Planning and Design.* New York: Macmillan.

Mendelsohn, H. N. (1987). *A Guide to Information Sources for Social Work and the Human Services.* Phoenix, AZ: Oryx Press.

Powers, G. T., Meenaghan, T. M. and Toomey, B. G. (1985). *Practice Focused Research: Integrating Human Service Practice and Research.* Englewood Cliffs, NJ: Prentice-Hall.

Reid, W. J. (1978). *The Task-Centered System.* New York: Columbia University Press.

Rosen, A. and Proctor, E. K. (1978). Specifying the treatment process: The basis for effectiveness research. *Journal of Social Service Research*, 2, 25–26.

Seltzer, M. M. and Bloksberg, L. M. (1987). Permanency planning and its effect on foster children: A review of the literature. *Social Work*, 32(1), 65–68.

Wiehe, V. R. (1987). Empathy and locus of control in child abusers. *Journal of Social Service Research*, 9 (2,3), 17–30.

Four

Single System Designs

Practitioners who do not want to do research on a large scale, but who may be interested in getting immediate, inexpensive, and practical feedback on whether their individual client has improved can make use of single system designs. (A system can be a community, an organization, a family, a couple, or an individual.) This type of research is also known as N = 1 research, case studies, single case and single subject designs. These designs typically require very little research expertise. In fact, they are attractive to social workers because they are so easy to use and understand—even with a very limited understanding of research methodology.

Single system designs are also useful because they focus on the individual client, unlike classical research of groups of clients which aggregates data and describes what happened to the "average" client after termination. Advocates of single system designs argue that in grouped-data studies information about specific clients is often obscured, that one might learn little about an individual client—perhaps only whether a client did better or worse than average. Single system designs "personalize" the research by looking at a particular individual's behavior over time. This allows for ongoing monitoring of progress so that one may determine the amount of improvement at any point in time. Before we begin with procedural concerns, let's first consider the history of single system designs.

The Origin of Single System Designs

The study of individual cases has long been a part of the richness of the social sciences. Thomas (1978) noted that for over a century case studies have been conducted in behavioral research. Bromley (1986) has stated that, in fact, the case study method goes back even farther, to "remote origins in human social history" (p.39). Prior to the development of statistics for group comparisons, research in the social sciences consisted almost entirely of descriptive case studies and reflections upon them. Case studies were useful for illustrating to one's colleagues and students how problems requiring remedial action could be approached or solved with specific theories or interventions.

Although these studies seldom employed any quantification of dependent variables, a number of important discoveries have come, not from the use of large groups of subjects commonly associated with social science research, but from the observations of single individuals. Several examples will serve to demonstrate this. Using nonsense syllables and himself as the subject, Ebbinghaus made major discoveries regarding principles of human learning. (We learn more efficiently in the morning than in the evening, for instance.) Pavlov's basic findings were obtained from single organisms and later reproduced (replicated) with other organisms (Hersen and Barlow, 1976). Piaget's theories derived from observations of his own children. From Freud's discussion of specific cases to eleven-month-old little Albert becoming conditioned to fear a white rat, generalizations from single subjects have played significant roles in helping us to understand human behavior.

Individual case studies have appeared with some frequency all through the social science literature (Dukes, 1965), and case examples or vignettes of cases are not uncommon today in medical and other journals, such as the *American Journal of Psychiatry, Hospital and Community Psychiatry*, the *Journal of Nervous and Mental Diseases*, and in social work journals such as *Social Casework* and the *Clinical Social Work Journal*. However, case studies have tended to vary greatly in their format, content, and organization. As statistical tests of comparison were developed and widely accepted, case studies fell out of favor by "sophisticated" researchers in the social sciences. This led to an era when research with single subjects was viewed by many as being elementary and somewhat inferior. The use of control groups and group statistical comparisons have now become firmly established in the social sciences, and the objective or quantitative methods of measurement used with these group studies has led to changes among those conducting case studies.

The emergence of single system designs in the 1960s and 1970s has been attributed to their use by B.F. Skinner and other practitioners of behavior modification (Zimbalist, 1983; Kazdin, 1982). With a focus on a specific target behavior, single system designs were well-suited for practitioners interested in demonstrating that their interventions were effective. Unlike the descriptive case studies of prior years which relied heavily upon subjective assessments of change, single system studies today often use objective measures to document that change has occurred. In fact, they may be very quantitative in appearance, and do not resemble the heavily narrative case studies of previous years except for the fact that they focus on one individual.

Single system designs were developed primarily in response to dissatisfaction with group research designs for clinical practice situations (Nelsen, 1988). Single system designs today provide a needed alternative to the group research designs usually associated with the conduct of research in the social sciences.

Single System Designs and Practice

Single system designs have been said to bridge the gap between research and practice (Dean and Reinherz, 1986). How is this possible? Imagine for a moment that it is sometime in the future. You have made it through the social work program and are now employed as a therapist in a mental health agency. Your next appointment is a college student in her twenties. As she explains why she has sought counseling, you begin to see a pattern of symptoms suggestive of depression. You have worked with depressed persons before and feel that you can work with this woman. Go forward in time another ten weeks. The young woman is now interested in terminating treatment. How would you determine whether your counseling was successful? Would you calculate the number of times she smiled during your last several sessions? Would her body posture indicate her level of depression? Her plans for the future? While you might have an intuition that you had helped her, could you empirically document this for a supervisor or program director? How would you go about evaluating your own practice?

This example of the depressed young woman comes from Berlin's (1983) description of a practitioner involved in both research and practice with the same client. In her article, Berlin describes how a single system design was employed by the practitioner to evaluate intervention. Because the client's symptoms suggested depression, the therapist asked the client to complete a short twenty item standardized scale that measured depression at the end of the first session. The client also completed one of these scales at each treatment session and one month after termination. When one views the test results from the depression scale on a graph over the several weeks of treatment, it is easy to see that the client's level of depression fell dramatically during this time and remained low one month after termination. Figure 4.1 demonstrates this visually in the graph used by Berlin.

Even a cursory glimpse at this graph or at the others in this chapter will convince you that single system graphs are intuitively obvious and easy to comprehend. This is the essence of single system designs—the visual presentation of a client's progress.

A Closer Look at the Single System Design

If you look closely at figure 4.1, the several component parts needed for a single subject design can be detected. Note that a single **target behavior** (the dependent variable) was identified. In this instance, the problem was the client's depression, and the practitioner's interven-

Figure 4.1: A Graph from a Single System Study

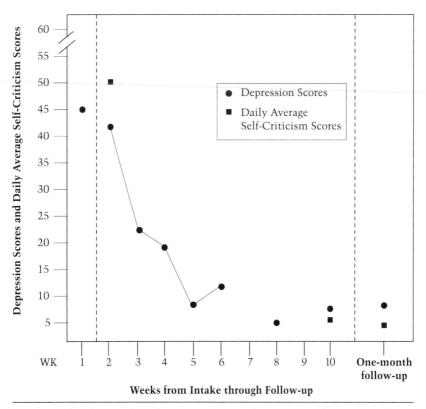

CES-D Depression Scores and Daily Average Self-Criticism Scores

Source: *Social Work Research & Abstracts*, 19(1). Copyright 1983, National Association of Social Workers, Inc. Reprinted with permission.

tions were oriented toward reducing that depression. Of course, depression may manifest itself in many forms. Berlin chose an objective instrument to measure the level of depression being experienced by the client. It would also have been possible to have monitored improvement with behavioral measures of depression, depending upon the client's presentation of the problem and the worker's assessment. The client may have had crying spells, restless sleep, poor appetite, and loneliness. The selection of a target behavior, such as frequent crying spells, could have been used had there been no objective instrument available for detecting changes in the depression.

Note that no complicated statistical procedures were used—just a simple graph to record (with repeated measurements) the client's improvement over time. (Although it is possible to use statistical procedures to check for statistically significant differences in improvement, this is not a requirement or a necessity for most single system designs.) The arrangement of the data chronologically on the graph is easy to interpret and follows from the research design. Ideally, data are collected before the intervention begins. The preinterventive data are called the **baseline** and allow for comparisons to be made with the behavior during and after intervention.

Starting a Single System Study

The first step in developing a single system study is to choose a behavior to monitor. This may be a difficult decision, but sometimes it is obvious which behavior needs to be targeted. If you have a client who has been arrested for driving while intoxicated and this is the second arrest in six months, it is clear that you have a client who needs to change his or her drinking behavior. Similarly, it would be apparent that a child with school phobia needs to decrease the number of days absent from school. Some clients need to demonstrate greater assertiveness; others need to learn to handle their destructive anger. Generally speaking, you will be working with clients to either increase or decrease certain behaviors. However, there can be as many as five different ways to think about how to modify behavior. Sundel and Sundel (1975) have suggested that we can help the client to: (1) acquire a behavior; (2) increase the strength or frequency of a behavior; (3) maintain a behavior; (4) decrease a behavior; or (5) completely suppress a behavior.

There will not be one target behavior that can be selected for all clients. Behling and Merves (1984) have provided fifty suggestions of behaviors that can be monitored (e.g., increasing positive interaction with co-workers, reducing fear of being alone, increasing positive use of time, maintaining therapy). Behaviors to be monitored in a single

system study must necessarily follow from the treatment plan prepared for that individual client. Even though most social workers are
not behaviorists, and the goals for their clients are fairly global or
long-range, single system designs can be used in nonbehavioral treatment providing that the client's final goals can be stated in measurable terms (Nelsen, 1981).

The selection of the appropriate problem to be influenced by the
intervention is obviously very important. When choosing a target behavior, there are several considerations that should be kept in mind:

1. *Target behaviors should come from the client.* As Hepworth
   and Larsen (1986) have noted: "the presenting problem . . . is the
   focal point of clients' motivation for seeking help" (p.173). To
   select problems that are not attuned to clients' perceptions of
   their problems risks premature termination. Although some
   clients may have a secret agenda for seeking help or other problems that may be revealed after a trusting relationship has been
   established, the best place to start is with the problem the client
   has identified as being most significant. This may require some
   prioritizing of the client's problems.

   Along this line, it may be helpful to use the following criteria to help rank the problems mentioned by clients: (1) problems
   that are the most immediate expressed concern of the client; (2)
   problems that have the most negative consequence for the client, significant others, or society if not handled immediately; (3)
   problems that have the highest probability of being corrected
   quickly, thus providing an experience of success; and (4) problems that require handling before other problems can be dealt
   with (Sundel and Sundel, 1975). Ideally, there should be mutual
   agreement between the social worker and the client regarding
   the major concern and focus of the intervention.

2. *Vaguely stated problems are difficult to measure.* Select behaviors that are concrete and observable. Avoid any behavior that
   might be difficult to detect or about which there might be disagreement as to whether it was happening or not (e.g., Johnnie
   says his parents don't respect his individuality). Choose behaviors that can be counted, observed, or quantified. You may have
   to help your client to move from an ambiguous description of
   the problem to a more precise definition. For instance, "ner-
   vousness" is a vague complaint, but associated with it may be
   several observable behaviors such as nail biting, overeating,
   stuttering, episodes of gastro-intestinal attacks, or excessive use
   of antacids that could be used as surrogate measures of the ner-

vousness. One could count the number of antacids consumed in a day, the number of stuttering episodes, or the number of calories ingested per day. Whenever possible, target behaviors should be so well defined that others would have little difficulty in observing or recording them.

Start with the presenting problem, and then explore how that problem manifests itself. Let's say that a woman tells you that her husband doesn't respect her. You cannot use "lack of respect" as a target behavior, because the term is too broad and not immediately associated with any specific behaviors. You need to find how this problem is expressed or detected by the client. What specific behaviors illustrate the problem of lack of respect? It could mean that her husband walks away while she is talking. It might seem that he is always late for supper. You want to identify the actions that indicate to the woman that her husband does not respect her. From these specific behaviors, choose one or two to focus on during the intervention.

In Berlin's example, a short standardized instrument was available for use. What happens if the therapist knows of no instrument suitable for measuring a problem like depression, anxiety, or other vaguely stated concerns? The therapist has only two choices, review the literature and attempt to find such an instrument or work without an instrument and select specific target behaviors suggested from the client's particular set of problems.

For instance, suppose a married couple comes to you because they are arguing almost daily. They are interested in saving their marriage; however, both are assertive, strong-willed individuals. The obvious target behavior is the number of arguments that they have. What led the couple to therapy? The wife (who happens to be a bookkeeper) kept a record of the number of arguments that the couple had over the past fourteen days. The frequency of these arguments was disturbing to both of them, and they agreed to seek help.

In this instance, the baseline was readily available to the therapist, and the couple were in agreement that they wanted to reduce the number of arguments that had been occurring. While an instrument would not be needed, one that measured marital satisfaction (Hudson, 1982) could be used if it were known to the therapist. If the marital counseling is successful, then it is reasonable to assume that a graph illustrating the number of arguments would show fewer arguments after intervention than during the baseline period.

Figure 4.2

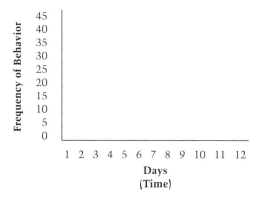

Frequency is not the only way of measuring the couple's arguments. In a different situation the therapist might have suggested that the length (or duration) of the arguments be monitored. Or, the intensity (magnitude) of the arguments might have been recorded. Minor verbal disagreements might not be counted; only those of the foot-stomping, door-slamming variety would qualify. The practitioner has quite a bit of freedom in choosing what to measure, how to measure, and even who should do the recording. However, the target behavior should always suggest itself from the client's description of the problem. The behavior should be an activity that a client agrees is important to count or record. Clients should be able to see how change in the target behavior contributes to improving their problem situation.

3. *Target behaviors are monitored over time.* Graphs are useful tools to portray changes in behavior. Graphs need not be drawn on engineering or graph paper; you can draw vertical and horizontal lines that intersect at a right angle and calibrate or demarcate the lines in a way that has meaning and indicates how much of the activity is occurring during the observation period (See figure 4.2).

On the vertical line (or axis), plot the number of times (frequency) the target behavior occurs. You need to have a rough idea how often the behavior is occurring in order to devise a scale to show its pattern.

The horizontal line is used to portray the behavior as it occurs over time. Whether you decide to use hours, days, or weeks as the unit of time is dependent upon the behavior itself. If you were working with a twelve-year-old who was having stomachaches because of school phobia and this tended to happen once a

60

day (ten minutes before the school bus arrived), it would be better to count the number of times a week that the stomachaches occurred than to keep hourly records. A baseline graph of the stomachaches in a month prior to the intervention might resemble the one in figure 4.3.

This graph shows that the child had stomach problems five times (corresponding to the five school days) the first week that a record was kept, five times the second and fourth weeks, but only four times in the third week when there was a school holiday because of snow. In this example, we know that the symptoms are occurring every schoolday. The child missed having a stomachache only once on a schoolday during a twenty-eight-day period. This is a well-established or *stable pattern* of behavior. If intervention is effective, a pattern of improvement will be readily observable. Contrast this with a target behavior that is unpredictable (where there is no discernible pattern). Suppose that the child had one stomachache the first week, none the second week, five stomachaches during the third week, and none during the fourth week. This would be an erratic pattern. In this case, we might want a longer baseline to help us understand what is going on. Instead of school phobia, the child's stomach problems might be due to food allergies that are triggered by specific foods that are not eaten every week.

It is necessary that the behavior prior to intervention (the baseline) be observed long enough so that you can predict about how often it occurs, on average. The purpose of the baseline is to provide data so that you can make "before and after" comparisons. Baselines record the frequency, intensity, duration, or magnitude of some behavior that will become a target for modification during intervention.

It is difficult to provide a rule about how long the baseline

Figure 4.3

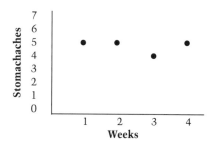

Figure 4.4

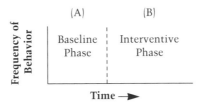

period should be. Much depends on how often the behavior is occurring and how stable this pattern is. A behavior that occurs relatively infrequently probably is not a useful behavior to choose for monitoring because it will be hard to see any patterns. Similarly, behavior that varies a great deal will not make a good target behavior. Choose a behavior that is fairly dependable in its occurrence. There can be some variation in the frequency of the behavior, but this variation should not have "wild swings." It would be ridiculous to monitor a behavior that occurred twenty times in one day and then did not occur at all during a three week observation period. As a rule, stable patterns are sometimes evident by the sixth or seventh observation period. However, the length of the baseline must be tempered by the availability of data and concern for not unduly delaying intervention. Also, the very act of counting or measuring a behavior during the baseline phase may serve to change or affect the client's behavior (especially if the client is involved in the counting) even before the intervention is implemented.

Various ways may be used to gather baseline data. You might find that there is ample reference to the occurrence of the target behavior in progress notes, the client may have kept some informal records or have a good memory, or there may be official records (e.g., elementary school absences). In our society, documentation is often readily available. A baseline for a spouse whose drinking behavior results in days missed from work, for example, might be obtained by looking at paycheck stubs. In some instances, clients can keep logs or self-report on the occurrence of the target behavior. In other situations, someone else will need to monitor the behavior. These are individually determined by a knowledge of the client's abilities and situation.

As can be seen in the graph in figure 4.4, the behavior during the baseline period is usually separated from the behavior during the intervention phase by a vertical dotted line.

4. *The last step in developing a single system study is selecting a design.* Of the many single system designs from which to choose, only a few of those judged to be the most useful to practitioners are presented here. As you read the balance of this chapter, you may find yourself liking some designs because you feel that you could comfortably use them. Other designs may strike you as impractical (or worse) because they seem more suited for experimental labs and require greater control over the client system than you feel that you have or ought to have. One design (the AB) is likely to meet most of your needs. But other designs may be more appropriate for specific cases or when you want greater assurance that it was your intervention that had the desired effect.

The Case Study or *B* Design

The case study (which has already been briefly discussed) is the design most familiar to students because it is used frequently in the social sciences. Case studies are sometimes called uncontrolled case studies because they lack baseline measures and use anecdotal information rather than objective measures of the target behavior. These designs are therefore seriously limited in that they do not permit conclusions that the intervention caused the change in the client's behavior. (There may have been other forces or influences at work in addition to the intervention.)

However, these designs are simple to conceptualize, don't require preplanning, and are possible to use once intervention has begun. In spite of their limitations, they are able to show that the client has made progress. (It is just that they can't rule out competing explanations.)

The practitioner begins keeping records with the beginning of intervention regarding how the client changes or improves. No attempt is made to compare the behavior at the end of the intervention with its baseline (because there was none). This design can be used with any theoretical orientation, and its value is the feedback it provides. For the reasons previously discussed—lack of systematization, no baseline measures or objective measurement, and little control of the treatment variable (e.g., the intervention may involve several simultaneous procedures)—this is a weak design that does not allow confidence in drawing conclusions about the effect of the intervention.

Case studies generally are not regarded as formal research strategies (Yin, 1984). A good example is the case described by Ashley

Montagu (1971) in his book *The Elephant Man: A Study in Human Dignity.* A case study is interesting to read and to discuss because of the rich description it provides about generally rare or uncommon occurrences. As a research strategy, its weakness comes from the fact that there is no basis for comparison. However, we can take an interesting case and construct a basis for comparison. This approach is discussed next.

The **AB** Design

The basic design by convention referred to as the **AB** design is the "workhorse" of the single system designs and the one most often used by beginning social work practitioners and researchers (Nelson, 1988, p.367.) There are two main features to this design: observation of the behavior prior to treatment (the baseline) and observation of the behavior after intervention has begun. The **A** portion of the design is the baseline measurement (e.g., administration of an instrument at intake to measure depression). The **B** part of the design is the data collected during the treatment phase. Because of its simplicity, the **AB** design is virtually unlimited in its applicability in social work. This is perhaps its greatest strength. It reveals changes in behavior—if they occur. Unfortunately, changes in behavior that are detected with this design do not "prove" that the intervention was responsible. There could be alternative explanations such as the occurrence of other events during intervention (e.g., leaving a stressful job, the birth of a child, over-the-fence counseling by a neighbor, or maturation of the client) for changes in the client's behavior. These alternative or rival explanations are difficult to rule out with the basic **AB** design. Most practitioners, however, would be happy with the client's success and would not worry about alternative explanations. While the **AB** design may not adequately control for competing explanations, it provides a useful way of examining whether there has been an improvement since intervention began.

The **ABA** and **ABAB** Designs

These two designs are sometimes called withdrawal, reversal, or experimental single system designs because they allow the client's behavior to return to its preinterventive level (the baseline condition) in order to show that the intervention was responsible for the observed effect on the target behavior. These designs are concerned with whether the effect of the intervention will continue or be maintained. After the intervention (**B**) has been completed or substantially

Figure 4.5: Illustration of an **AB** Design Graph

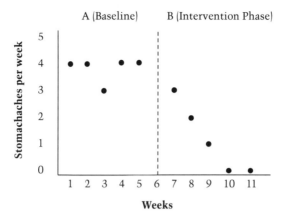

delivered, treatment is withdrawn or stopped, and the target problem is monitored to see what direction it takes.

The second (**A**) phase in an **ABA** design is like the first **A** phase in that behavior is recorded during a period of no intervention. This is not to suggest that you as a practitioner should purposely withdraw treatment for "research" purposes; that would be an unethical practice. The second **A** phase could legitimately come about following termination (Berlin mailed a depression scale to the client as a follow-up measure one month after treatment. Look back to figure 4.1 for an example of this graph).

Because of practice-related concerns about ending client contact during a nonintervention phase, Bloom and Fischer (1982), do not recommend this design for most practice situations. However, if the second **A** phase comes about as a follow-up to intervention, or for other therapeutically sound reasons, this design might be useful and ought not be overlooked.

Each phase of the classical single system design (**AB**) is repeated twice in the **ABAB** design. As in the **ABA** design, treatment is withdrawn or removed in the second baseline (**A** phase) in order to see if the target behavior will return to its original level (prior to intervention). There may be valid reasons for a second period of nonintervention, both practical, for example, the therapist's vacation, and therapeutic, for example, a trial period of three weeks between appointments to wean a "dependent" client away from intervention. After the second baseline period, the treatment is reintroduced. Unlike the **ABA** design, the study ends during an intervention phase, which makes it more appealing from an ethical standpoint.

Because the client serves as his or her own control, the **ABAB** design is an experimental design and provides some assurance that the intervention actually was responsible for any changes in behavior. In this sense, the **ABAB** design is a stronger and more powerful design than the **AB** and **ABA** designs. If the same effects are shown during the second **AB** (replication) phase, then there is less likelihood that outside influences (alternative explanations) were responsible. The **ABAB** is an "ideal" design for those who are interested in contributing to our knowledge base by experimentally demonstrating that some intervention is effective—especially if they want to show generality by replicating the treatment with other clients (Howe, 1974).

However, use of the **ABAB** design is not always practical. In fact, if the first treatment phase reduced the behavior to acceptable levels for the client and others concerned, it is likely that all involved persons would feel that the intervention was a success. Termination would occur, and the therapist would be given a new client to add to his or her caseload. There would be little reason to introduce intervention again unless the client made another request. In fact, the more successful the intervention, the less likely it will be that the behavior would return to its initial baseline (**A**) level.

The **ABAB** design may not feel comfortable to many practitioners because they are painfully aware of the shortage of staff or the long lists of clients patiently waiting for help with their problems. Even though the second baseline could come about naturally (vacations, hospitalizations, etc.), the **ABAB** design may still seem excessive or a luxury unavailable to many practitioners.

The **ABAB** design is best thought of as a design to be used for knowledge-building. It is a design that enables thorough testing of an intervention and reduction of alternative explanations for the client's improvement. This design is what you would use if you were sure that a given intervention worked and you wanted to document or publish your success in some sort of formal way.

The *ABC* and *ABCD* Designs

Practitioners know well that sometimes the intervention that you start with doesn't work, is not valued by the client, or does not appear to be working as fast as it should. In these situations, major changes are made in the treatment plan. Another intervention might be started or multiple modalities employed.

The **ABC** or "successive interventions" design allows the practitioner to respond with different interventions when needed and still allows for monitoring the effects of these interventions. In this scheme, the effects of the second intervention are identified as (C). The effects of the third intervention are (D), and so on. (It is also possible to think of the C phase as a period when the client is taught how to maintain the behavior achieved during the intervention (B) phase.)

Since there is no return to a baseline between the second and third (or even fourth) interventions, these successive intervention designs do not allow the practitioner to determine which interventions caused the changes in the behavior. Even though it might appear that the first intervention (B) didn't work, but that the second intervention (C) did, it could be that the accumulative or interactive effects of both B and C resulted in the change. Although one's colleagues and the client may be duly impressed with these changes, strictly speaking, conditions were not controlled enough for any sort of formal statement of causality.

Even if this design tends to fall short of the experimenter's expectations, it is appealing to practitioners, because intervention is often modified in practice and different techniques are used in the course of therapy. If everyone is happy that the behavior has changed in the desired direction, and success is in the air, neither client nor practitioner may need greater "proof" that the interventions worked. Figure 4.6 shows an example of an **ABCD** design found in the social work literature (Nuerhring and Pascone, 1986).

Multiple Baseline Designs

Single system designs known as **multiple baseline designs** may be used when you want to apply the same intervention with a client having two, three, or more problems. For instance, Taber (1981) has described the use of a multiple baseline design with an eleven-year-old boy who was referred to a residential treatment center for impulsive fighting, hitting and swearing. When there is more than one target behavior, a baseline is needed for each. After the desired change has been achieved with the first behavior, the intervention is then applied to the second behavior, and so on. The shorthand notation for a **multiple baseline design across behaviors** for two problems and one intervention would be A_1A_2B. The design for three target behaviors and one intervention would be $A_1A_2A_3B$.

The multiple baseline designs are variations of the basic **AB** design, except that monitoring of all the behaviors continues until the desired change has been reached with the last target behavior. Practitioners may find these designs more useful than the **ABA** or **ABAB** designs because no withdrawal of intervention is required.

The multiple baseline design can also be used when you are

Figure 4.6: Treatment Progress of a Businesswoman with Early-Phase Alcoholism

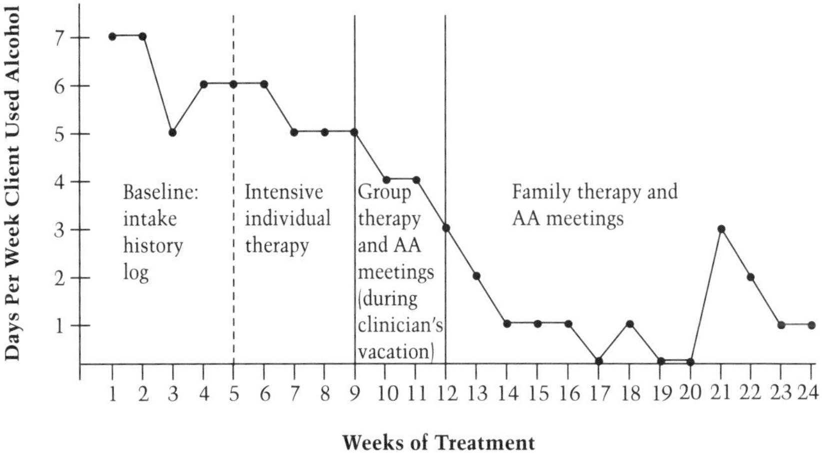

Weeks of Treatment

Source: *Social Work*, 31(5), 361. Copyright 1986, National Association of Social Workers, Inc. Reprinted with permission.

working with several clients having the same problem and receiving the same intervention. (Then it is called a **multiple baseline across subjects design**.) For instance, you might be a social work consultant to several nursing homes and find similar cases in need of intervention at three different homes. Treatment is begun with one individual at a time, and baseline data are gathered on the other clients. When the first individual begins to show a change in behavior, intervention is applied to the second client.

A recent example of a multiple baseline across subjects design is found in Pinkston, Howe, and Blackman's (1987) description of a treatment procedure for the problem of urinary incontinence in three wheel-chair-bound nursing home residents with organic brain disorders. Following the intervention of praise and cookies for appropriate urination, there was a decrease in urinary incontinence and an increase in appropriate toilet behavior.

You can see in figure 4.7 that multiple baseline designs have baselines of unequal length and that intervention does not begin in the second graph until change has been recorded in the first. This holds true whether the design involves one subject with multiple target behaviors (The Taber example) or multiple subjects having a single target behavior (the Pinkston, Howe and Blackman example). One of the strengths of the multiple baselines design is that it is useful in testing the external validity (generalizability) of an intervention (Be-

Figure 4.7: Illustration of Multiple Baselines Across Subjects

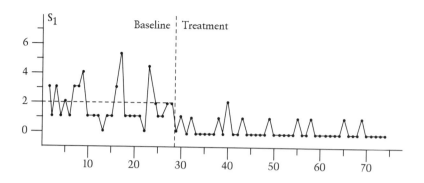

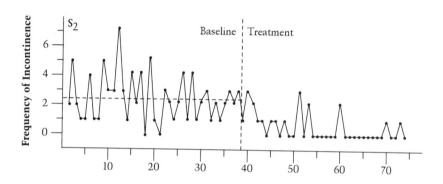

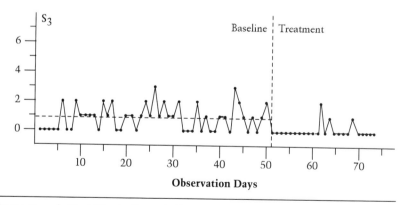

Observation Days

Source: *Journal of Social Service Research*, 10 (2,3,4), 188. Copyright 1987, Haworth Press, Inc. Reprinted with permission.

hling and Merves, 1984) and for demonstrating causality (Bloom and Fischer, 1982). This is because multiple baselines show that specific changes in problems or in clients are related to the onset of intervention. Change is produced only after intervention and is not due to other factors.

Statistical Analysis

Statistics usually are not needed with single system designs. Because these designs rely upon graphs and visual inspection, "eyeballing" and clinical significance are all that is usually needed to establish that improvement occurred. However, for those situations where it is important to establish that there was a statistically significant change in behavior, or where it is impossible to determine whether there was a change by visual inspection, there are a number of statistical tests that can be computed fairly easily. These procedures are outlined elsewhere (Jayaratne, 1978; Jayaratne and Levy, 1979; Bloom and Fischer, 1982; Kazdin, 1982, Gingerich, 1984). These sources provide detailed presentations on the use of statistical tests with single system designs. The *Journal of Applied Behavior Analysis* or *Behavior Modification* also provide examples of these designs in a scholarly format. Persons working with single system designs may also be interested in computer software that provides diagnostic and interpretive functions and allows for progress monitoring and evaluation of service effectiveness (Nurius and Hudson, 1988). Existing software can store data, draw graphs, and compute statistical tests when desired (Bronson and Blythe, 1987).

Advantages and Disadvantages of Single System Designs

Single subject designs are popular with social workers for several reasons. Some of these may be more apparent than others. Bloom and Fischer (1982) have listed twelve advantages, and I have condensed these into what I think are the major advantages. First of all, single system designs readily lend themselves to clinical practice situations. If a social worker wants to objectively evaluate his or her practice, single system designs do not require either control groups or large groups of clients in order to demonstrate that the intervention is working.

Secondly, single system designs are not disruptive to the treatment process. In fact, they support and complement practice nicely by focusing on specific treatment goals or problems. Often, they serve to clarify or confirm a worker's initial assessment of a client.

Further, these designs are constructive in that they provide continuous feedback to the practitioner as well as the client. There is no need to wait until the treatment has ended to determine progress. Many clients have "failure" identities and need to be reassured that they are progressing. Single system designs can visually demonstrate the progress that has been made.

Thirdly, single system designs do not normally require computers, knowledge of statistics, or clerical help in compiling data. These designs do not require that you develop a hypothesis to test. In short, they are not burdensome to one's practice. They are easy to use and understand. Lastly, they are theory-free. That is, they can be applied regardless of the worker's theoretical application. For social workers who are interested in some form of accountability, but not in larger empirical research projects, there is much to recommend single system studies.

Nuehring and Pascone (1986) have suggested that single system designs should be used by social work department heads for peer reviews. If a client is not making progress, this is readily detected, and suggestions for corrective action can be made.

On the other hand, these designs have some major limitations. A considerable one is the problem of generalization. Even though one uses a rigorous single system design and clearly demonstrates that the intervention worked, there will still be those skeptics who say, "So? Maybe you worked well with this one client. Show me that your approach works with lots of clients." The skeptic makes a good point. A social worker or counselor could be very effective with a single client and yet ineffective with the rest of the caseload. It is possible to make your results have greater generalization by replicating (repeating) single subject designs with other clients. However, practically no replications have been reported in the literature (Reid, 1987).

A number of practical problems sometimes emerge when using single system designs. Ideally, all phases should be of equal length, yet realistically an intervention might be longer than the baseline or longer in one phase (the **B** phase) than another phase (**C**) phase. In actual practice, is is unlikely that all phases would be the same length. Other problems are encountered when we know the baseline behavior is not stable but must start intervention immediately or when several interventive techniques have to be applied simultaneously. Another problem is that even experienced practitioners may be hard-pressed to think of situations in which they would deliberately withdraw or remove an intervention that is working just to show that it is the intervention that was responsible for the change in behavior. As a consequence, some of the more experimental single system designs (e.g., **ABAB**) may be viewed by practitioners with disdain or lack of interest.

The Choice and Use of Single System Designs

This chapter has presented several different single system designs. Some of these designs are more powerful (e.g., the **ABAB** design) than others (e.g., the **AB** design) for demonstrating that the intervention and not some other factor was responsible for the change in behavior.

The single system design that is "best" to use depends upon how much evidence you feel that you need to rule out alternative explanations for improvement; it is also dictated by the target behaviors or problems identified in the treatment plan. Knowledge of the client and his or her problems is an important consideration in the choice of a design. For instance, you wouldn't want to attempt an **ABAB** design with a client who agrees to a maximum of three contacts. With another client, you may feel that it is important to monitor three or more target behaviors. Sometimes you might combine such behaviors as hitting and fighting and refer to the commission of either as "assaultive acts", then you could use only one graph instead of two. With single subject designs, you have a great deal of flexibility. As a general guideline, however, let your knowledge of the client dictate the design rather than choosing a design and attempting to find a client that conforms to it. If we were all to wait for the "ideal" client to come along before beginning to evaluate our practice, not much evaluation would get done.

It is important not to forget that the purpose and best use of single system designs is to identify whether a client is progressing. These designs cannot explain why an intervention isn't working. Their purpose is only to inform you whether the intervention is working.

It requires a certain amount of self-discipline to conduct research. One has to be conscientious about keeping records or monitoring changes in behavior. For many practitioners whose agencies do not require formal evaluation, it is easier to use subjective determinations ("I think the client is doing better"; "The client is acting more appropriately"; "I feel that the couple is getting along better.") However, subjective determinations do not advance the profession or build practice knowledge. Single system designs can allow you to discover what works under which circumstances. A study by Campbell (1988) indicates that clients prefer the use of some single system evaluation procedure over practitioners' opinions of effectiveness of treatment. Campbell went on to note that "concern over client reactions to the use of single system evaluation procedures does not appear to be a valid reason for not using them" (p.22).

Single system designs have practical value and can benefit you and your clients. You may find that if you make use of them, you gain an appreciation for empirical research and are more willing to engage in it. (However, this is an untested hypothesis.)

QUESTIONS FOR CLASS DISCUSSION

1. Look again at the discussion of the twelve-year-old who had stomachaches. Besides graphing the stomachaches in terms of the number of times they occur per week, is there another way? Why wouldn't you want to graph the behavior in terms of times per day? (Hint: make a graph on the blackboard showing the reduction from one episode a day to none per day at the end of the intervention.)

2. Gingerich (1984a) has conducted research examining why single system research is not widely used by practitioners. Prior to reading this article, make a list of the reasons likely to be given in the study as to why social workers don't make greater use of single system designs. Vote as a class to determine the "most popular" explanations. Arrange these in descending order and then compare with the data presented in the articles.

3. In how many different ways can graphs show lack of improvement? Choose a target behavior and draw suggestions from the class that demonstrate lack of improvement.

4. Why is the ability to operationalize variables important for single subject designs?

5. What would be a good argument for monitoring more than one target behavior with a client?

6. Think about how to set up a graph for a particular target behavior; would there be advantages in graphing positive behaviors (e.g., number of days on the job) rather than negative behaviors (e.g., days of work missed)?

7. A co-worker tells you that she has just completed a single system design on a family that has received intervention for seven months. She is pleased with what she has done and brings a graph to show you.
    a. What would be your initial reactions about her competence?
    b. Would you conclude that she did a good job with this par-

ticular family without knowing more about its history and the treatment plan?

    c. Why would it be important to know the presenting problem and other major issues?

    d. Can single subject design "prove" that your co-worker is an excellent social worker?

8. With a multiple baseline across subjects design, what is the reason for waiting for a change in the behavior of the first subject before beginning intervention on the second? Why not begin intervention on all three subjects at the same time?

MINI-PROJECTS FOR EXPERIENCING RESEARCH FIRSTHAND

1. Choose a client with whom you have worked or are working. (Or, make up a fictitious client.) Describe the presenting problem, and then select a target behavior that follows from the client's description of major concerns. Construct a graph for a single system design to monitor the client's progress. Be sure to address the following:

    a. What is the target behavior?

    b. How long a baseline will you need? What units will you use to measure the time intervals? How will you measure the target behavior (e.g., frequency of the behavior, percentage of completed tasks)?

    c. What design would you use? It should be apparent on the graph.

    d. Have the graph show that the intervention was successful.

    e. What other explanations for the change could there be?

2. Find an article that reports the use of a single system design.

    a. What additional information do you think should have been included? Do you have enough information to replicate the study?

    b. Could another design have been used? If so, what design?

    c. How convincing were the findings? Do you think replication should be attempted?

    d. Were alternative explanations adequately discussed?

    e. What are the implications for social work practice?

3. Using the scenario below, construct a graph or graphs to use with a single system design to monitor the couple's progress. Mr. and Mrs. Jones have been having terrible arguments. Mrs. Jones, a college graduate, has quite a bit more education than her husband, (a high school graduate). He has been spending

time away from home, and often finds excuses to work late and on weekends. They are not having meaningful discussions. Generally, the arguments start when Mr. Jones finds fault with something that Mrs. Jones has either done or not done. Sometimes she doesn't get up when the alarm clock rings, and he must fix breakfast for their kids. She does not like to do housework, and clutter greatly bothers Mr. Jones.

On the other hand, Mr. Jones does not often sit down and listen when his wife is talking. Mr. Jones is very conscious of time and most often will be doing something else while she is talking. She complains that he doesn't spend enough time with the family, but Mr. Jones feels that it is more stressful than enjoyable when they do something together. When she complains about this, Mr. Jones finds some problem with her housekeeping. The zip seems to have gone out of this marriage, and the number of arguments each week is escalating. With your single system design, be sure to address:

a. the target behavior(s)
b. the design
c. the baseline

Briefly summarize the intervention and the client's progress after eight weeks.

4. Using the scenario below (modified from Taber, 1981), construct a graph or graphs for monitoring the client's progress. Steve, an eleven-year-old boy living in a residential treatment center, was referred there because of his outbursts of temper, which involved fighting, hitting, and swearing. Steve verbally abused or hit his peers in response to slight provocations. When child-care workers tried to direct his activities, Steve would become enraged, grabbing and hitting workers with intensity. Steve showed no sign of thinking before he acted. These problems persisted during his first year in residence, despite the efforts of child-care workers to modify his anger through "life-space interviews," use of time-outs, and a token economy system. Steve was anxious to go to a foster home. Since this was contingent upon control of his anger, he was eager to work on the problem.

With your single system design, be sure to address:

a. the target behavior(s)
b. the design
c. the baseline

Briefly summarize the intervention and the client's progress after eight weeks.

RESOURCES AND REFERENCES

Behling, J.H. and Merves, E.S. (1984). *The Practice of Clinical Research: The Single Case Method.* New York: University Press of America.

Berlin, S.B. (1983). Single-case evaluation: Another version. *Social Work Research and Abstracts,* 19, 3–11.

Bloom, M. and Fischer, J. (1982). *Evaluating Practice: Guidelines for the Accountable Professional.* Englewood Cliffs, NJ: Prentice-Hall.

Blythe, B.J. and Briar, S. (1985). Developing empirically based models of practice. *Social Work,* 30, 483–488.

Bromley, D.B. (1986). *The Case-Study Method in Psychology and Related Disciplines.* New York: Wiley.

Bronson, D.E. and Blythe, B.J. (1987). Computer support for single-case evaluation of practice. *Social Work Research and Abstracts,* 23 (3), 10–13.

Campbell, J.A. (1988). Client acceptance of single-system evaluation procedures. *Social Work Research and Abstracts,* 24 (2), 21–22.

Dean, R.G. and Reinherz, H. (1986). Psychodynamic practice and single system design: The odd couple. *Journal of Social Work Education,* 22, 71–81.

Dukes, W.F. (1965). N + 1. *Psychological Bulletin,* 64(1), 74–79.

Gambril, E. and Barth,R. (1979). Single-case study designs revised. *Social Work Research and Abstracts,* 16 (3), 15–20.

Gingerich, W.J. (1978). Procedure for evaluating clinical practice. *Health and Social Work,* 4, 104–130.

Gingerich, W.J. (1984). Generalizing single-case evaluation from classroom to practice. *Journal of Education for Social Work,* 20, 74–82.

Gingerich, W.J. (1984). Meta-Analysis of applied time series data. *Journal of Applied Behavioral Science,* 20, 71–79.

Hepworth, D.H. and Larsen, J.A. (1986). *Direct Social Work Practice: Theory and Skills.* Chicago, IL: Dorsey.

Hersen, M. and Barlow, D. (1976). *Single Case Experimental Designs.* Elmsford, NY: Pergamon Press.

Howe, M.W. (1974). Casework self-evaluation: A single-subject approach. *Social Service Review,* 48,1–24.

Hudson, W.W. (1982). *The Clinical Measurement Package: A Field Manual.* Homewood, IL: Dorsey.

Jayaratne, S. (1978). Analytic procedures for single-subject designs. *Social Work Research & Abstracts,* 14 (3), 30–40.

Jayaratne, S. (1977). Single-subject and groups designs in treatment evaluation. *Social Work Research & Abstracts,* 13 (3), 35–42.

Jayaratne, S. and Levy, R. (1979). *Empirical Clinical Practice.* New York: Columbia University Press.

Kazdin, A.E. (1982). *Single-Case Research Designs: Methods for Clinical and Applied Settings.* New York: Oxford University Press.

Levy, R. and Olson, D. (1979). The single-subject methodology in clinical practice: An overview, *Journal of Social Service Research,* 3, 25–49.

Montagu, A. (1971). *The Elephant Man: A Study in Human Dignity.* New York: Dutton.

Nelson, J.C. (1978). Use of communication theory in single-subject research. *Social Work Research and Abstracts,* 14 (4), 12–19.

Nelsen, J. (1981). Issues in single-subject research for nonbehaviorists. *Social Work Research and Abstracts,* 17, 31–37.

Nelsen, J. (1984). Intermediate treatment goals as variables in single-case research. *Social Work Research and Abstracts,* 20, 3–10.

Nelsen, J. (1988). Single-subject research. In Richard M. Grinnell (Ed.), *Social Work Research and Evaluation.* Itasca, IL: Peacock.

Nelsen, J. (1985). Verifying the independent variable in single-subject research. *Social Work Research and Abstracts.* 21 (2) 3–8.

Nuehring, E.M. and Pascone, A.B. (1986). Single-subject evaluation: A tool for quality assurance. *Social Work,* 31 (5), 359–365.

Nurius, P.S. and Hudson. W.W. (1988). Computer-based practice: Future dream or current technology? *Social Work,* 33 (4) 357–362.

Pinkston, E.M., Howe, M.W., and Blackman, D.K. (1987). Medical social work management of urinary incontinence in the elderly: A behavioral approach. *Journal of Social Service Research,* 10, 179–183.

Reid, W.J. (1987). Research in social work. In Ann Minahan (Ed.), *Social Work Encyclopedia.* 18th ed. Silver Spring, MD: National Association of Social Workers, p. 482.

Robinson, E.A.R., Bronson, D.E., and Blythe, B.J. (1988). An analysis of the implementation of single case evaluation by practitioners, *Social Service Review,* 62, 287–301.

Ruckdeschel, R., and Farris, B. (1981). Assessing practice: A critical look at the single-case design. *Social Casework: The Journal of Contemporary Social Work,* 62, 413–419.

Sundel, M. and Sundel, S.S. (1975). *Behavior Modification in the Human Services: A Systematic Introduction to Concepts and Applications* New York: Wiley.

Taber, S.M. (1981). Cognitive-behavior modification treatment of an aggressive eleven-year-old boy. *Social Work Research & Abstracts,* 17 (2), 13–23.

Thomas, E. (1978). Research and service in single-case experimentation: Conflicts and choices. *Social Work Research and Abstracts,* 14 (4), 20–31.

Welch, G. (1983). Will graduates use single-subject designs to evaluate their casework practice? *Journal of Education for Social Work,* 19, 42–47.

Witkin, W. and Harrison, D. (1979). Single-case designs in marital research. *Journal of Social Service Research,* 3, 51–66.

Yin, R.K. (1984). *Case study research.* Beverly Hills, CA: Sage.

Zimbalist, S.E. (1983). The single-case clinical research design in developmental perspective: Mainstream or tangent. *Journal of Education for Social Work,* 19, 61–66.

Five

Research Designs
for Group Comparisons

Some years ago an educator described a series of events he had undoubtedly observed firsthand, events you may also have observed. He characterized the events by what he called the "law of the hammer": if you give a young child a hammer, the child will find many things that "need" hammering. Few of us would want to hire a carpenter who has only a hammer in his toolchest. While it is important to know what and when to hammer, it is also essential to have the various tools that different jobs require as well as knowledge of how to use them.

Single system designs may not always be the right "tool" for every research occasion. They provide only one tool to use in a very complex world of clients and their problems and agencies and their programs. There are times when we need to aggregate our data in order to understand phenomena or to conduct an evaluation at a group, program, or community level. When we move beyond a single client focus, we use research designs that allow us to make comparisons with groups or clusters of individuals.

Hudson (1978) suggests that the teaching of single system designs should be targeted to those students who wish to have careers in counseling or direct-service delivery (microsystems), but that those wanting to work with macrosystems (administration, social policy, planning, and community organization) ought to know the traditional research methodologies. He states that these methodologies (the experimental and quasi-experimental designs, field studies, and social surveys) are more useful for dealing with the types of problems experienced when one works with institutions, systems, agencies, communities, and advocacy groups. Macrosystem practitioners, he argues, need to know methodologies that use group comparisons and data aggregation.

While all of this may be sobering news for those interested in

79

macrosystems, microsystem practitioners are not off scott-free. Many who never considered the possibility of doing anything but direct practice while they were in school often are promoted to management positions and find themselves having to evaluate their staff, to determine whether one treatment modality is better than another, to decide whether one group of clients averages a longer length of stay than others, or to conduct surveys of clients or of the community. Some phenomena are best studied not on the individual level, but with group data. Evidence to support the notion that social workers need to know more than single subject designs comes from a study by three social workers (Gentry, Connaway and Morelock, 1984) who mailed questionnaires to members of the National Association of Social Workers asking about their involvement with research. They found that 91 percent engaged in at least one research activity. Eighty-five percent had given a formal presentation; 81 percent had planned a new program; 73 percent had evaluated an agency program; 66 percent had conducted a needs assessment; 58 percent had prepared a paper; 49 percent had systematically compared a group of cases; 36 percent had written a grant proposal; 35 percent had conducted a research project; 31 percent had developed a research proposal; 28 percent had submitted a manuscript for publication; and 19 percent had had an article published.

You may find it somewhat comforting to learn that students in sociology, psychology, education, and the allied health disciplines learn the same designs when they study research methodology.

Choosing the Right Design

Numerous research designs can be used to guide research projects. Choosing the right design is somewhat analogous to picking out a new car. The primary consideration when deciding on a car is how much money you have or how big a monthly payment you can manage. The researcher must also consider how much has been budgeted for the research. Design issues related to finances are: use of staff time (e.g., making follow-up contacts with clients in person or by phone); postage, telephone, or travel expenses; purchase of copyrighted instruments or scales; computer processing of the data; use of consultants; and so on. These and other variables contribute to the cost of the project.

While the car buyer considers whether the car's optional equipment is really necessary, the researcher decides which facets of the study are essential. Some procedures or features of the proposed study, the researcher may believe, are definitely needed. The investigator may have firm ideas about how the "success" of the intervention should be determined. This could require expensive personal interviews or involve less costly examination of existing data.

Having made decisions to this point, the car buyer usually begins to choose among models. Some models may strike the buyer as more prestigious than others, or as enhancing his or her reputation. Some cars are chosen because they provide the basics without any frills. Similarly, some research designs are more respected than others; these are the classic experimental research designs. However, because social workers almost always view experimentation with clients with great suspicion, no-frill designs (pre-experimental or quasi-experimental designs) with less rigorous requirements may have greater appeal or relevance.

In summary, various motives or considerations have a bearing on the choice of a research design. No one design will be applicable or correct in every situation. The design is dependent upon the nature of the problem being investigated, the availability of clients or other data, monetary and staff resources, the amount of time one has to complete the project, and the purpose of the research (is it for internal agency use or do you need to convince skeptical colleagues outside of the agency?).

Research strategies are most often developed from the specific objectives of the study and the nature of the presenting problem. Social work researchers generally move from interest in a problem to the selection of a design. Seldom would one choose a design and then look for a problem to investigate.

Experimental Research

The classic experimental design is valued as the model to which other research designs are compared (Nachmias and Nachmias, 1981). Even though the opportunities to conduct true experiments may not often come your way, the experimental design remains the standard or "ideal." Other designs in this chapter are discussed in terms of how close they come to the "ideal."

For many social workers, the notion of experimentation involving human subjects brings to mind misconceptions about unethical, painful, or presumably painful stimuli (e.g., the controversial Milgram experiments) being inflicted upon unsuspecting persons in a climate-controlled laboratory. These notions are best forgotten. Today there is much greater concern for and widespread protection of the rights of persons participating in research than there was twenty-five to thirty years ago. For instance, the federal government requires institutional review boards to oversee research being funded with federal money and involving human subjects. (See chapter 12 for a discussion of ethical guidelines for researchers.) Further, these old stereotypes do not facilitate our thinking about how experimental designs can be of benefit to us in our practice.

It will be helpful at this point to briefly discuss several examples of experimental research to broaden our understanding of the practical benefits of experimentation. Since the concept of the medical community testing the effects of medication on persons with certain illnesses is probably familiar to you, let's start with an example from a medical experiment.

With the rapid adoption of aspartame (NutraSweet) by food processing companies as a substitute for sugar came a number of complaints of headaches, which supposedly were caused by the sweetener. The Duke University Medical Center enrolled forty people with these complaints in a carefully controlled study. Subjects were given identical capsules that contained either aspartame or inert cellulose (a placebo). Two days later, those who received the aspartame were given the placebo and vice versa. A double-blind procedure was used so that neither the researchers nor the subjects knew who got the placebo. Subjects were monitored for the onset of headaches during the course of the study. The investigators found that fourteen of the subjects who got the aspartame did get headaches; however, eighteen subjects reported headaches when they got the placebo (which would not have caused the headaches). The experiment showed that it was not the aspartame that caused the headaches (Schiffman, Buckley, Sampson, Massey, Baraniuk, Follett, and Warwick, 1987).

In the field of social work, experiments have made valuable contributions to practice and have affected the way services are delivered to clients. Cox, Brogan, and Dandridge (1986) reported on a study that attempted to find the best way to reduce payment errors to recipients of Aid to Families with Dependent Children. Clients were randomly assigned to one of three groups. One group was never visited by a caseworker; those in the second group were visited only during the application process; and those in the third group were visited at both intake and in the fourth month of program participation. The authors found that there were no statistically significant differences in error rates or payment amounts among the three groups.

In another study using an experimental design, Goodstadt and Sheppard (1983) report on the effectiveness of three different approaches in an alcohol education program for school-age children. Students were randomly assigned to one of four groups. The group approaches used for alcohol education were: cognitive, decision making, and values clarification. The fourth group, a control group, received no intervention. The researchers found that a cognitive program was more positively received than the decision-making or values-clarification approaches and did the best job of raising levels of knowledge.

Some social policies have been shaped by the outcomes of social experiments. Hausman and Wise (1985) estimate that the government spent over $500 million on social experiments during the 1970s. These experiments ranged from Experimental Housing Allowance Program (EHAP) to negative income tax experiments and prevention of coronary heart disease.

One of the longest and most sophisticated social experiments ever carried out in the United States, the New Jersey Graduated Work Incentive Experiment, ran from 1968 to 1972 and cost $8 million. This experiment was set up to determine if a negative income tax (cash paid to those below the poverty line to bring them up to a guaranteed income level) would reduce the incentive to work. As families' incomes rose from outside earnings, the negative tax would be reduced, but always less than the earnings, so that there was an incentive for a family to improve its financial situation. The experiment found that the negative tax did not reduce the participants' propensity to work. In fact, black families in particular worked harder and earned more as a result of the guaranteed income. There were no significant effects on health, fertility, marital dissolution, or school attendance (Bulmer, 1986).

The Classic Experimental Research Design

Experimental designs are the most rigorous of research designs and the ones that best permit casual inferences to be made. These designs have two main features that distinguish them from other designs: clients (or subjects) who participate in the experiment are randomly selected (defined as the absence of bias; allowing chance to play the role of selecting clients) and assigned to either the group that gets the intervention (the *experimental group*) or the group that gets no intervention (the *control group*).

The shorthand notation for the classic **Pretest-Posttest Control Group Design** is often written as follows:

$$R \quad O_1 \quad X \quad O_2$$
$$R \quad O_3 \qquad \quad O_4$$

The **R** in this notation scheme stands for the random assignment of clients to either the experimental or the control group; the **X** represents the intervention. Observations, measurements, or assessments of each group are made twice. The first observation (O_1) is called the **pretest,** and the second observation (O_2) is called the **posttest.** This design provides information not only about changes in the group that receives the intervention, but also comparable information from the group that does not get intervention.

This is a strong design because the group that receives no intervention provides a "control" for possible alternative explanations for the effect on the experimental group. Random selection of subjects makes the groups equivalent before the intervention begins. For instance, if clients tend to make better decisions because they grow wiser with the passage of time (maturation) and not because of the intervention, then the control group would also show similar improvement or outcome. There would be little reason to believe that the intervention was responsible for any changes if the same changes were also found in the control group.

As an example of this design, suppose you are a medical social worker assigned to a dialysis clinic. Let's further assume that the management of anxiety is a major problem for patients in the clinic. You decide to start a support group for anxious patients because you believe it will help to alleviate some of their health concerns. Because you are limited in the amount of time you can allocate for this project, you want to start small with about twenty-five patients. Since this is a large dialysis clinic with hundreds of patients, there is no problem in finding willing participants. In keeping with the experimental Pretest-Posttest Control Group Design, you randomly select twenty-five dialysis patients for the support group and randomly assign an approximate number to the control group. Next, you use a standardized measure to determine the anxiety level of both groups prior to the start of the intervention. The support group begins and runs its normal course (six to eight weeks). Afterwards, you administer the instrument a second time to both groups and make comparisons. Has the average level of anxiety in the experimental group decreased? Has the average amount of anxiety in the control group remained about the same or increased? Finally, is the level of anxiety in the experimental group less than in the control group? If so, then you have some evidence that the intervention was effective.

Posttest Only Control Group Design

A second experimental design, the **Posttest Only Control Group Design** is handy for those situations where a pretest might affect the posttest results or when it is not possible to conduct a pretest. This design is also useful in situations where anonymity is paramount—where it would not be possible to compare an individual's pretest and posttest scores.

Campbell and Stanley (1963) note that there is a common misconception that pretests are always needed in an experimental design. Not so, they say. Early experimental designs in agriculture did not make much use of pretests. As with the previous design, random selection and assignment of subjects establish the initial equivalence between the experimental and control groups. Measurement of the control group (O_2) then serves as a pretest measure for comparison with the experimental group's posttest (O_1).

$$R \quad X \quad O_1$$
$$R \qquad O_2$$

As an example of this design, consider the following problem. Counseling agencies often find that 30 percent or more of scheduled appointments result in "no-shows" or last minute cancellations. Productive or "billable" time is lost, which can seriously affect the revenue needed to operate an agency. Suppose you have a hypothesis that the 30 percent no-show rate could be reduced by the agency's receptionist calling clients to remind them of their scheduled appointments. The group receiving the phone calls would constitute the experimental group. Those clients who do not receive a reminder constitute the control group. Membership in either the experimental or control group would be randomly determined. (For instance, even-numbered clients scheduled for an appointment during the first week of March would be assigned to the experimental group and would get a reminder. Odd-numbered clients would be assigned to the control group.) At the end of the study period, the cancellation rates for the two groups could be compared.

The Solomon Four-Group Design

The third experimental design is called the **Solomon Four-Group Design.** As you can see from the notation below, it is composed of the basic experimental design plus the Posttest Only Control Group Design. This is an elaborate, sophisticated design that social workers may not often have the opportunity to utilize.

This design provides two opportunities for the treatment effect to be demonstrated. The design's strong point, however, is that the investigator can maximally control for alternative explanations and thus increase the confidence that can be placed in the findings. While this is a rigorous design and provides greater confidence that the intervention produced any observed changes, the tradeoff for this certainty is greater difficulty in coordinating and implementing the design.

$$R \quad O_1 \quad X \quad O_2$$
$$R \quad O_3 \quad \quad O_4$$
$$R \quad \quad X \quad O_5$$
$$R \quad \quad \quad O_6$$

Internal and External Validity

To keep the explanation of the single system design in chapter 4 uncomplicated, I used the terms alternative explanations and competing explanations to refer to those unplanned or unexpected variables that might have had an effect upon the observed outcome. However, now we will examine the internal and external validity of studies to more fully understand the strengths and weaknesses of the various research designs for group comparisons. The following section is presented to help you think about the variables that can influence your study and make it difficult to determine if your intervention was effective. As you learn more about research, you will develop an appreciation for factors (not limited to those below) that can interfere with your study. Keep in mind that this discussion of internal and external validity is equally applicable to the single system designs.

Campbell and Stanley (1963) and Cook and Campbell (1979) are prominent in social science research because of their conceptualization of research designs. Their books are classic texts on the topic, and few research methodology texts have not cited their work. Besides identifying a host of experimental, quasi-experimental, and pre-experimental research designs (more about these a little later), these authors contributed to our understanding of internal and external validity.

Threats to the **internal validity** of a study (that is, whether the intervention was truly responsible for the observed differences in the experimental group) come from extraneous variables (those not purposely incorporated into the experiment).

1. **Maturation:** Growing older or different rates of growth within two comparison groups are examples of an influence that researchers should be cognizant of and attempt to control as much as possible. A client's criminal activities may cease not because of intervention from a concerned therapist, but because the client has grown too old to hustle or no longer has the same athletic quickness needed to avoid capture.

2. **History:** This refers to the specific events that occur between the pretest and posttest that were not part of the researcher's design and that could influence the results (e.g., national crises, tragedies, or historical events, or, on a local level, a large factory laying off hundreds of employees—including some of those in your study).

3. **Testing:** Taking a test on more than one occasion can affect later test scores. Repeated testing provides practice and is in itself a unique experience that may influence subsequent scores (e.g., the subject gets bored with the test and does not pay as much attention to the test the second time, or the subject's score improves not because of an intervention, but due to the results of practice on the test).

4. **Instrumentation:** This refers to changes in the use of the measuring instrument, in the way the instrument is scored, or in the way observers are scoring the behavior (e.g., as a result of a lot of observation, the observers modify or give fewer extreme scores than they did initially).

5. **Selection of respondents:** This threat to internal validity stems from any bias that causes the control and experimental groups to be different because of the way they were selected (e.g., your experimental subjects volunteer to participate, while an incentive was used to attract the control group).

6. **Statistical regression:** This refers to the selection of subjects who were chosen because of extreme scores. There is a tendency for extreme scores to move toward the group average on a second testing.

7. **Mortality:** Also known as attrition, this threat to internal validity refers to the loss of respondents (e.g., they terminate services, move out of town, get sick, or simply just drop out of the study). The loss of subjects may change the overall group complexion (especially if a large number of clients are involved or if they have extreme scores) and may produce differences in the

data at the posttest that have nothing to do with the intervention.

8. **Interaction effects:** This occurs when any of the extraneous variables interact with one another. In a selection and maturation interaction, the subjects in one group may mature at a faster rate than those in the comparison group. The example Powers, Meenaghan, and Toomey (1985) use of a maturation and mortality interaction is clients who improve from maturation and then drop out of the control group. In such situations, the researcher would have difficulty in understanding the true effect of the intervention.

The use of any experimental design will help you gauge the extent of any of these threats to the internal validity of your study. It is the use of randomization and a control group that allows the investigator to determine if any extraneous variable has exerted an unexpected influence. For instance, if you notice an unexpected improvement in the control group, you might suspect that an extraneous variable (such as history, maturation, or testing) had an effect upon the study. You might want to correct for that influence by subtracting the gains made by the control group from those of the experimental group when computing the benefits of intervention.

When you have considered these eight threats and ruled them out as having produced an effect, then you have established that your study has internal validity. You can now conclude with some confidence that the intervention was responsible for (caused) the observed changes. Then, if you want to insure that the findings from your study can be generalized to different subjects or settings, you should consider the threats to the external validity of the study.

Campbell and Stanley (1963) must also be given credit for identifying several ways in which the **external validity** (the generalizability or representativeness of the study) can be threatened.

1. *Reactive or interactive effect of testing:* This occurs when a pretest affects the respondent's sensitivity or awareness to important variables associated with the study. The pretest could make the subjects unrepresentative of the population from which they were drawn by raising their consciousness or by stimulating new learning, or simply because they realize that they are involved in a study. This threat should seem familiar to you because it is the same as the internal validity threat of testing.

2. *Interaction effects of selection biases and any research stimulus.* These occur when there are problems getting a random sample. If you are conducting a study that required in-depth interviews of two or three hours in duration, the majority of persons you contact might turn you down and not participate. Those who agree to the interview may not be representative of the larger population—they have volunteered when most others have not. They may have some traits or characteristics (e.g., they are lonely) that make them less representative and therefore affect the generalizability of the study.

3. *Reactive effects of arrangements:* This has to do with the experiment being conducted in a setting that is different from the subject's usual experience. Subjects' behavior may change because of the different environment. Subjects may be more productive or more wary and nervous. They may behave in a way not indicative of their normal style. Would your behavior change if you knew that you were being video-taped or observed through a two-way mirror?)

4. *Multiple-treatment interaction:* This becomes a problem when there is more than one intervention. The researcher needs to be sure that the same timing, sequence, or order is followed for each subject. Multiple treatments may have a cumulative effect, which could make reaching conclusions about a specific intervention difficult.

In those situations where you are evaluating a local or specific program, it might *not* be important to you to demonstrate external validity. In this instance, you are concerned only with whether treatment worked in a specific program—you may not be interested in generalizing your results to other communities or subjects because your program is not like any others.

On the other hand, if you are concerned with generalization, you may want to consider threats to your study that this brief overview has not covered. Grinnell and Stothers (1988) cite six threats to external validity, Kazdin (1982) discusses nine, and Cook and Campbell (1979) cite thirteen.

In summary, there are always distinct threats to a study's internal and external validity. Think of the threats to the internal validity as the alternative explanations that can be offered to explain why it wasn't the intervention that produced the observed changes. Experimental research designs use random selection and assignment of subjects to comparison groups to help the researcher monitor and understand the threats to internal validity. As a rule, the more control you have over the situation or experiment, the greater the internal validity. However, there is a corresponding cost in terms of external validity.

With more control comes the problem of making the experimental setting or situation unlike those familiar to the subjects. Even the best research project has some weaknesses, and the researcher must realize that every study has its limitations. While generalizability may be more limited than you had initially hoped, your study may still reveal that an innovative procedure worked with your clients!

Pre-Experimental Designs

Suppose you are a counselor in an agency and are working with a group of shy individuals. You have developed an approach that, over the course of ten meetings, significantly alleviates shyness. You administer a shyness inventory to the group on its first meeting, and the average score for the group is 135. From the scores and your clinical impressions, you know that this group is extremely shy. Your group meets ten times, and you administer a posttest on the last session. You find that the group's average score has gone down to 62, which indicates major improvement.

This type of design does not have the complexity of an experiment. Since subjects are not randomly selected or assigned to either a treatment or a control group, this design is popular and often used in evaluations of social service programs. This design (which is similar to the **AB** design) is called the **One-Group Pretest-Posttest Design** and can be designated with the notation:

$$O_1 \quad X \quad O_2$$

Here, again, the (O_1) represents the pretest measurement or observation and the (O_2) the posttest.

Even though you, as a clinician, have seen major improvement in the individuals of the group, this design cannot rule out alternative explanations for the changes. It cannot rule out the internal validity threats of history, maturation, testing, instrumentation, or the interaction of selection and maturation. Any of these extraneous variables may have produced the changes in the shyness inventory. Without a control group, it is impossible to say that these threats did not have an effect. The researcher, however, may be able to rule out some of these threats because of the particular situation or context within which the study occurred. Although this is a weak design, it serves a purpose when no control group is available for comparison.

If there were no pretest data associated with the earlier study of shy individuals, the resulting design would be the **One-Group Posttest Only Design.**

$$X \quad O_1$$

With this design, an intervention is delivered, and later, observations are recorded in order to determine the intervention's outcome. This design stipulates only that you take a reading or observation after the intervention. If you were working with the group of shy individuals described above, this design would require only a posttest after the intervention. Since there would have been no pretest for comparison, the average posttest score of 62 does not provide much information. With no data available for comparison, any perceptions of a reduction in shyness are unsubstantiated. Instead of the intervention having an effect on shyness, extraneous variables such as selection, history, maturation, or mortality may have contributed to any perceived effect after treatment.

With the One-Group Posttest Only Design there is the presumption of an effect. Sometimes, however, you can see an effect more clearly—especially if you are conducting a study of a problem that is behavioral (e.g., you have a group of clients who are trying to quit drinking). If the group reported after ten weeks that they weren't drinking, you would be pleased and willing to take the credit. Indeed, your colleagues probably would have no difficulty attributing the cessation of drinking to the intervention. However, the "success" might have been due to spouses or mates threatening to leave if loved ones didn't stop drinking, from bosses threatening to fire inebriated clients, court appearances for driving while intoxicated, or a combination of several factors. Again, without a control group, it is difficult to know the extent to which extraneous factors are influencing the outcome.

A third pre-experimental design is called the **Posttest-Only Design with Nonequivalent Groups.** It is expressed:

$$X \quad O_1$$
$$O_2$$

This design is an improvement over the previous two in that the control group functions as a pretest condition and can be compared with the group that receives the intervention. While it may seem logical to infer that any observed differences are due to the intervention, this is debatable, since we cannot assume that the two groups were similar prior to the intervention (there was no random assignment to the groups). As a consequence, differences between O_1 and O_2 may be due to their nonequivalence in the beginning and not to the effect of intervention.

By way of example, think of the population of women who have been battered by husbands or boyfriends. Assume we want to know if service programs connected with a shelter for battered women are instrumental in helping these women to avoid returning to abusive situations. Of the battered women who contact the shelter, some request shelter services, while others request information about child custody, jobs, police protection, etc.) and attempt to leave abusive situations on their own without spending time in the shelter. There are, then, two groups of women with the same basic problem. One group gets the intervention (the shelter), while the other group does not. For the purpose of follow-up research to determine how many women were living in abusive situations one year from their contact with the shelter, would these two groups be equivalent? I think not. They may differ in the amount of financial resources at their disposal (those who don't stay at the shelter may have more money), in the extent of family or social support systems, and possibly with regard to the severity of the abuse experienced.

These two groups of women may seem to be convenient groupings in terms of trying to determine the impact of a battered women's shelter. If it were later found that a greater proportion of the women who used the shelter's services than women who didn't were still in abusive situations, what does this say about the shelter's services? It would be risky to conclude that the shelter was in someway responsible for its clients returning to abusive situations. While it may appear that women who avoid the shelter are more successful in not returning to abusive situations, we must keep in mind that the two groups of women may not have been equivalent even though they shared a common problem. If we were to select these two groups for our study, we might expect differences in the two groups even before our data are aggregated. Of course, the more similar (or homogeneous) the two groups are, the more comfortable everyone will be that the intervention did have an effect. The absence of randomization makes this design weak; we are unable to rule out such internal validity threats as those of selection, mortality, and interaction among variables (such as selection and maturation).

Kidder and Judd (1986) say that these three pre-experimental designs are examples of how *not* to do research if there are alternatives.

Fortunately, alternatives exist—they are called quasi-experimental designs.

Quasi-Experimental Designs

Quasi-experimental designs are those which fall a little short of the "ideal." Often in agency settings, it would not be acceptable or possible to randomly assign clients to one of several treatment modalities (or to a control group receiving no intervention). When randomization cannot be done, the researcher should consider quasi-experimental designs.

The **Nonequivalent Control Group Design** has been called the "archetypal quasi-experimental design" because it is the most internally valid design that can be implemented in most applied settings (Judd and Kenny, 1981). It is also one of the most commonly used quasi-experimental designs.

The notation for Nonequivalent Control Group Design is:

$$O_1 \quad X \quad O_2$$
$$O_3 \qquad O_4$$

In this design, a control group is used, just as with the experimental design. However, there is no randomization. Usually a convenient natural group (e.g., another class of fifth graders, another AA group, another group of shy clients) is selected that is similar but may not be equivalent to the group receiving the intervention. Just as with the previous design, the control group consists of clients who have the same characteristics. The control group can come from those clients on a waiting list for service, clients receiving alternative services from the same agency or from another similar agency, or even from nonclients.

Researchers often attempt to match the two groups on important variables (e.g., age, socio-economic status, drinking experience). As you can imagine, matching is difficult because of the number of variables that could be involved. A major problem with matching is that observed differences between the control and intervention groups at the end of the experiment may have been due to the influence of unmatched variables. When you must match, the best advice is to match the groups on as many of the relevant variables as possible. Equivalence is not guaranteed with matching, but it does serve to approximate equivalency. When random assignment is not possible, matching is a good alternative.

With this design, it is usually plausible to assume that the treatment produced the effect. Like the experiment, this design does provide the investigator with the ability to monitor internal validity threats such as those from testing, maturation, instrumentation, history, and mortality. The main threat to this design's internal validity comes from interaction of selection with maturation, with history, or with testing, since random assignment wasn't used (so there was no guarantee of equivalency). Still, this design is better than the pre-experimental designs because of the use of a control group. The more similar the control and the experimental groups, the more confidence you can have in your findings.

As an example of this design, consider the problem of relapse among the chronically mentally ill. You want to know whether those patients who are served by your state-run hospital stay as long in the community as those in a similar institution in a different part of the state. With the cooperation of both hospital administrators, you make comparisons of such variables as staff-to-patient ratios, percentage of first-time admissions, and average age of patients in order to establish that the patients and the facilities are roughly equivalent.

Suppose you find out that the patients from your hospital do seem to have longer stays in the community than patients of the other hospital. You might conclude that the programming or staff at your hospital is better. However, this design cannot unequivocally demonstrate this. It could be that more of the clients in the other hospital return to rural areas, where there is not the same level of community support services (aftercare) as are available to the patients from your hospital (who tend to remain in an urban area). There could be differences in staff morale at the two hospitals (which might affect the treatment received by patients) or in the ease of readmission or screening procedures. Could differences in the physical facilities be a factor? (What if one hospital had been built in 1824 and the other in 1984?) So, while you can be somewhat reassured that your hospital is more successful than another, the lack of control over potentially very important factors prevents you from *conclusively* determining that the intervention at one hospital is the main reason for the patients' longer stays in the community.

Another quasi-experimental design is called **Time-Series** or **Interrupted Time Series.** This design is one of the older designs used in the natural sciences, but it has not been utilized extensively in the social sciences. The Time-Series design is an extension of the One-Group Pretest Posttest design, where there are a series of measurements taken before and after an intervention. This allows the researcher to understand trends and patterns in the data before the intervention is applied and then provides for continued monitoring for major changes. Notation for a Time-Series design is:

$$O_1 \quad O_2 \quad O_3 \quad X \quad O_4 \quad O_5 \quad O_6$$

With this design, the researcher is able to get a grasp on incremental changes (if any) in the study group's behavior prior to the intervention and then to determine if the change after intervention is greater or not. Where possible, an equal number of measurements should be made before and after the intervention. Also, the period of time between the measurements should be comparable. Note that the period of time between intervals is determined by the researcher; it is not imposed from the design. The amount of time between O_1, O_2 and the other observations could be seven days, two weeks, or three months.

This type of design is probably best understood in terms of historical or archival data. For instance, you might monitor the number of suicides or homicides from handguns before and after passage of federal legislation that requires a seven day "cooling off" period before purchase of a handgun. Or, you might look at agency productivity before and after a new executive director revises scheduling procedures. As with any baseline, it is important to insure that a stable period is established. With the last example, such things as seasonal variations in agency productivity (e.g., lower productivity in the summer months and around the Christmas/New Year holidays) make it important to insure that you have enough observation periods to help you understand seasonal (or other) fluctuations.

When the data from time series are graphed (recall the **AB** designs in the last chapter), the slope of the line is often of assistance in understanding whether the observed effect was caused by the intervention. On a graph, you can readily determine if the magnitude or frequency of a behavior is increasing prior to and after an intervention. Because the measurements are obtained over an extended period of time, history is the chief threat to the internal validity of this design. A threat from instrumentation might also be apparent in some instances.

This Time-Series design provides even better information if a corresponding control group can be added:

$$O_1 \quad O_2 \quad O_3 \quad X \quad O_4 \quad O_5 \quad O_6$$
$$O_1 \quad O_2 \quad O_3 \qquad\quad O_4 \quad O_5 \quad O_6$$

This new design with a control group is called the **Multiple Time-Series Design.** It resembles a stretched out Nonequivalent Control Group Design. Campbell and Stanley (1963) recommend this design for research in school settings. It is a strong quasi-experimental design with no serious internal validity threats. The investigator can use the control group to check for the influence of history and to understand the effects of testing, maturation, mortality, and instrumentation.

For instance, prior to the passage of federal legislation to require a seven day "cooling off" period before purchase of a handgun, an investigator could examine the number of homicides in a sample of cities or states with such legislation and compare this data to a control group of cities or states that did not have such legislation. You would expect fewer homicides, over time, in the sample having the greater regulation of handgun sales. Use of a control group allows the investigator to determine whether a decrease in homicides is part of a national trend towards less violence or whether it could be attributed to the legislation.

Design and Validity Considerations

The main reason that researchers often choose experimental over pre-experimental or quasi-experimental designs is because they make causal inference easier (Cook and Campbell, 1979). As a social work practitioner, you may have a notion that a certain intervention employed by you or your agency is more effective with clients than others. To test this hypothesis, you would probably choose one of the designs described in this chapter. Sometimes, however, social workers have questions like, "Are parents of disabled children more likely to abuse their children than other parents?" Or, "Is alcoholism primarily responsible for the problem of homelessness?" Such basic research questions as these do not require experimental research designs. Rather, they are more likely to be explored using secondary data analysis (chapter 8) or a survey research design (chapter 6). The designs in this chapter are commonly used to determine the impact or effect of an intervention used with groups.

As previously discussed, pre-experimental and quasi-experimental designs are susceptible to problems of internal validity. Yet, useful information and valuable studies can come from designs that are not truly experimental. Quasi-experimental designs should not be quickly dismissed, particularly in those settings where randomization is not possible. In order to make your study as strong as possible, careful planning is required. Some threats to the internal validity of your study can be eliminated or minimized by following the suggestions of Mitchell and Jolley (1988):

1. Keep the time between the start and the end of the study short. This helps to minimize the threat of *history*. (Note that this suggestion does not apply to time-series designs.) Also, keeping the study period short can help minimize the threat of *maturation* (especially a problem when studying children and youth), as well as any interaction of maturation with selection.
2. Test subjects only once, use different versions of the same test, or give the subjects opportunity to extensively practice prior to collecting the pretest data so that any gains occurring at the posttest are not an effect of the second test. This helps to minimize the threat of *testing*.
3. Administer the instrument the same way, every time. (This helps to minimize the threat of *instrumentation*.)
4. Use innocuous or placebo treatments, brief treatments, or mild incentives so that subjects do not drop out of the study. Keep in touch with those participating in your study—especially with those in the control group when there is a long period in-between observations. (This helps to minimize the threat of *mortality*.)
5. Be careful with choosing subjects on the basis of one extreme test score. (This helps to minimize the threat of *statistical regression*.)
6. Randomly assign where possible. If you must match, match on as many key variables as is practical. (This helps to minimize the threat of *selection*.)

Thinking about ways of preventing extraneous variables from influencing (or explaining away) the effect of your intervention will result in a stronger study. While the selection of a good research design is important, it is no substitute for good planning. Even a strong design can be poorly implemented and go awry when little attention is paid to details. If, for instance, you lose most of your control group through neglect, even an experimental design will be of little assistance in helping you to infer that the intervention caused the observed changes in the treatment group.

Research designs are only guides to the research process. They structure a problem-solving process and provide an outline for how data will be collected. Choice of a particular design is a complex decision often hinging upon feasibility considerations. Should you be faced with having to use a group research design sometime in the future, remember that there are numerous other designs (and multiple variations of the designs in this chapter) available to you. Regardless of the design you choose, devote time to considering how extraneous variables may affect the internal and external validity of your study.

QUESTIONS FOR CLASS DISCUSSION

1. What are the different pretest-posttest comparisons that can be made with the Solomon Four-Group design?
2. Do you think it is possible to conduct research in the social sciences without a research design as discussed in chapter 4 or this chapter? Why or why not?
3. What kinds of experimental research do you think are needed or would you like to see conducted? Make a list of these.
4. Consider the threats to internal validity as presented in this chapter and discuss how they also may pose threats to single system designs.
5. Discuss how pragmatic considerations (the agency setting, its clientele) influence the choice of a research design. How do the possible implications or findings of the study affect the choice of a design?
6. Which two designs discussed in this chapter are identical except for the use of randomization?
7. How might the use of experimental designs in social service agencies involve ethical considerations?
8. Do you think practitioners who want to do research start with a specific research design that they want to use or start with an intervention they want to evaluate and then seek a research design that fits the situation?

MINI-PROJECTS FOR EXPERIENCING RESEARCH FIRSTHAND

1. Briefly describe a feasible experiment that could be conducted in a social service agency using one of the three experimental designs.
2. Think about some controversial social problem (e.g., homelessness, teen pregnancy, drug abuse) and describe a grand social experiment that might test a hypothesis or a notion you have about how to ameliorate the social problem. Specify a hypothesis, the research design, and threats to the internal validity of your study.

3. Identify some recent legislation and describe how a time-series quasi-experimental design could be used to study the effects of the legislation. Be sure to identify the type and source of the data that you would need for the study.
4. Imagine you are the new director of a small agency that is not well known in the community. You direct a staff member to coordinate a number of activities that worked in your former agency and that you think will increase contacts and referrals from the community in your new agency. How will you know if the public relations intervention made any difference? Specify a research design.
5. Read the reports of the Milgram (1963, 1965) experiments and write a brief report arguing why you think the experiments were or were not important and whether they were ethical.

RESOURCES AND REFERENCES

Bulmer, M. (1986). *Social Science and Social Policy*. London: Allen & Unwin.

Campbell, D.T. and Stanley, J.C. (1963). *Experimental and Quasi-Experimental Designs for Research*. Skokie, IL: Rand McNally.

Cook, T.D. & Campbell, D.T. (1979). *Quasi-Experimentation: Design and Analysis Issues for Field Settings*. Skokie, IL: Rand McNally.

Cox, G.H., Brogan, D.R., and Dandridge, M.A. (1986). The effectiveness of home visitation in reducing AFDC case payment errors. *Social Service Review*, 60 (4), 603–618.

Gentry, M.E., Connaway, R.S., and Morelock, M. (1984). Research activities of social workers in agencies. *Social Work Research and Abstracts*, 20 (4), 3–5.

Goodstadt, M.S. & Sheppard, M.A. (1983). Three approaches to alcohol education. *Journal of Studies on Alcohol*, 44 (2), 362–380.

Grinnell, R.M. and Stothers, M. (1988). Utilizing research designs. In Richard M. Grinnell (ed.), *Social Work Research and Evaluation*, Itasca, IL: Peacock.

Hausman, J.A. and Wise, D.A. (1985). *Social Experimentation*. Chicago, IL: University of Chicago Press.

Hudson, W.W. (1978). Research training in professional social work education. *Social Service Review*, 52 (March), 116–21.

Judd, C.M. and Kenny, D.A. (1981). *Estimating the Effects of Social Interventions*. Cambridge: University Press.

Kazdin, A.E. (1982). *Single-Case Research Designs: Methods for Clinical and Applied Settings*. New York: Oxford University Press.

Kidder, L.H. & Judd, C.M. (1986). *Research Methods in Social Relations*. New York: Holt, Rinehart and Winston.

Milgram, S. (1963). Behavioral study of obedience. *Journal of Abnormal and Social Psychology, 67*, 371–378.

Milgram, S. (1965). Some conditions of obedience and disobedience to authority. *Human Relations,* 18, 57–76.

Mitchell, M. and Jolley, J. (1988). *Research Design Explained.* New York: Holt, Rinehart and Winston.

Nachmias, D. & Nachmias, C. (1981). *Research Methods in the Social Sciences.* New York: St. Martin's Press.

Powers, G.T., Meenaghan, T.M. & Toomey, B.G. (1985). *Practice Focused Research.* Englewood Cliffs, NJ: Prentice-Hall.

Schiffman, S.S., Buckley, C.E., Sampson, H.A., Massey, E.W., Baraniuk, J.N., Follett, J.V., and Warwick, Z.S. (1987). Aspartame and susceptibility to headache. *New England Journal of Medicine,* 317 (19), 1181–1185.

Six

Survey Research

If the topic of experimental design was strange or alien to you, survey research should be familiar. Social work literature abounds with surveys. Surveys have been conducted to explore such varied problems as why battered wives return to their husbands (Aguirre, 1985), teen dating violence (O'Keeffe, Brockopp, and Chew, 1986), menopause (Berkun, 1986), and shoplifting (Ray, 1987). Our understanding of the human condition and of human diversity has been extended by such surveys as those exploring stress in black, low-income, single-parent families (Lindblad-Goldberg, Dukes, and Lasley, 1988), effectiveness of casework services with Chicanos (Gomez, Zurcher, Farris, and Becker, 1985), the marital and parental behavior of lesbian wives and mothers and gay husbands and fathers (Wyers, 1987), and coverage of women's issues in social work journals (Quam and Austin, 1984).

Practically every issue of *Social Work* contains at least one article that has used a survey methodology. To support this statement, I did a little survey of my own. I examined the first four 1988 issues of *Social Work* for articles containing surveys. Sure enough, each of the four issues carried at least three articles that used some form of survey methodology. The diversity of topics explored with surveys in these issues was just as broad as the above examples. Surveys were used to examine the effect of plant closings on older workers (Beckett, 1988), the medical and psychiatric needs of the homeless, the parent-child relations in children with sickle-cell anemia (Evans, Burlew and Oler, 1988), the psychosocial impact of AIDS on gay men (Stulberg and Smith, 1988), the social networks of the poor (Auslander and Litwin, 1988), the parenting or adopting decisions of pregnant adolescents (McLaughlin, Pearce, Manninen, Winges, 1988), and attitudes about performance standards for social workers (Harkness and Mulinski (1988).

Surveys may well be the most common research methodology used by social workers. If you think of all the times you have been asked to participate in a survey, or the numerous occasions where surveys or polls have been reported in the mass media, you know that most Americans are familiar with the survey approach to obtaining information. Moreover, their popularity seems to be increasing.

Surveys can be thought of as photographs or portraits of attitudes, beliefs, or behaviors at one point in time. Using a predetermined set of questions or issues, they reveal what a group of respondents is thinking, feeling, or doing at the time during which the survey is conducted. Social workers and social scientists use surveys, as do market researchers, who poll the public about consumer purchases, and professional pollsters, who predict the outcomes of elections, assess the popularity of an elected official, and discover the public's views on certain issues.

How important are surveys? In a report for the National Research Council, Adams, Smelser, and Treiman claim that the sample survey is "the single most important information gathering invention of the social sciences" (cited in Fienberg, Loftus, and Nanur, 1985). We see the truth in this statement as we think about the various ways in which surveys provide us with information about the world around us.

Social workers use surveys to identify community needs or the needs of special client groups (e.g., chronic schizophrenics or persons with dual diagnoses). Sometimes these surveys are called **needs assessments** and may include interviewing direct-service personnel and referral sources, as well as clients or their families. Even individuals randomly selected from the larger community may be interviewed. Social workers also use surveys conducted by others (e.g., the Bureau of the Census) to understand how the population is distributed and to help determine such things as areas within a city where there are concentrations of the elderly or the impoverished.

Surveys can be used for program evaluation activities. (See, for example, Vinokur-Kaplan, 1986.) Surveys are sometimes conducted to see how satisfied clients are with an agency's services. As an administrator, you might be interested in surveying client admission data to see if your agency is currently serving a greater percentage of minority or elderly clients than in a previous year. You might survey your staff to determine the extent of feelings of burnout, or you might have your staff evaluate you as an administrator or the agency as a whole. You might even survey the community to ask what perceptions they have of your agency.

Surveys are also conducted to gather data about special problems or concerns where little information is available. We conduct surveys to learn more about phenomena that are not well understood, for example to determine the extent of a condition in a group or target population so that appropriate intervention can be applied. Surveys are not limited to providing basic information for research; their uses are more varied than can be fully elaborated here. For instance, public opinion surveys have been used to try and change the venue of highly publicized criminal cases and to exclude persons from jury service because of their attitudes about the death penalty (Turner and Martin, 1984).

The multiple varieties and uses of surveys can be summarized by noting that they fall into three broad categories. Where there is little data, **exploratory surveys** provide beginning information so that more rigorous studies can be implemented. **Descriptive surveys** provide information on the characteristics of a given population. For example, a descriptive survey of juvenile status offenders might examine and describe them in terms of average age, parents' income, number of prior offenses, attendance in school, and so on. Neither exploratory nor descriptive surveys require hypotheses. In **explanatory surveys** the researcher collects data in an attempt to show that some stimulus (independent variable) caused or had an effect on something else (the dependent variable). However, surveys cannot establish causal connections between variables.

Because they can be creative in designing questions and can easily tailor existing questionnaires to specific settings or clientele, social workers tend to like surveys. If a committee or group is developing the questionnaire, everyone can participate either by suggesting items or by pointing out ways specific items might be misinterpreted or could be improved. Other reasons for the popularity of surveys are that they are quickly implemented and convenient to administer. Once the survey instrument has been chosen or designed and a sample identified, the survey can often be handled by a clerical person (for instance, with a mail survey), thus freeing the researcher to attend to other matters until a sufficient number of survey questionnaires have come in for analysis. Sometimes, the investigator can coordinate the collection of data from personal or telephone interviews. Each of these approaches has its own set of advantages and disadvantages.

The Mail Questionnaire

The advantages of the mail questionnaire have been well expressed by Dillman (1983):

> What could be easier and more efficient than conducting surveys through the mail? The researcher simply has to write the questionnaire and then prepare it for mailing. The otherwise time-consuming legwork of locating respondents is done by the U.S. Postal Service; respondents interview themselves at their own convenience. Interviewer salaries and travel costs, the major expenditures incurred in face-to-face interviews, are thereby eliminated making it feasible to survey thousands of people for the same cost as a few hundred interviews. Further, since postage rates do not increase with geographic dispersion, the data collection costs for national surveys may approximate those for city and county surveys. (P. 359)

The mail questionnaire also allows greater anonymity for the respondents when the topic of the study involves private or sensitive issues (e.g., illegal or sexual behavior).

A final advantage of the mail questionnaire is that it reduces errors that might occur from the process of interviewing. Not all interviewers are equally skilled, and some may have traits that annoy, offend, or cause those being interviewed to be less than honest.

On the other hand, there are a number of specific disadvantages to the mail questionnaire: first of all, unlike personal or telephone interviews, researchers experience some loss of control over the survey process once the questionnaire has been mailed. Although the questionnaire may be delivered to the proper address, there is no guarantee that the intended recipient will be the one who completes the questionnaire. An eleven-year-old child could respond for his or her mother or father even though the researcher intended the survey form to go to adults. A related problem is that the survey could be completed under less than optimal conditions (e.g., when the respondent is ill or intoxicated, or completes the questionnaire while the television is blaring or a party is going on in the living room).

Second, investigators cannot assume that all recipients of the survey will be literate or will be able to comprehend complex issues. While college student are accustomed to questionnaires and multiple choice response sets, individuals with lower levels of educational attainment may find structured response sets (e.g., Strongly Agree, Agree, Undecided, Disagree, Strongly Disagree) confusing or too confining for the responses they want to give.

Third, mail questionnaires tend to be highly structured and relatively short. These questionnaires may not provide the detail that could emerge from a face-to-face contact. In personal interview situations, the interviewer is able to ask for additional information (to probe) if the respondent says something exceptionally interesting or if the interviewer is not sure of the response or thinks the respondent did not understand the question.

Mail questionnaires have become a popular gimmick with some businesses (e.g., an official-looking survey form arrives asking information about how much you travel or take vacations, but its real purpose is selling real estate or vacation time-sharing plans). Consequently, some Americans see surveys as a form of soliciting or as junk mail. Even if a survey form arrives in an envelope carrying first-class postage, it can be seen as an invasion of privacy and thrown away. Individuals with good intentions can put the survey form aside until "later" with the result that questionnaires get lost, thrown out, or put in the parakeet's cage.

Another problem is that Americans are a highly mobile population and are constantly changing addresses, last names, and places of employment. Your survey will be seriously disadvantaged if your mailing list is inaccurate or out of date. The post office may not be able to deliver or to forward mail—especially if the intended respondent is trying to avoid creditors or legal authorities.

These factors directly affect the number of people who complete and return survey questionnaires. It is not uncommon for only 25 to 35 percent of those who were mailed a questionnaire to return it. (Alreck and Settle, 1985, say that the response rates for mail surveys are often only 5 to 10 percent, and response rates over 30 percent are rare.) Of course, if your addresses are recent and the topic is one that interests the respondents, response rates will improve, but will seldom reach response rates of telephone or face-to-face interviews. However, these rates apply only to those who receive one mailing. With a reminder postcard and the mailing of a second questionnaire to those who did not initially respond, these rates can be improved quite a bit—to 70 percent or more. This is discussed in the next section.

Getting the Most Out of Mail Questionnaires

Designing a mail questionnaire is not so simple as it may first appear. Extensive research exists on all aspects of the mail survey. It is known, for instance, that using first-class postage results in better response rates than using bulk mail. Similarly, personalized cover letters are thought to provide better response rates than "Dear friend" or comparable salutations.

Dillman (1983) has provided an overview of steps that contribute to what he calls the "Total Design Method." He suggests that the questionnaire be photo-reduced and designed as a booklet to make it more appealing and less imposing (preferable size is 6.5 inches by 8.25 inches). The first page is designed as a cover with an interesting title and illustration; the back page is left blank for additional comments. The booklet should be printed on white paper (preferably sixteen-pound weight) and arranged so that the most interesting questions appear first. The whole questionnaire should be designed so that lower-case letters are used for questions and upper-case letters for responses. Visual clues (arrows, indentations, and spacing) are used to their fullest advantage to help respondents answer in a straight vertical line rather than going back and forth across the page. (See figure 6.1.)

Considerable thought and research has also gone into the implementation of the survey procedures. Dillman (1983) suggests a one-page cover letter on letterhead stationery explaining that a socially useful study is being conducted and why each respondent is important. Individual names and addresses are typed on the cover letter and the envelope (which is then mailed first class). One week after the first mail-out, a reminder postcard is sent to all recipients. Three weeks after the first mail-out, a second cover letter, questionnaire, and return envelope are sent to all those who have not responded. Seven weeks after the first mail-out, another cover letter and ques-

Figure 6.1: An Example of a Well-Designed Questionnaire

Child Abuse Survey

1. How serious a problem is child abuse and neglect in our community?

   _____ VERY SERIOUS

   _____ SOMEWHAT SERIOUS

   _____ NOT VERY SERIOUS

   _____ NOT A PROBLEM AT ALL

2. Have you ever had reason to suspect that a child living in your neighborhood has been emotionally abused?

   _____ NO

   _____ YES

2a. Have you ever reported a case of suspected emotional abuse?

   _____ YES

   _____ NO

3. Compared to ten years ago, do you think there is now more, less, or about the same amount of child abuse?

   _____ MORE

   _____ LESS

   _____ ABOUT THE SAME

tionnaire are sent by certified mail to all those who have not responded.

The Total Design Method greatly improves the response rates ordinarily found with mail surveys. Dillman (1978) stated that the average response rate for forty-eight surveys using his procedures was 74 percent, with no survey receiving less than a 50 percent response. Response rates of 77, 79, and even 92 percent have been reported in social work literature in connection with the use of prepaid postcard surveys and a single follow-up letter (Weinbach, 1984). Another study reported that an overall response rate of 66 percent was obtained with a seven-page questionnaire when social workers used a lottery approach with incentives to reward respondents (Blythe, 1986).

Whether or not you use an approach like the one advocated by Dillman, the success of your mail survey will rest largely upon three considerations: (1) insuring that the mailing list is current and accurate; (2) keeping the questionnaire as short as possible (preferably one to two pages); and following up with another copy of the questionnaire to all nonresponders.

The Telephone Survey

The chief advantage of the telephone survey over the face-to-face interview is that it is less expensive (one avoids all expenses associated with traveling to the respondent). Telephone surveys can also be conveniently run from an office. Bulk user rates (WATS lines) help to reduce the costs of numerous calls. Telephone surveys allow the interviewer to have control over the choice of the respondent and give the interviewer the ability to probe when questions or responses are not understood. (However, Blankenship, 1977, has noted that too much probing can be a source of annoyance to the respondent and result in a terminated interview.)

Telephone surveys allow interviewers access to individuals who cannot or will not open their doors to strangers for the purpose of an interview (e.g., persons confined to bed because of illness or injury). Another advantage is that when timeliness is important, special issues can be explored and data gathered almost immediately. A final advantage is that telephone interviewers can be closely monitored and the quality of their work frequently evaluated to insure that questions are asked correctly and responses are coded satisfactorily.

A disadvantage of the telephone survey is that the interviewer cannot see the respondent. This means that some items such as the person's race or the condition of the house cannot be observed. If these are important to the investigator, they must be asked of the respondent. When the phone is used, the interviewer misses facial expressions, which indicate such states as confusion or the beginning of an emotion like anger or sadness. Not everyone can be a successful telephone interviewer; he or she must be articulate, personable, and a good conversationalist. The quality of the interviewer's voice ("telephone voice") is important (Blankenship, 1977). An interviewer must quickly interest the potential respondent in cooperating and establish rapport before the respondent loses interest. If open-ended questions are used, the interviewer must be able to write down the responses quickly and accurately.

Another disadvantage of telephone surveys is that they must be kept short. Telephone interviews should be under twenty minutes long, and the shorter the better (there are exceptions—much longer surveys have been successfully completed by phone.) As a general rule, the more interesting the topic is for the respondent, the greater the probability that the respondent will complete the interview even if it is lengthy.

Some believe that interviewing by telephone is unacceptable because of built-in bias associated with the inability to interview persons who do not have telephones. While telephone surveys may somewhat underrepresent the poorest of the poor, 92.5 percent of all American households have telephones (U.S. Department of Commerce, 1988). The Rand Corporation concluded in 1977 that the number of telephones in the United States was so high that exclusion of those without phones was no longer a liability for telephone surveys in most parts of the country: "For most purposes, the evidence that the universe of telephone households is an acceptable representation of all households is now rather compelling (Lucas and Adams, 1977, p. 5).

The use of a telephone directory to produce samples for telephone surveys could lead to biased data. Some professionals (therapists, doctors, judges) do not have listed phone numbers, and separated and divorced persons often have unlisted phone numbers. To compensate for unlisted numbers, most large-scale telephone surveys use such procedures as random-digit or added-digit dialing. In random-digit dialing, there is intentional selection of the first three digits for the desired local exchanges, and the last four digits are randomly generated by a computer. In added-digit dialing, a legitimate "seed number" is provided for those local exchanges from which the samples are to be drawn, and then consecutive digits are added to the last digit or the last two or three digits. While these procedures result in some phone calls to businesses or others who are not target respondents, it provides a good way of accessing households with unlisted numbers and thus getting a representative sample of all households with phones.

With telephone surveys you can expect refusal rates to range from 20 to 28 percent (Frey, 1983). Dillman (1978) notes that telephone surveys using his Total Design Method have an average response rate of 85 percent.

Getting the Most Out of the Telephone Survey

Interviewers need to be trained in the conduct of the survey. This training should include role-plays and interviewing other trainees to insure that the purpose of each question is well understood. All interviewers should be given standardized introductory statements that move quickly to the survey questions. Some texts advise against asking the respondents' permission to interview them or if they have a few minutes to answer some questions (Alreck and Settle, 1985; Institute for Social Research, 1976). A brief introduction might go something like this:

> Hello. My name is _____ . I'm calling from the _____ Survey Research Center. We're conducting a survey this month of people randomly selected from across the state. The survey will take about fifteen minutes. We have only a phone number and not any names, so all of your responses will be anonymous. If I have your permission, let me begin by asking how many years you have lived in this state . . .

It is strongly recommended that the questionnaire and interview procedures be tested (a pilot survey) to determine if there are any unforeseen problems.

Personal Interviews

The personal interview provides the interviewer with more control than either mail or telephone surveys. The interviewer can read facial expressions and moods, monitor environmental distractions, and determine if the interview should move to a quieter room or be continued at a later date. See for example, the following report from an interviewer:

> It was a three-ring circus—the respondent had five children ranging from one to eight years and they all had a great time climbing all over the furniture. One child stood on her head on the couch

next to me. I managed to hang onto my pencil, the questionnaire, my purse—but it wasn't easy! (Converse and Schuman, 1974, p. 3)

Observational data (such as the respondent's race or affect) can also be determined from the personal interview without requiring questions to be asked of the respondent. Further, visual aids can be used to help a respondent. This is particularly advantageous if there is a need for a complex response set. In such situations, the respondent can be handed a card from which to choose a response. Another advantage is that the personal interview usually achieves a higher response rate than either mail or telephone surveys.

The prime disadvantage of the interview is that it is much more expensive than the two other approaches. While interviewers can be paid either by the hour or by the number of interviews completed, there must also be allowances for travel time to the respondents' homes. Occasionally, multiple trips must be made when appointments are broken (because they have been forgotten, friends drop in, or minor emergencies arise). Interviewers can get lost, find it difficult to locate the respondent's residence, or have car trouble. Further, comments hurriedly scrawled in the margin of the questionnaire can become difficult to discern hours later in the office. The safety of interviewers can also be a major concern, and sometimes interviewers must be assigned in teams of two. Supervision and quality control of the interview process can be more difficult to assure than with the telephone survey.

Getting the Most from Personal Interviews

The Survey Research Center at the University of Michigan is one of several well-known institutions that have many years of experience in conducting surveys. (Another is the National Opinion Research Center at the University of Chicago.) Anyone seriously considering conducting a large number of personal interviews for research purposes should start by reading the Survey Research Center's *Interviewer's Manual: Revised Edition.* This very practical publication outlines, in a step-by-step format, what the interviewer should and should not do. Suggestions are provided for such concerns as securing the interview and responding to such questions as "How did you pick me?" and "What good will all this do?" With regard to the first question, the interviewer briefly explains the sampling process. To answer the second question, it is helpful to pull out newspaper or periodical clippings to show the respondent how information from surveys is used.

The Survey Research Center also recommends that the interviewer ask questions exactly as they are worded and in the order in which they appear on the questionnaire. Interviewers are not to assume that they know the respondent's position or response. Every question should be asked, even if a preface is needed ("I know that we have already touched on this, but . . ."). The Center recommends that the interviewer repeat questions that are misunderstood or misinterpreted, and probe where necessary. (You can probe by repeating the question, by being silent for a few seconds and giving the respondent time to expand his or her thoughts, by repeating the respondent's reply, by making a neutral comment such as "Can you tell me a little more?" "Anything else?" or by simply stating that you do not understand.)

Babbie (1986) has composed a list that he calls general rules for interviewing. His recommendations are: the interviewer should dress in a fashion similar to what would be found in the respondent's neighborhood; he or she should not over- or underdress. He says that middle-class neatness and cleanliness are expected by the largest number of respondents. Further, the interviewer must be familiar with the questionnaire so that he or she doesn't stumble over words or phrases. Responses should be recorded exactly. He also recommends that an interviewer's first five completed questionnaires should be reviewed by a supervisor to insure that there are no major problems, and then some random reviewing and checking should be employed later on.

Comparison of the Three Approaches

Mail surveys have the advantage of generally being less expensive than telephone or personal interviewing. Tradeoffs are the low response rate and the tendency for respondents to skip questions they don't understand, which seem to require too much thought or writing, or for which they don't want to give a response. On the other hand, both mail and telephone surveys can allow the respondent to reply somewhat anonymously. Respondents may not feel anonymity to the same extent in personal interviews.

Complicated questions are more easily handled by a personal interview than with the other two approaches, but when time is an important consideration, the telephone survey has the advantage. Mail surveys and face-to-face surveys can easily take three to four months to complete (Frey, 1983). Both telephone and face-to-face surveys are labor-intensive and require personnel with good social and conversational skills.

Which is the best approach to use? Each approach has its own particular set of strengths as well as weaknesses. Dillman (1978) has listed twenty-four factors that could be considered in choosing among the three approaches. These range from the obvious desire to keep costs low, to speed of implementation, and to such issues as contamination by others in the household and success with boring or tedious questions. Dillman concludes by stating that any final decision "requires the subjective weighing of one consideration against another" (p. 76). In short, the best approach is the one that has the fewest limitations and the most advantages at a cost you can afford. See table 6.1 for further assistance with the decision of which approach is best for your project.

Table 6.1   Comparison of Mail, Face-to-Face, and Telephone
Survey Methods

Factor	Mail	Face-to-Face	Telephone
1. Cost	1	4	2
2. Personnel requirements: interviewers	N/A	4	3
3. Personnel requirements: supervisors	2	3	4
4. Implementation time	4	4	1
5. Sample coverate	3	1	1
6. Response rate—general public	4	2	2
7. Refusal rate	Unknown	3	3
8. Noncontact/nonaccessibility	2	3	2
9. Ability to obtain response from an elite	4	1	2
10. Respondent within household	4	2	2
11. Interviewer control	N/A	3	1
12. Socially desirable response	1	4	3
13. Item nonresponse	3	2	3
14. Length of questionnaire—impact or response	3	1	2
15. Confidentiality	4	4	4
16. Ability to ask sensitive questions	2	1	2
17. Ability to probe	4	1	2
18. Ability to clarify	4	1	2
19. Ask complex questions	3	1	3
20. Use of open-ended questions	4	1	1
21. Use of visual aids	2	1	4
22. Avoid opportunity for consultation by respondent with others	4	1	1

Key: 1 = Major advantage; 2 = Minor advantage; 3 = Minor disadvantage; 4 = Major disadvantage
Source: Frey (1983). Reprinted by permission of Sage Publications, Inc.

Sampling Theory

Virtually everyday you are involved in sampling. On cold winter days you may stick your foot out from under the covers and decide that it is too cold to get up right then. Later on, you test your bath or shower water to see if the temperature is right. You might take a sip of coffee and decide it is too strong. You sometimes walk into a clothing store, glance at a few price tags, and decide the store has more expensive items than you can afford. If you donate blood, a tiny sample of your blood is tested to see if you have sufficient iron content in your blood.

In each of these instances sufficient information came from sampling. It was not necessary to experience the *whole* of the phenomenon. You didn't have to drink the whole cup of coffee to realize it was too strong. One sip served as a sample of the whole cup. You didn't have to examine every article of apparel in the clothing store to know that the store catered to an exclusive (and rich) clientele. The people at the blood center didn't have to draw blood from every part of your body, because your blood (whatever its characteristics) is pretty much the same regardless of whether it is in your arm or foot or ear.

The notion behind sampling theory is that a small number of **sampling units** (a few price tags) can tell you something about the total population (all the items of apparel sold by the clothing store).

Let's say that you have been elected to a schoolboard in a town with 50,000 registered voters. If there is a movement to raise taxes to build a new high school, you wouldn't have to talk to all 50,000 registered voters to get an accurate notion of whether the majority of the adults in the community were in favor of this tax. A telephone poll of several hundred randomly selected registered voters could provide you with an accurate assessment of support for a new tax. Polling 50,000 individuals is impractical, if not impossible. But more importantly, it is unnecessary. Sampling is best applied when large populations or numbers are involved and when economy is a consideration.

Sampling works because trends or tendencies within a large population can be discovered from a much smaller number of individuals. For instance, if 90 percent of the registered voters in the above example were going to vote for an increase in their taxes, an indication of support for the tax issue should be apparent whether you sample 75 or 475 of the registered voters (if these voters were randomly selected). The larger sample merely allows for greater confidence and precision in estimating the "true" level of support or nonsupport for the tax issue. It is possible that if you sample only a handful of individuals, these few may not feel, act, or believe as the majority of the larger population. But if the sample is large enough (something akin to a critical mass), and there is no bias in the selection of the individual sampling units, then the pattern or characteristics found in the sample should match what you would find if you could contact everyone in the total population. Later in this chapter we will discuss the important issue of sample size.

The Accuracy of Samples

The Gallup organization is one of several nationally recognized professional survey research organizations. Even though the population of the United States is in excess of 200 million, Gallup is able to develop representative samples of the U.S. adult civilian population with interviews of approximately fifteen hundred respondents. That sample size allows them to be 95 percent confident that the results they obtain are accurate within plus or minus 3 percentage points. Their accuracy is impressive. As can be seen in Table 6.2 in twenty-five national elections, their samples differed from the actual election results by an average of only 2 percentage points.

Although there may be times when a researcher would want to interview every person in a given population, it rarely would be necessary. If sampling is conducted without bias, then smaller representative samples can be used quite adequately to gauge or predict the larger population. A sample is representative when all individual units of the population have an equal chance of being selected.

Nonprobability Sampling Designs

There are two basic approaches to sampling. The first we will discuss is known as **nonprobability sampling.** These designs generally are selected because of availability, convenience, or economy. If you were, for instance, to poll ten friends about some matter instead of randomly selecting a sample from the 50,000 registered voters in your town, you would be taking a **sample of convenience.** When we draw a convenience sample, we do so because it is easy or quick, and we think it will provide us with some information as to what the larger population might think. But this type of sampling is prone to error. Your friends, for example, knowing how strongly you feel on an issue such as the tax for a new high school may not be completely honest in telling you how they would vote. Since there is some reason they are your friends, the common interests you have (your friends may all be social workers, have about the same income, and have children in school) may also influence how they would vote. In other words, your ten friends may not be representative of the other

114

49,990 voters in your town who are not social workers, who make more or less than you do annually, and who may or may not have children.

Accidental or **availability sampling** are terms often used synonymously with convenience sampling. An example of accidental sampling is television, radio, or newspaper reporters stopping people on the street and asking about their opinions on some issue. In this form of sampling, those who happen to pass close by are selected (as op-

Table 6.2   Gallup Poll Accuracy Record

Year	Gallup Final Survey		Election Results		Deviation
1988	56.0%	Bush	53.9%	Bush	− 2.1
1984	59.0	Reagan	59.1	Reagan	− 0.1
1982	55.0	Democratic	56.1	Democratic	− 1.1
1980	47.0	Reagan	50.8	Reagan	− 3.8
1978	55.0	Democratic	54.6	Democratic	+ 0.4
1976	48.0	Carter	50.0	Carter	− 2.0
1974	60.0	Democratic	58.9	Democratic	+ 1.1
1972	62.0	Nixon	61.8	Nixon	+ 0.2
1970	53.0	Democratic	54.3	Democratic	− 1.3
1968	43.0	Nixon	43.5	Nixon	− 0.5
1966	52.5	Democratic	51.9	Democratic	+ 0.6
1964	64.0	Johnson	61.3	Johnson	+ 2.7
1962	55.5	Democratic	52.7	Democratic	+ 2.8
1960	51.0	Kennedy	50.1	Kennedy	+ 0.9
1958	57.0	Democratic	56.5	Democratic	+ 0.5
1956	59.5	Eisenhower	57.8	Eisenhower	+ 1.7
1954	51.5	Democratic	52.7	Democratic	− 1.2
1952	51.0	Eisenhower	55.4	Eisenhower	− 4.4
1950	51.0	Democratic	50.3	Democratic	+ 0.7
1948	44.5	Truman	49.9	Truman	− 5.4
1946	58.0	Republican	54.3	Republican	+ 3.7
1944	51.5	Roosevelt	53.3	Roosevelt	− 1.8
1942	52.0	Democratic	48.0	Democratic	+ 4.0
1940	52.0	Roosevelt	55.0	Roosevelt	− 3.0
1938	54.0	Democratic	50.8	Democratic	+ 3.2
1936	55.7	Roosevelt	62.5	Roosevelt	− 6.8

Trends in Deviation

Elections	Average error
1936–1950	3.6
1952–1960	1.7
1962–1970	1.6
1972–1988	1.4

Average deviation for 26 national elections: 2.2 percentage points
Average deviation for 19 national elections since 1950, inclusive: 1.5 percentage points
Source: *The Gallup Report*, no. 279, Dec. 1988.

posed those who cross the street to avoid being interviewed). This sampling design is weak and prone to errors.

Nonprobability sampling is often done when the extent of the population is not known. For instance, I once conducted exploratory research to find out how much money trash pickers make each day from gathering and selling aluminum beverage cans (Royse, 1987). I did not know the true population (the actual number) of trash pickers in the city or the state, so I arbitrarily chose a nonprobability sample of fifty. This group may have been somewhat unrepresentative of the larger population of all trash pickers, but there was no way of knowing this. (I tried to make the study a little more representative by interviewing trash pickers in two different cities.) This type of sampling is also known as **purposive sampling,** because the respondents had to have certain characteristics in common in order to be selected for an interview (in my study, they all had to be trash pickers).

One respondent leading you to another respondent (e.g., the mother of an autistic child gives you the name of another mother of an autistic child) is sometimes referred to as **snowball sampling**. The sample grows by referrals to other potential respondents.

Quota sampling involves knowing certain characteristics of a population (e.g., the proportion of an agency's clientele who are under thirty, middle aged, and sixty or older) and then striving to obtain the same proportions in the selected sample. With this approach, screening is often done early in the interview so that interviewers will not have to continue with those who do not have the desired characteristics. Although the final sample may match the population in terms of the proportions of respondents having certain characteristics, the sample may be unrepresentative in other areas because of characteristics for which they were not screened. For example, although the quota sample may resemble the population by containing an identical proportion of those who are over age 60, a poorly designed quota sample could reveal that the majority of the respondents over sixty were retired or disabled, while in actuality this characteristic was found in only 20 percent of those sixty and older in the actual population. With this approach, interviewers have greater flexibility in deciding whom to reject or include, and for this reason the potential for interviewer bias is a major concern.

The problem with all nonprobability sampling designs is not knowing how representative or how closely the sample resembles the "true" population. The nonprobability sample could be very biased, yet it would be difficult for the investigator to know this without drawing additional samples.

Probability Sampling Designs

With **probability sampling** the investigator has a good idea of both the number of people or units in the target population and their characteristics. With these parameters the researcher can determine if a sample is representative. There are several probability sampling designs to consider. The first one we will examine is the **simple random sampling design,** where each sampling unit in the population has the same probability (an equal chance) of being chosen.

Suppose the president of your university is retiring, and the board of trustees is interested in selecting a former governor for the new president. You think it is a good idea, but you want to know what the rest of the student body thinks. You find out from the registrar that there are 19,787 students enrolled in the university. Knowing the population of university students, you can begin to make some decisions about how many to contact and which survey approach to use.

If the registrar provides you with a listing of all the enrolled students as well as their phone numbers and addresses, you could use a table of random numbers (see Appendix A) to find a starting place and randomly select a sample of students to contact. This listing would be known as the **sampling frame.** You choose to contact a sample of 100 students. If you have a good list and you randomly select from it, the names you draw for your sample should be representative of the population enrolled at the university. Your sample should be a microcosm of the population of university students. The proportion of males and females in the sample should reflect their proportion at the university, as should the proportion of freshmen, sophomores, juniors, and seniors. (For example, if you find that 42 percent of your sample are seniors and yet seniors make up only 18 percent of the student body as a whole, then you should suspect something is wrong with either your sampling procedure or your list of students.)

Sometimes researchers talk about **systematic sampling.** What they mean by this is best explained by way of example. Let's say that you plan to take a 10 percent sample of the 19,787 university students. However, a quick calculation shows that this would require almost 2,000 interviews. Since you plan to conduct the telephone survey in a week's time, you decide that 2,000 would be far too many students to attempt to contact. As you think about the realistic constraints on your time, you decide that 200 interviews is much more feasible. If you divide the proposed sample size of 200 by the university's population of 19,787, you get a **sampling ratio** of .01—which means that your sample will draw one name for every hundred students enrolled in the university.

In this example of systematic sampling, the next thing you need to do is to number all of the students on the listing you received from the registrar. Then you refer to the random number table (Appendix A) and find a random starting place (any number between 1 and 100), for example 6. The first student selected from the list would be 6, followed by 106, 206, 306, 406, 506, 606, 706, 806, 906, 1,006, 1,106, 1,206, and so on through the entire list of 19,787 students. If the list were not numbered and since numbering all 19,787 students would be very time-consuming, you could count out the first 100 names, measure that distance with a ruler, and then use that distance to locate the next name to be selected.

Both systematic and simple random sampling approaches tend to provide representative samples as long as the lists you work from are not organized in such a way as to bias the sample. For example, suppose you choose the first name on the list, then the one hundredth, the two hundredth, and so on, but you aren't aware that a computer program inadvertently placed students with the highest grade point averages in every hundredth position. In this case, your sample would contain only those students most likely to make Phi Beta Kappa and would not be representative of the larger student body.

While probability sampling is the best insurance against a sample being unrepresentative, it is no guarantee that every group will be well represented. Sometimes bad luck or some form of bias will produce a random sample that is not representative. For example, 48 percent of the university population may be female, but 54 percent of those drawn for your sample could be female. If you play cards, you understand how this could happen. Even though the deck is shuffled many times, luck (chance) plays a role in which cards you are dealt—it is possible to get all hearts or four aces. Similarly, any sample from a population is by definition only an approximation of the total population. Numerically large samples are the best guarantee against obtaining unrepresentative samples.

Some researchers try to guard against a freak or fluke sample by using **stratified random sampling.** When certain important characteristics of the population (e.g., the percentage of men and women) are known, exact proportions are obtained by dividing the study population into subgroups or subsets called strata and sampling the appropriate proportion from each stratum.

For instance, suppose that instead of sampling from the whole student body, you want to interview only seniors and freshmen.

You already know that there are twice as many freshmen as seniors and that you want to interview 200 students. You again approach the registrar and ask for a listing of just freshmen and seniors. Once again you number each of the freshmen and seniors, choose a random starting place, and begin selecting. Since there are twice as many freshmen as seniors, you decide to select 65 seniors to interview and 130 freshmen. This keeps the proportion of seniors to freshmen in your sample the same as it is in the university, and you have retained the sample size that you think is manageable. While quota sampling and stratified random sampling may seem similar, remember that quota sampling does not involve random sampling. Quota sampling is more concerned with obtaining a certain number or percentage of subjects with a given characteristic than with how they were obtained.

Cluster sampling is another design available to researchers. Used primarily for convenience and economy, cluster sampling randomly selects natural groups or clusters instead of individuals from the population. For example, suppose you want to explore the extent of community responsibility felt by individuals who belong to civic organizations. It would be impossible to get a national mailing list of every person who belongs to some civic organization. However, it would be possible to randomly select eight or ten states and to contact the national or state offices of several civic organizations to learn which communities within the states have chapters. You could then randomly select chapters or cities from within the states where these organizations have members. In this illustration, one cluster consists of the states that were chosen and another cluster consists of the communities or chapters within those states.

An example of a **one-stage cluster sampling** is dividing the population of a town into households (households would be the clusters because they usually contain more than one individual) and then taking a sample of households and obtaining information from *all* the members of the household. **Two-stage cluster sampling** involves dividing the population into households or clusters and then taking a *sample* of members from each selected household (Jolliffe, 1986).

One of my students used a **multistage cluster sampling design** in connection with a research project. She had been reading about transracial adoption and found that there was little information about blacks' attitudes toward this topic. Since she was not interested in whites' attitudes, but only in blacks' attitudes, a random community survey would have been inefficient. Instead, a multistage cluster sampling design was selected.

We first identified the nine census tracts in the city containing the highest concentrations of blacks. From these nine tracts, three were randomly selected (since she was doing the interviewing all by herself, there was no need to walk her legs off). From these three tracts, forty city blocks were randomly chosen. Finally, every sixth household was selected from these blocks (after getting a random starting place) until 150 interviews had been completed (Howard, Royse and Skerl, 1977).

Additional Survey Designs

In addition to the probability and nonprobability survey designs, several other designs may be useful. The term **cross-sectional survey design** is used to refer to the probability sampling designs. The term indicates that a one-time survey is made with a randomly selected sample. The cross-sectional design allows a broad representation of the population and thus involves persons of all ages, incomes, and educational levels.

In contrast, **longitudinal surveys** may not be representative of the population. These surveys are conducted on multiple occasions over an extended period of time. Change is measured through a succession of surveys. There are three types of longitudinal surveys: **trend surveys, cohort surveys,** and **panel surveys.** Trend studies require multiple samplings from the same population over months or years in order to monitor changes or trends. The same individuals are not repeatedly interviewed. For a good example of trend survey research, see the National Institute on Drug Abuse Publications, *Drugs and American High School Students, 1975–1983.*

A cohort is a group of persons who have some critical or significant experience in common (e.g., Vietnam veterans). Cohort studies involve only persons who fit into these subgroups. Persons who are born, married, or graduated from high school in a given year could be used to form cohorts by birth, marriage, or graduation, respectively. Cohort studies involve multiple samples from the cohort(s) of interest. Comparisons by cohorts are most commonly found in sociological studies of the population.

Panel studies are studies of the *same* group of persons over an extended period (e.g., the survivors of Hiroshima). Panel studies are used to detect changes in individuals over time.

Table 6.3 shows the three types of longitudinal surveys. Each study began with interviewing fifteen-year-old runaways in Chicago. In a trend survey, the investigator is interested in differences in fifteen-year-old runaways over time. Do their characteristics change? Do the reasons they run away change? An investigator using a cohort

Table 6.3   Comparison of Trend, Cohort, and Panel Longitudinal Surveys

Type	Subjects' Age in 1990	Subjects' Age in 1995	Subjects' Age in 2000
Trend	15 yrs. old	15 yrs. old	15 yrs. old
Cohort	15 yrs. old	20 yrs. old	25 yrs. old
Panel	15 yrs. old	20 yrs. old	25 yrs. old

survey would want to interview any person who was fifteen years old and a runaway in 1990. The panel surveyor would want to interview the 1990 runaways interviewees in 1995 or 2000.

Determining Sample Size

How big a sample is necessary for a good survey? This is a major question in the minds of many would-be researchers. Unfortunately, there is no simple response to this question. Sample size is related to the researcher's objectives, monetary and personnel resources, and the amount of time available in which to conduct the research. A precise sample size cannot be determined until you are able to state your expectations in terms of the accuracy you need and the confidence that you would like to have in the data.

You may have heard that a minimum sample size is 10 percent of the population. But the accuracy of your survey is much more dependent upon the size of the sample than on the population size. In order to be confident that your findings are reasonably accurate, you need to interview proportionately more of those who compose small populations than of those making up large populations.

Prior to determining sample size for a study where statistical probability statements can be made about the findings, several terms must be understood. **Margin of error** refers to the precision needed by the researcher. A margin of error of 5 percent means that the actual findings could vary by as much as 5 points either positively or negatively. A consumer satisfaction survey, for instance, with a 5 percent margin of error associated with a finding of 65 percent of clients "highly satisfied" with services would mean that the true value in the population could be as low as 60 percent (65 − 5 = 60) or as high as 70 percent (65 + 5 = 70). If you believe that greater precision is needed (e.g., plus or minus 2 points), then you must plan on obtaining a larger sample to support that precision. This can be seen in table 6.4 by comparing the sample sizes in the .05 column with those in the .02 column.

The other term that is important to understand is **confidence level.** A confidence level (or level of confidence) is a statement of how often you could expect to find similar results if the survey were to be repeated. Since every survey varies slightly (depending upon who is selected to be in the sample), the confidence level informs about how often the findings will fall outside the margin of error. For example, in a sample developed to have a 95 percent confidence level with a 5 percent margin of error, the findings could be expected to miss the actual values in the population by more than 5 percent only five times in one hundred surveys. (In the example above, findings that less than 60 percent or more than 70 percent of the clients were "highly satisfied" would be expected to occur no more than five times in one hundred surveys.) The use of a 95 percent confidence level and 5 percent margin of error is pretty standard in the social sciences.

Table 6.4 will help you decide how large a sample to select in your own surveys. This table is used when you do not have a firm notion about the proportion of a population that would be in favor of or opposed to a specific issue. In order to be confident that the same findings would have occurred in 95 surveys out of 100, and to be accurate to within plus or minus 5 percentage points, you would need to interview 79 persons in a population of 100. However, in a population of 1 million, you would have to interview only 384 persons. The greater the precision you require, the larger your sample must be. Note that for a permissible error of 1 percent with the same population of 1 million, you would need a sample of 9,513. Few issues are worth the increase in sample size necessary when one goes from plus or minus 5 percentage points to plus or minus 1 point. For example, if you are 95 percent confident, plus or minus five percentage points, that 80 percent of the sample supports a tax increase, then it really doesn't matter whether the "true" level of support is 75 percent or 85 percent. The tax issue would pass comfortably with anything over a 51 percent majority.

It is possible to find other tables that allow you to use smaller samples if you can accept less confidence (e.g., permissible error of 10 percent), or if you have some evidence (prior surveys) of how the sample might respond (e.g., 90 percent opposed to a tax increase).

Mistakes to Avoid

The American Statistical Association published a small brochure in 1980 entitled *What Is a Survey?* Contained within the brochure is some helpful information regarding "shortcuts" to be avoided in survey research. These are: (1) failure to use a proper sampling procedure; (2) failure to pretest the instrument and procedures; (3) failure to follow-up nonrespondents; and (4) inadequate quality control.

If you are in the position of not being able to interview all of the individuals in a given population, draw a sample based on probability design. Be alert to any limitations that could result in your sampling

Table 6.4 Appropriate Sizes of Simple Random Samples for Specific Permissible Errors Expressed as Absolute Proportions When the True Proportion in the Population Is 0.50 and the Confidence Level Is 95 Percent

Population Size	Sample size for permissible error (Proportion)				
	0.05	0.04	0.03	0.02	0.01
100	79	86	91	96	99
200	132	150	168	185	196
300	168	200	234	267	291
400	196	240	291	343	384
500	217	273	340	414	475
600	234	300	384	480	565
700	248	323	423	542	652
800	260	343	457	600	738
900	269	360	488	655	823
1,000	278	375	516	706	906
2,000	322	462	696	1,091	1,655
3,000	341	500	787	1,334	2,286
4,000	350	522	842	1,500	2,824
5,000	357	536	879	1,622	3,288
6,000	361	546	906	1,715	3,693
7,000	364	553	926	1,788	4,049
8,000	367	558	942	1,847	4,364
9,000	368	563	954	1,895	4,646
10,000	370	566	964	1,936	4,899
15,000	375	577	996	2,070	5,855
20,000	377	583	1,013	2,144	6,488
25,000	378	586	1,023	2,191	6,938
30,000	379	588	1,030	2,223	7,275
40,000	381	591	1,039	2,265	7,745
50,000	381	593	1,045	2,291	8,056
75,000	382	595	1,052	2,327	8,514
100,000	383	597	1,056	2,345	8,762
500,000	384	600	1,065	2,390	9,423
1,000,000	384	600	1,066	2,395	9,513
2,000,000	384	600	1,067	2,398	9,558

Source: *Sampling and Statistics Handbook for Research in Education* (National Education Assn., 1980). Copyright by Chester McCall. Reprinted with permission.

frame being less inclusive than you had planned. Be particularly alert to sample selection bias that could occur because of the order in which the sample units are listed, incomplete listings (e.g., the omission of employees who work less than forty hours per week), and the tendency of respondents to self-select.

No matter which approach you select to conduct your survey, it is important to **pilot test** (or pretest) your procedures and instrument. Generally, pilot testing is informal and can involve giving the survey instrument to a few friends or co-workers to see if they understand the questions and respond in the ways you anticipate. Administer the survey instrument to a group of persons as similar as possible to the population that you will be surveying. The major purpose of the pilot test is to determine if the type of information you want is supplied by the respondents. Pilot testing need not involve more than twenty persons if the respondents have no problems understanding the questions or recording their responses. Pilot testing provides estimates of the time required to complete the questionnaire and, in the case of telephone and face-to-face interviews, provides useful data for estimating the cost of the survey.

Allow sufficient time to follow-up on nonrespondents. Reminder postcards and mailing second and third questionnaires to nonrespondents greatly increases response rates. In telephone and face-to-face interviewing, unless you follow-up on those who are not home when you call, you run the risk of having a bias against those who work during the hours that you attempt to reach them.

A low response rate is just as problematic as too small of a sample. If less than a majority of the respondents reply, one is left wondering about the attitudes or characteristics of those who chose not to respond. Are the data biased when only 20 percent respond? Would a different pattern of findings emerge if the response rate could be raised from 35 percent to 70 percent by following-up the nonresponders? There is no way of knowing unless nonresponders are given more than one opportunity to reply. It has been said that the response rate is "probably the most important single indicator of the reliability of a survey" (Shipman, 1981, p. 67–68). If you have a response rate of 50 percent or less, it is not possible to extrapolate the findings with any confidence to the larger population (Posavac and Carey, 1985).

If you need to employ interviewers, train them well to prevent careless errors in the field or in the recording of responses. Let them know that you will be recontacting a portion of their respondents to validate their answers. A nationally prominent sociologist once told me that as a student he sat in a coffee shop and made up information for a community directory when he should have been going door-to-door to obtain accurate data. Falsification of data is not a major difficulty with most surveys, particularly if you screen your interviewers well.

QUESTIONS FOR CLASS DISCUSSION

1. You want to conduct a national survey of social workers. What are three ways in which you might stratify the sample? Why might you want to stratify the sample?
2. Assume that you have a budget of $3,500 (exclusive of your own time) with which to conduct a national survey of social workers. What survey approach would you use? Why?
3. Give an example of a topic that might best be explored with the following:
   a. Snowball sampling
   b. Cluster sampling
   c. A longitudinal design
4. Assume that you are the director of a staff of twenty-five. You suspect that they are so overworked that they are fast approaching burnout. You decide to conduct a survey of the staff. How many of the staff should you interview?
5. How have surveys advanced our understanding of human nature or improved our lives? Cite examples where possible.
6. Cite examples of surveys in which you have participated or personal encounters you have had with surveys.
7. Your agency has asked you to conduct a random sampling of clients to determine how satisfied they are with the agency's services. After some discussion, it is decided that a telephone survey is the most sensible approach. If the agency closed approximately three thousand cases last year, how big a sample would be needed in order to have 95 percent confidence in the findings, plus or minus 5 percent? If the agency decides to use a mail approach, how many persons would you have to contact in order to get the same level of confidence and accuracy? (Keep in mind that about 30 percent of the respondents in a mail survey respond on the first mailing.)

MINI-PROJECTS FOR EXPERIENCING RESEARCH FIRSTHAND

1. List the steps you would go through to draw a random sample of 50 from a population of 350 using the table of random num-

bers. Draw the sample of 50 and record the numbers of those who would be selected.

2. Look through past issues of the *Gallup Report* and find an example of trend research. Respond to the following questions:
   a. What is the topic of the research?
   b. What does the survey data show about trends?
   c. What period of time is covered?
   d. From the time of the first survey to the most recent one, how much fluctuation can be observed?
3. Browse through back issues of *Social Work* and find five articles that report the use of a survey methodology. What is the average size of the samples reported? In how many instances did the sample size seem to be too small to allow 95 percent confidence and plus or minus 5 percent accuracy? Were most of these studies exploratory studies?
4. Skim through old magazines and newspapers in order to locate survey data. Try to find the following:
   a. an advertisement reporting survey data
   b. a magazine article citing or using survey data
   c. a newspaper article citing survey data
   Describe what each of these reveals with regard to how the survey was conducted. What else would you like to know?

RESOURCES AND REFERENCES

Aguirre, B.E. (1985). Why do they return? Abused wives in shelters. *Social Work*, 30 (4), 350–353.

Alreck, P.L. and Settle, R.B. (1985). *The Survey Research Handbook*. Homewood, IL: Irwin.

Auslander, G.K. and Litwin, H. (1988). Social networks and the poor: Toward effective policy and practice. *Social Work*, 33 (3), 234–238.

Babbie, E. (1986). *The Practice of Social Research*. Belmont, CA: Wadsworth.

Beckett, J.O. (1988). Plant closings: How older workers are affected. *Social Work*, 33 (1), 29–33.

Berkun, C.S. (1986). In behalf of women over 40: Understanding the importance of the menopause. *Social Work*, 31 (5), 378–384.

Blankenship, A.B. (1977). *Professional Telephone Surveys*. New York: McGraw-Hill.

Blythe, B.J. (1986). Increasing mailed survey responses with a lottery. *Social Work Research and Abstracts*, 22 (3), 18–19.

Bradburn, N.M. and Sudman, S. (1988). *Polls and Surveys: Understanding What They Tell Us*. San Francisco: Jossey-Bass.

Converse, J.M. and Schuman, H. (1974). *Conversations at Random: Survey Research as Interviewers See It.* New York: Wiley.

Dillman, D.A. (1983). Mail and other self-administered questionnaires. In P.H. Rossi, J.D. Wright, and A.B. Anderson (Eds.), *Handbook of Survey Research.* New York: Academic Press.

Dillman, D.A. (1978). *Mail and Telephone Surveys: The Total Design Method.* New York: Wiley.

Evens, R.C., Burlew, A.K., and Oler, C.H. Children with sickle-cell anemia: Parental relations, parent-child relations, and child behavior. *Social Work,* 33 (2), 127–132.

Fienberg, S.E., Loftus, E.F. and Tanur, J.M. (1985). Cognitive aspects of health survey methodology: An overview. *Milbank Memorial Fund Quarterly/ Health and Society,* 63 (3), 547–564.

Frey, J.H. (1983). *Survey research by telephone.* Beverly Hills, CA: Sage.

Gomez, E., Zurcher, L.A., Farris, B.E., and Becker, R.E. (1985). A study of psychosocial casework with Chicanos. *Social Work,* 30 (6), 477–482.

Harkness, L. and Mulinski, P. (1988). Performance standards for social workers. *Social Work,* 33 (4), 339–344.

Howard, A., Royse, D., and Skerl, J.A. (1977). Transracial adoption: The black community perspective. *Social Work,* 22 (3), 184–189.

Institute for Social Research, Survey Research Center. (1976). *Interviewer's Manual.* Rev. ed. Ann Arbor: University of Michigan Press.

Jolliffe, F.R. (1986). *Survey Design and Analysis.* New York: Halsted.

Lindblad-Goldberg, M., Dukes, J.L., and Lasley, J.H. (1988). Stress in black, low-income, single-parent families: Normative and dysfunctional patterns. *American Journal of Orthopsychiatry,* 58 (1), 104–120.

Lucas, W.A. and Adams, W.C. (1977). *An Assessment of Telephone Survey Methods.* Prepared under a grant from the National Science Foundation (Report R-2135-NSF). Santa Monica, CA: Rand Corp.

McLauglin, S.D., Pearce, S.E., Manninen, D.L., and Winges, L.D. (1988). To parent or relinquish: Consequences for adolescent mothers. *Social Work,* 33 (4), 320–324.

O'Keeffe, N.K., Brockopp, K., and Chew, E. (1986). Teen dating violence. *Social Work,* 31 (6), 465–468.

Posavac, E.J. and Carey, R.G. (1985). *Program Evaluation: Methods and Case Studies.* Englewood Cliffs, NJ: Prentice-Hall.

Quam, J.K. and Austin, C.D. (1984). Coverage of women's issues in eight social work journals, 1970–81. *Social Work,* 29 (4), 360–365.

Ray, J. (1987). Every twelfth shopper: Who shoplifts and why. *Social Casework,* 68 (4), 234–239.

Royse, D. (1987). Homelessness among trash pickers. *Psychological Reports,* 60, 808–810.

Schuman, H. (1985). *Racial attitudes in America: Trends and interpretations.* Cambridge, MA: Harvard University Press.

Shipman, M. (1981). *The Limitations of Social Research.* New York: Longman.

Stulberg, I. and Smith, M. (1988). Psychosocial impact of the AIDS epidemic on the lives of gay men. *Social Work*, 33 (3), 277–281.

Turner, C.F. and Martin, E. (1984). *Surveying Subjective Phenomena.* Vol. 1. New York: Russell Sage Foundation.

U.S. Department of Commerce, Bureau of the Census. (1988). *Statistical Abstract of the United States: 1988.* Washington, DC: U.S. Government Printing Office.

Vinokur-Kaplan, D. (1986). National evaluation of in-service training by child welfare practitioners. *Social Work Research & Abstracts*, 22, (4), 13–18.

Weinbach, R.W. (1984). The prepaid postcard survey: Enhancing brief research. *Social Work Research & Abstracts*, 20 (4), 5–6.

Wyers, N.L. (1987). Homosexuality in the family: Lesbian and gay spouses. *Social Work* 32 (2), 143–148.

Seven

Questionnaire Design

Social workers are familiar with the use of questionnaires. In almost every social service agency, initial data collection is conducted before new clients are admitted for services. This process is called "intake," "screening," completing the "face sheet," or "taking the client's history." To collect data, social workers follow a set of previously determined questions in an established order and sequence. Although most agencies' admission forms may not have been designed for research purposes, they have enough in common with research questionnaires that we can use them to increase our knowledge about questionnaires.

Think for a moment about an agency's admission form (or any other questionnaire with which you are familiar). Someone (or perhaps a committee) may have spent a considerable number of hours in deciding which questions were important to ask and which ones were not. One of the purposes of the questionnaire is to insure that the same set of questions is asked each time information is required. From the agency's perspective, this standard set of questions provides the minimal level of information required of each client. The social worker does not have to guess or anticipate what information the agency needs, because it has already been predetermined on the printed form. The social worker is also freed from worrying about wording the question the same way each time. If the social worker had to decide with each new client how to phrase the questions, there is the possibility that these questions would be unclear or confusing and not generate the same type of information each time. With a standard set of pretested questions in a carefully designed admission form, problems with clients providing erroneous information are minimized.

Similarly, research questionnaires use a set of carefully selected questions that standardize the way the information is asked for and structure the respondents' responses (e.g., instead of asking the respondent to state his or her age, the questionnaire asks for year of birth). Through careful wording and attention to such matters as the sequence and order of questions, researchers attempt to remove opportunities for recording inaccurate data.

Questionnaire design requires more precise statements and questions than we use in ordinary conversation. In casual conversation between two individuals, vague areas either become clear later in the conversation, or more specific information is not needed. One person may say to another, "I've noticed that Martha has a pretty low self-esteem." Seldom will the other party say, "How are you operationalizing self-esteem?" However, in the conduct of research the concepts we use must be operationalized and focused. Ambiguities and vague terms in questionnaires can cause problems for respondent and researcher alike. Such problems will be discovered and eliminated during pretests of the questionnaire. The resulting final product should provide each respondent with a clear notion of what is being asked.

DeVaus (1986) articulates well the importance of specificity in developing useful items for questionnaires:

> It is not enough to say, "I'm interested in getting some answers about inequality." What answers to what questions? Do you want to know the extent of inequality, its distribution, its causes, its effects, or what? What sort of inequality are you interested in? Over what period? (P. 27)

Designing research questions that are clear, concise, and result in data that can be used by the researcher is not an easy task. Questions that seem to be straightforward to their developers might be described as confusing or circuitous by others. In an effort to become precise, it is possible to become too wordy so that the intent of the question is hard to comprehend. Questions may also inadvertently omit important response choices or contain overlapping response choices. And, there is always the problem of unconsciously biasing the responses simply by the way the questions are phrased.

Beginning the Development of a Questionnaire

First and foremost, you must have a clear idea of what data the questionnaire should provide. What is it that you want to find out? What are the specific content areas to be covered? Concurrently, you must decide which survey approach will be used to present the questions to the respondents. Some formats (e.g., questions requiring many response options) work better in mail surveys than in telephone surveys. In mail surveys, respondents can simultaneously view all of the response categories (e.g., "Strongly agree," "Agree," "Undecided," "Disagree," "Strongly disagree") before choosing one. In telephone surveys, respondents find it difficult to keep the question as well as all of the response options in mind. Sudman and Bradburn (1982) have noted that even five categories can stretch a respondent's ability to keep a whole scale in mind at once. Consequently, respondents may remember some but not all of the responses, and their responses may have a narrower range of variation ("Agree" or "Disagree"). Another consideration is that when recall and recognition questions are vital to the survey, interviews work better than mail surveys (Berdie, Anderson and Niebuhr, 1986).

The nature of the content, the intended survey approach, and the nature of the population being surveyed affect the final form that the questionnaire takes (Blankenship, 1977). Only after consideration has been given to these areas should further conceptualizing of the questionnaire begin.

A review of the literature can provide questions or examples of ways that researchers have approached the topic of interest. It is not unethical, but rather good research practice to use questions that have worked well for other researchers (Sudman and Bradburn, 1982). Do not, however, "borrow" items that are protected by copyright without the author's permission. Customarily, one writes the author of the instrument for permission to use it and requests any additional information that the author may have on the instrument. Sometimes the author can refer you to other researchers who have recently modified or used the instrument with interesting results. Besides the possibility of saving time in questionnaire design, another advantage of using questions that have already been employed by other researchers is that you can then compare your findings to those from existing studies. The literature review may also reveal methods or approaches that were not successful.

As you begin selecting and composing questions for the first draft of a questionnaire, you will have to give some thought to whether your research topic requires **closed-ended questions** (multiple choice type responses) or **open-ended questions** (unstructured responses).

Closed-Ended Questions

Closed-ended questions area those that have their own predetermined response set. (Look again at the items on the Drug Attitude

Questionnaire in the Appendix.) The major advantage of closed-ended questions is that a great deal of time is saved in the tabulation of the data and coding it for computer analysis. Since the response choices are supplied (e.g., "Yes," "No," or "Strongly agree," "Agree," etc.) the person who is tabulating the responses does not have the problem of deciphering lengthy, illegible responses. Virtually no interpretation is required of what the respondent intended or whether a response is more like an existing set of responses or deserves a whole new category. Another advantage is that since closed-ended questions list response options, their greater specificity communicates the same frame of reference to all respondents (Converse and Presser, 1986).

Closed-ended questions are used when it is known how respondents might reply. If their responses are difficult to anticipate, open-ended questions can be used in a pilot study to find out what terms or language respondents tend to use in responding. It is then possible to identify frequent or common responses as well as the range of responses so that closed-ended questions can be developed.

Closed-ended questions can be used effectively in practically all areas of interest to social workers. For example, perhaps you are interested in specific dimensions of nursing home life. One area that you feel is important is how the residents evaluate the food prepared by the nursing home. You might construct a closed-ended question that allows for ratings of "Excellent," "Good," "Fair," or "Poor." However, a "fair" rating does not provide a wealth of information about the food. It doesn't tell you, for instance, whether hot oatmeal is served every day for breakfast, whether it arrives barely warm, or whether there is a wide variety of breakfast foods available. A number of closed-ended questions might be used to follow the initial question and to further help assess the quality of meals provided at the nursing home. Additional closed-ended questions can be used to examine residents' perceptions of other facets of nursing home life.

Open-Ended Questions

Open-ended questions have no prepared response choices. This form of question allows respondents to communicate without having to choose from a set of prepared response categories. Open-ended questions are best suited for those occasions when the researcher intends that direct interviewing be employed. Few respondents take the time to elaborate their thoughts or feelings when they must write them out on paper. Whether respondents are self-conscious about their writing skills or do not wish to create so personal a written document, mailed questionnaires that rely heavily on open-ended questions have a poorer response rate than those that use closed-ended questions. There is some evidence (Sudman and Bradburn, 1982) that open-ended questions result in greater reporting of sensitive or socially disapproved behavior than closed-ended questions. One possible explanation for this is that respondents will avoid placing themselves in categories that include high levels of socially unacceptable behavior when there are categories with more acceptable levels of behavior from which to choose.

There are times when the researcher wants greater detail than closed-ended questions typically provide. For example, if you wanted to know more about the quality of life in a nursing home as the residents experience it, closed-ended questions are not likely to provide you with much insight into their personal reflections. Open-ended questions supply you with quotes from residents—if this is of interest. On the other hand, a respondent can ramble; it requires a skillful interviewer to bring the respondent back to the topic of interest.

In any given survey, it is possible to combine both closed-ended and open-ended questions. In the example of an evaluation of a nursing home, one could rely chiefly upon closed-ended questions for rating various facets of the nursing home (e.g., courteousness of the staff, noise level, social and recreational opportunities) and still employ an open-ended question such as: "Is there anything else you would like to tell us about how it feels to live in this nursing home?" Alternatively, you could use these open-ended questions: "What is the *best* thing about living in this nursing home?" and "What is the *worst* thing about living in this nursing home?" Your use of open- or closed-ended questions (or a mixture of the two) is dependent upon the goals of your research and the type of information you require. Keep in mind that open-ended questions are easier to develop than closed-ended ones, but they are harder to analyze. While closed-end questions are more difficult to construct, they are easier to analyze.

Whether you adopt questions that have been used by other researchers or write your own, circulate a rough draft of the proposed questionnaire among your colleagues for comments and suggestions. Use their responses to revise the questionnaire before it goes out for a pilot test. After the pilot test, scrutinize the questionnaire again for questions that might have been misunderstood, biased items that suggest responses, insufficient response categories, typographical errors, and similar problems. Only after several revisions should the questionnaire be printed and distributed.

133

To assist you in developing good questionnaires, a number of specific guidelines have been elaborated. These guidelines are suggested in order to help you recognize the subtle ways in which bias can creep into your questionnaire items. Ill-conceived questions can produce error. However, more important than memorizing a series of rules is that you understand why hastily constructed questions can result in worthless data. Examples of poorly phrased or constructed questions appear in this chapter; consider each of the examples and decide for yourself why it is flawed before reading the discussion accompanying it.

Guidelines for Writing Good Questions

Double-Barreled Questions

Example: Have you donated blood or gone to the dentist this month?

( ) Yes
( ) No
( ) Don't know

This question is poorly constructed because it asks about two different behaviors (donating blood and visiting the dentist) but is structured so that only one response is expected. In the minds of most people, these two events are not connected in any way. A response of "Yes" could mean that the respondent had donated blood and been to the dentist. It is also possible that some respondents might respond "Yes" when they had visited the dentist but not donated blood, and vice versa. Some respondents will indicate "No" when they have done one but not the other. Some "No" responses will mean that the respondent has neither donated blood nor gone to the dentist. In this example, it is impossible to interpret what any response means.

As a rule, a question should ask about one issue, thought, or event at a time. If more information is desired, more questions should be asked. In this example, two separate questions should be constructed—each one focusing upon a single issue. Avoid asking two questions in one item.

Leading Questions

Example: Don't you agree with the President that the federal government should not overspend?

( ) Agree
( ) Disagree
( ) Don't know

This question clearly leads the respondent into thinking along certain lines. Most of us want to be agreeable and to get along with others. And most Americans believe it is important to respect the office of the President and would generally want to support that office (by agreeing with the President where possible). This example is a leading question because its suggests the desired response.

The question, "Don't you agree that the federal government should spend more on social services and less on germ warfare research?" is an example of a double-barreled leading question. Besides begging for an "Agree" response, it also asks for information about two different items. First, it wants to know if the government should spend more money on social services. Second, it wants to know if the respondent thinks the government should spend less on germ warfare. Again, the respondent could agree with one of these two thoughts and disagree with the other and be confused about how to respond. The two separate ideas can be constructed in the format: "As you think about the amount the federal government spends on social services programs in this country, would you say that amount is: (a) adequate, (b) inadequate, or (c) excessive?"

Unavailable Information

Example: How many hours of television did you watch last year?

Respondents should not be asked for information that is not available to them. Since most of us do not keep records of this kind of thing, it would be unlikely that the response we give would be anything more than a wild estimate. It would be better to ask about the average number of hours of television watched daily (and perhaps on weekends).

Another example of asking for information not generally available to the respondent would be: "What was your favorite color when you were five years old?" The flaw in this question is that it asks for information that most people could not reasonably be expected to have. Recall of distant events is always problematic, because human memory is subject to error. Converse and Presser (1986) note that recall of even important events, such as hospitalizations, can erode with time. When one asks questions about events or situations several years after they have occurred, one should not assume that reli-

135

able information has been given. Avoid asking for information that is unavailable to the respondent.

Asking for information that might not be available to *all* respondents can present another problem. Consider the following question: "Do you agree or disagree with the philosophy of the state's Commission on Literacy?" This question is a poor one *if* the philosophy of the state's Commission on Literacy is not well known. If, on the other hand, the Commission has recently been in the news because of some unusual or controversial philosophy, then it would be quite reasonable to ask this question. However, it might be better to ask in one question if there is a Commission on Literacy; then ask those respondents who answer "Yes" to describe the Commission's philosophy. A third question in this series might ask if they agree or disagree with the Commission's philosophy. This approach involves the use of **contingency questions** (branching questions). Those respondents who answer "Yes" to the first question are directed to the second and third subquestions. Those who respond "No" to the first question are guided to another set of questions. See figure 7.1 for an example of a contingency question.

Use of Jargon and Technical Terms

Example: Do you feel that Freud's structural hypothesis is an improvement over his topographic hypothesis?

Like the previous question relating to respondents' favorite color when they were five years old, this question asks for information that most people could not be expected to have. Furthermore, it uses terms that are not familiar to most adults. In fact, even those who are familiar with psychoanalytic theory may not know how to answer this question. It is too technical, and it uses jargon.

Use the simplest terms and vocabulary possible—the language that we use in everyday speech (sometimes called Standard English). Avoid slang, colloquialisms, abbreviations, and foreign phrases. Some texts (Alreck and Settle, 1985) recommend using words that an average eighth grader would understand. Sentences should not be long and complex; keep them short and simple.

Insensitive Language

Example: How do you people feel about apartheid in South Africa?

You may be interested in discovering how a certain ethnic or racial group feels about an issue. But a question like this may make

Figure 7.1: Illustration of Transition and a Contingency Question in a Personal or Telephone Interview Schedule

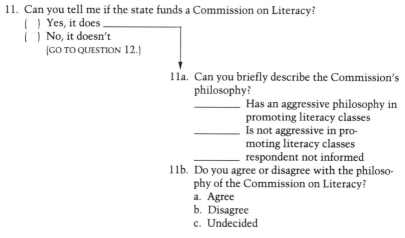

We have discussed several self-help groups found in our area. Now we would like to examine some additional services that may be available statewide.

11. Can you tell me if the state funds a Commission on Literacy?
( ) Yes, it does _____
( ) No, it doesn't
    (GO TO QUESTION 12.)

11a. Can you briefly describe the Commission's philosophy?
    _____ Has an aggressive philosophy in promoting literacy classes
    _____ Is not aggressive in promoting literacy classes
    _____ respondent not informed

11b. Do you agree or disagree with the philosophy of the Commission on Literacy?
a. Agree
b. Disagree
c. Undecided

some people uneasy because it is suggestive of racial bias. It accentuates differences among respondents by saying, in effect, that the respondent is a member of a group that is dissimilar from others (possibly the majority of Americans). Instead of asking questions in the format of "How do *you blacks* (or *you Indians*) ...," simply ask, "How do *you* feel about apartheid in South Africa?" Or, present a statement about apartheid in South Africa and ask the respondent to choose a response that reflects his or her feeling about the situation there. Later, when analyzing the data, you will be able to determine if racial groups differ in their attitudes regarding South Africa (if you collect data on the respondent's racial group as part of your questionnaire). Avoid using any language in a questionnaire that is suggestive of racism, sexism, or insensitivity.

Inflammatory or "Loaded" Terms

Example: Are you a religious fanatic?

Social desirability is a term used to describe the tendency of people to want their behavior to be perceived as socially acceptable. It is a strong motivation, and response bias can easily occur as respondents avoid categories or labels that are stigmatizing. Few of us want to be labeled fanatic, zealot, or any other term that has socially undesirable connotations. Even though a respondent may have very strong convictions, he or she would likely deny having tendencies toward fanaticism. Examples of loaded terms that should be replaced with more neutral terms include "crisis," "innocent," "victim," "forced," and "coerced."

Just as the term "fanatic" is loaded, few people would want to be labeled alcoholic. Questions that get the information without labeling or stigmatization should be employed. A better way to explore the extent of problem drinking is to ask respondents about specific behaviors, for example, "How many times a week do you have a drink in the morning?" You might also provide a series of categories that give a respondent an opportunity to describe his or her pattern of drinking in more socially acceptable terms. Consider the set of response choices in the next example.

Mutually Exclusive Response Choices

Example: "Teetotaler," "Social Drinker," "I occasionally drink to excess," "I frequently drink to excess."

In our quest to avoid socially unacceptable labels, we create another problem. Consider the two response choices of "social drinker" and "I occasionally drink to excess." Are they mutually exclusive? Is it possible to be a social drinker and to occasionally drink to excess? If you agree, then this response set will not provide "clean" data. Since the categories overlap, some respondents will think of themselves as social drinkers even though they drink to excess. Being a social drinker is a more attractive response to some individuals than the more unacceptable possibility of revealing how often they drink to excess. Measuring the number of times a person drinks and the amount (volume) of alcohol he or she consumes in an average weekday are more precise ways of developing categories that help the investigator separate light drinkers from moderate or heavy drinkers. Behavioral measures such as these are much more useful than stigmatizing or labeling terms.

The problems of overlapping response categories and finding good behavioral measures are obvious examples of why you need to refer to the literature as part of the research process. It is very likely that other researchers have struggled with these problems and have developed response sets or categories (if not whole questionnaires) that you could use in your research. If your literature review is thorough, you may find that someone has already done the very research that you are proposing. This being the case, you may decide to go no further, or you may make modifications to pursue a slightly different hypothesis.

Vague and Ambiguous Terms

Example: How many times in the past year have you seen a social worker?

The problem with this question is that it contains language that is vague. Is the intent of this question to find out how many social workers are observed (seen) by nonsocial workers in a year's time? Or, to learn the number of appointments or sessions the respondent had with a social worker last year? To rephrase the question, "How many times in the past year have you talked with a social worker?" is not an improvement, since one can talk informally or socially with social workers (for instance, at a party or conference). It would be better to ask, "How many appointments have you made with your social worker in the last thirty days?" Or, since it is possible to make appointments but not keep them, "How many office visits have you had with your social worker in the last thirty days?" Even these two questions could be refined since an office visit could last ten minutes or two and a half hours. But, these questions omit the whole dimension of home visits. A more exact approach would be to ask, "In the past thirty days, about how much time (in hours and minutes) have you spent talking about your problems face-to-face with your social worker?"

The following question also uses a vague term that may cause problems: "Do you attend Alcoholics Anonymous (AA) meetings regularly?" The problem with this sentence is that "regularly" is one of those terms that means different things to different individuals. Some respondents may attend AA regularly—at the beginning and end of each school year. Other respondents may attend regularly the first Wednesday of the month. Some respondents may attend twice a week every week. A better way to ask for information of this type would be: "How many times a month do you attend Alcoholics Anonymous meetings?"

Another example of the use of vague terms is the question: "What is your income?" This question is problematic because the respondent must figure out whether the information sought has a yearly, monthly, or weekly referent. It also is unclear whether the respondent should report annual salary (gross income) or the amount after all the deductions have been made (net income). A further problem is that the question does not indicate whether combined family income is expected or whether the respondent should report only his or her personal income (even though others in the household may be working).

A final example of the use of vague terms can be seen in the question: "Are you employed?" This question may be difficult to answer because there are several responses that can be made in addition to "Yes" or "No." The status of being employed could include those who work full-time and those who work part-time. There may be respondents who have retired from one career and work sporadically in order to help out when other employees take vacations or when others are on sick leave. Respondents could be employed seasonally (e.g., migrant workers or college students who work full-time in the summer but not at all when school is in session). Finally, there are those who help with a family business (e.g., a spouse who keeps the books) but who do not receive a paycheck.

All-Inclusive Terms

Example: Are you always in bed by 11:00 P.M.?

The use of such terms as "always" and "never" creates problems for the respondent and for the researcher attempting to interpret the data. Does "always" allow for exceptions? For instance, what if you are in bed by 11:00 P.M. every night of the year except for New Year's Eve when you stay up until 12:01 A.M. Does that mean that you should respond with a "No" to the above question? "Always" and "never" imply that there are no exceptions. In my experience, researchers are more concerned with general patterns, for example, "On most week nights, about what time do you usually go to bed?"

Negatively Constructed Items

Example: Marijuana should not be decriminalized.

This item, borrowed from DeVaus (1986), is a good example of how the word "not" confuses the meaning of the statement. In this instance, it reverses the meaning of decriminalized so that a person agreeing to the statement is saying in effect that marijuana usage should be made illegal. A respondent disagreeing with the statement is saying that marijuana use should be made legal. It is much more clear and straightforward to ask, "Should the private use of marijuana be made legal?" Where possible, the term "not" should be avoided in questionnaires.

Kidder and Judd (1986) have suggested that **acquiescence,** a tendency some respondents have to agree with items regardless of their content, can be countered by constructing items so that the respondent will respond positively (e.g., "Agree") and negatively (e.g., "Disagree") in roughly equal proportions. With a little creativity, items can be prepared so that the respondent does not know which response is the one desired by the researcher. Figure 7.2 provides an example of wording questions so that a respondent sympathetic to AIDS victims could not respond either "Strongly Agree" or "Agree" to all four questions.

Sequence of Questions

There is general agreement that the first questions to be asked should be of interest to the respondent. Respondents need to "warm up" to the survey process and establish a sense of trust or rapport with the researcher or the researcher's representative (which could be the mailed questionnaire). Accordingly, the first several questions should be applicable to all respondents. Respondents seem to prefer closed-ended questions at the start of mailed questionnaires but open-ended questions when interviewed in person or over the phone. Information about potentially sensitive areas such as age and income should occur at the end of the questionnaire. Such information, if asked at the beginning of the interview or questionnaire, may result in a lower response rate. More important questions should be asked earlier than less important ones in case the respondent decides to terminate the interview or stop working on the questionnaire before all questions have been completed. Respondent fatigue can be a problem with especially long questionnaires.

There also seems to be consensus that topically related questions should follow one another in some sort of recognizable sequence as opposed to being interposed and spread throughout the questionnaire. Usually, some sort of "funnel sequence" is used, in which general questions are followed by more narrowly focused questions. A problem may occur if a question has an effect on subsequent responses because it creates some sort of expectancy or "mind-set." Some topics seem to be immune to this sort of problem, and others are sensitive to it. Little experimental research is available to help us anticipate this problem in advance. Frey (1983) has noted that broad, summary-type questions are more susceptible to contextual redefinitions than specific questions that have concrete responses. The best

Figure 7.2: Phrasing Questions to Avoid Acquiescence

	Strongly Agree	Agree	Undecided	Disagree	Strongly Disagree
1. Children with AIDS should be allowed to attend school.	( )	( )	( )	( )	( )
2. Persons having AIDS should be quarantined.	( )	( )	( )	( )	( )
3. Persons having AIDS should be allowed to eat in public restaurants.	( )	( )	( )	( )	( )
4. Persons who contract AIDS deserve what they get.	( )	( )	( )	( )	( )

advice that can be offered regarding order effects is to be alert to the possibility that questions can affect later responses.

Thinking about Guidelines

The problem with guidelines is that circumstances not covered sometimes present themselves. There are times when one might use a loaded question to try to determine the extent of some socially undesirable behavior. For instance, the implication that "everyone does it" may be useful in reducing the threat of reporting some behaviors. This approach is illustrated in the following example from Sudman and Bradburn (1982): "Even the calmest of parents get angry at their children some of the time. Did your child(ren) do anything in the past seven days to make you, yourself, angry?" (p. 75).

Other instances come to mind when guidelines are best ignored. If you are interviewing members of a street gang, you may want to use terms that they commonly use instead of those terms common to Standard English.

It is difficult to cover every situation with a guideline. Potential problems arise for which there seem to be no guidelines. However, it is possible to learn more about questionnaire construction than the space limitations of this chapter allow: When you, as a professional, have the responsibility of developing a questionnaire for a research project, you may want to consult some of the references at the end of this chapter for further assistance. Dillman (1978) has a particularly useful discussion of the questionnaire's format.

It has been shown, for example, that crowded, cluttered or difficult-appearing questionnaires result in lower response rates than those that appear interesting, inviting, or simple to complete. Mailed questionnaires should be visually attractive. Blank or white space should be used to full advantage. The responses should appear in the same area of the questionnaire so that the respondent can easily locate them. Instructions, questions, and response categories should be kept brief, and diagrams used to visually direct the respondent where necessary. Numbering the questions is also useful to both respondents and those who must process the data. Where there are various components or parts to the study, a sentence or two to indicate that a shift is occurring smoothes the transition (e.g., "Now we would like to change the subject just a bit and ask some health related questions"). (Alreck and Settle (1985), Rossi, Wright and Anderson (1983), and Sudman and Bradburn (1981) address some of the finer points of questionnaire construction not covered in this chapter.)

The Role of Questionnaires in Generalizing Results

Substantive generalization of survey results is dependent upon various assumptions. Jaeger (1984:19) has identified these as:

1. the questions were "construct valid";
2. the respondents understood the questions;
3. the questions were interpreted as intended;
4. the respondents were cooperative and willing to respond;
5. the respondents had the knowledge or information needed to respond;
6. the respondents were honest in their responses;
7. responses were recorded accurately;
8. responses were interpreted accurately;
9. responses were transcribed and aggregated accurately.

As you can see, developing a good questionnaire is necessary if one hopes to generalize the survey results. Even if the sampling design is sound, a poorly constructed questionnaire will result in little useful information. Good questionnaires do not result from a single draft. They come about from polishing, revising, pretesting, and revising again. If a concept is not operationalized well, the questionnaire needs to be redone. Dillman (1978) talks about doing eight, ten, or even twelve revisions before sending the final questionnaire to the printer. Don't be afraid to circulate your drafts among those whose opinions you respect. More times than not, they will be flattered that you asked for their assistance! Be sure to pilot test your questionnaire with persons who are similar to those who will be participants in your study. Make sure that the items are understood and that this is indicated in the responses they make. Pilot testing and revising are crucial steps in the construction of a good survey instrument.

Finally, it is vital that your questions not only be technically correct but also provide you with the information you need to prepare a response to some problem. Each question should give you some essential information, and all of the questions taken together should help you to conclude something about the topic of your investigation. Research is much more than formulating questions or devising questionnaires. Perhaps my relating of an actual experience will serve to reinforce this point: A group of local citizenry asked for my assistance in conducting a mental health needs assessment of their community. "Okay," I said, "tell me more." Their spokesperson indicated that they had found a book about needs assessment that included, in its appendix, a complete set of questions that could be photocopied and used with very little modification. As I looked at the needs assessment instrument, I saw a question that asked the respondents to list three problems in their neighborhood and another that asked for a ranking of the most serious problems in the community. In my mind, I saw respondents being concerned with street lights and potholes, police protection, and a great many other community concerns. I did not, however, believe the use of that particular questionnaire would produce much useable information about the mental health needs of the community. I asked the spokesperson, "What do you hope to learn from the community needs assessment?" "Well," she said, "we want to know about all the mental health needs in the community." Further questioning revealed that there wasn't anything more specific that they hoped to learn.

At that point I tactfully asked the group to meet together to determine what, exactly, they wanted to know about the mental health needs in the community. They met and discussed what they wanted to know, and to the best of my knowledge, that group never did conduct a community needs assessment. I strongly suspect one of the reasons that they didn't was that there was no agreement among them on what was important to learn about their community's mental health needs—or how the information would be used. As you can see, the point is not just to develop a set of questions—the questions we ask must have a clear focus and purpose. Each question should add another increment to that sum of information that we require. The well-designed questionnaire asks no less and no more than is needed for our research. Anyone can develop a questionnaire or conduct a survey. The "test" of a good survey is whether it produces useful data. Genuinely useful information seldom comes about just because someone happens to find a set of already prepared questions.

QUESTIONS FOR DISCUSSION

1. Why is it important that the questionnaire communicate the same frame of reference to all respondents?
2. Construct a closed-ended question (complete with response set) to record marital status.
3. Why is it important to decide upon the survey methodology before designing the questionnaire to be used?
4. What is wrong with each of the following questions? (Hint: watch for terms that are not operationally defined and may not mean the same to everyone.) Suggest a better way to phrase each question.
   a. Do you feel that individuals who are forced to have life support systems in order to continue existence should be given the choice to die?
   b. Do you feel that the feminization of poverty has come about due to the increasing divorce rate?
   c. What effect does dropping out of school have on employment opportunities?
   d. Is there a higher incidence of suicide among upper-middle-class teens than in the lower income levels?
   e. Are older men or women more likely to be abused?
   f. Is abuse of the elderly related to the emphasis of youth on television?
   g. Among teens who later become pregnant, why do you think they do not consistently use birth control?
   h. Do you think that higher levels of education result in a decrease in racist attitudes?
   i. Do you think there is not any more drinking among college students who live at home than among those who live away from home?

MINI-PROJECTS FOR EXPERIENCING RESEARCH FIRSTHAND

1. Iacono-Harris and Nuccio, in an article entitled "Developing the Macro Pool: Turning Undergraduates on to Macro Practice" (Administration in Social Work, 11 (2), Summer, 1987), state in their conclusions (p. 85), "We believe that macro practitioners are developed, not born."
   a. How would you test this hypothesis?
   b. What kinds of questions would you develop? Develop a ten to fifteen item questionnaire that would help you to test this hypothesis.

    c. Share your questions with another student who has also developed questions. Examine all of the group's questions and decide which ones could be used for research into this topic and which ones should be purged.

2. Develop a set of questions to use to interview nursing home residents to find out about the quality of their lives.
   a. List the important dimensions to be covered.
   b. Construct five open-ended and five closed-ended questions along with the corresponding response set.
   c. As you reflect over the questions you would ask, what would you learn about life in a nursing home? What wouldn't you learn from this set of questions?

3. Conduct a twenty-minute interview with a neighbor, friend, grandparent, or someone else you know. Ask respondents to relate a significant experience in their lives (e.g., living through the Depression, recovery from major surgery, running for political office). Use only open-ended questions. Keep notes, and transcribe your interview. Be sure to include the questions that were asked of the respondents and any remarks (such as transitional statements) you made along the way. Share in class what you learned from the experience. Be sure to include a brief description of the person whom you interviewed (e.g., female, eighty-three years of age, former journalist, etc.).

4. Develop a questionnaire that will help you learn why your fellow students have become social work majors.
   a. What hypothesis do you want to test?
   b. Develop ten to fifteen closed-ended questions and one open-ended question.
   c. Interview ten social work majors.
   d. What did you learn from this experience? Did you learn more from the open-ended or the closed-ended questions?

5. Review the article "Student Satisfaction with Field Placement" (Fortune, Feathers, Rook, Scrimenti, Smollen, Stemerman and Tucker, 1985) in *Journal of Social Work Education*, 21 (3), pp. 92–112. Look especially at the items used on their questionnaire (p. 95). If it were your responsibility to revise this instrument, what modifications would you make? Prepare a revised questionnaire to measure students' satisfaction with their field placements.

6. Review the article "Social Well-Being of Institutionalized Elderly Persons" (Reed and Washington, 1984) in *International Journal of Aging and Human Development*, 19 (4), pp. 311–318.

Examine the eleven-item Social Well-Being Scale. If it were your responsibility to review and possibly revise this instrument, what modifications would you make? Prepare a revised questionnaire to measure elderly persons' social well-being.

RESOURCES AND REFERENCES

Alreck, P.L. and Settle, R.B. (1985). *The Survey Research Handbook.* Homewood, IL: Irwin.

Berdie, D.R., Anderson, J.F. and Niebuhr, M.A. (1986). *Questionnaire Design and Use.* Metuchen, NJ: Scarecrow Press.

Blankenship, A.B. (1977). *Professional Telephone Surveys.* New York: McGraw-Hill.

Bradburn, N. and Sudman, S. (1979). *Improving Interview Method and Questionnaire Design.* San Francisco, CA: Jossey-Bass.

Converse, J.M. and Presser, S. (1986). *Survey Questions: Handcrafting the Standardized Questionnaire.* Beverly Hills, CA: Sage.

DeVaus, D.A. (1986). *Surveys in Social Research.* London: George Allen and Unwin.

Dillman, D.A. (1978). *Mail and Telephone Surveys: The Total Design Method* New York: Wiley.

Fink, A. and Kosecoff, J. (1985). *How to Conduct Surveys: A Step-by-Step Guide.* Beverly Hills, CA: Sage.

Frey, J.H. (1983). *Survey Research by Telephone.* Beverly Hills, CA: Sage.

Jaeger, R.M. (1984). *Sampling in Education and the Social Sciences.* New York: Longman.

Kidder, L.H. and Judd, C.M. (1986). *Research Methods in Social Relations.* New York: Holt, Rinehart and Winston.

Rossi, P.F., Wright, J.D., and Anderson, A.B. (1983). *Handbook of Survey Research.* New York: Academic Press.

Schuman, H. and Presser, S. (1981). *Questions and Answers in Attitude Surveys.* New York: Academic Press.

Sudman, S. and Bradburn, N.M. (1982). *Asking Questions: A Practical Guide to Questionnaire Design.* San Francisco, CA: Jossey-Bass.

Eight

Unobtrusive Approaches to Data Collection: Secondary Data and Content Analysis

The research approaches we have discussed thus far have one thing in common—they involve interaction with respondents in order to collect the needed data. Unfortunately, anytime interviewers interact with respondents there is the potential for producing unintended changes in them. For example, imagine that you are involved in presenting a workshop to your co-workers on the avoidance of sexism in language. A week before the workshop you send each participant a small questionnaire that asks if he or she uses certain terms or phrases in conversation. Suppose Robert Doe reads the questionnaire, briefly considers how he will respond, and then indicates on the form that he does not use any of those terms in his normal conversation. However, driving home from work that night, he reflects back upon the questionnaire and realizes that there are several other ways in which his choice of words or phrasing might be considered sexist. As a result of thinking about the pretest, he resolves to eliminate these terms and phrases from his speech and writing.

Your workshop is conducted as scheduled, and you administer the posttest. An examination of the data reveals a decrease in the use of sexist language at the time of the posttest. But if others in the agency had the same experience as Robert Doe, how would you know which had the most impact, the workshop or the pretest? Perhaps any reduction in sexist language was merely the result of respondents' reactions to the pretest questionnaire. It is conceivable that even as mild an interaction as testing can bring about changes in attitudes, behavior, or knowledge.

Even if we are considerate and polite about it, asking respondents to give us information about themselves is intrusive. This can be seen in the number of respondents who refuse to cooperate with interviewers or complete survey forms. Even with cooperation, there is the possibility that merely asking questions may have some inadvertent effect upon respondents.

One of the more famous examples of an unanticipated effect on research subjects has come to be known as the **Hawthorne Effect**. Prior to World War II, researchers at a Western Electric plant in Chicago found that employees in the study raised their production—no matter what physical changes were made in their work environment (e.g., the lighting was both increased and decreased). What researchers learned is that subjects may be significantly influenced by the knowledge that they are taking part in a research study. In fact, knowing that they have been chosen to participate in a research project has more influence on them than the independent variables.

One way to avoid having to rule out the Hawthorne Effect is to utilize data that already exist instead of collecting new data from respondents. Using existing data that does not involve interaction with research subjects fits into the category called **unobtrusive research**. The classic work in this area is that of Webb, Campbell, Schwartz, and Sechrest (1966), *Unobtrusive Measures: Nonreactive Research in the Social Sciences.*

Whether they are aware of it or not, social workers in performing their routine tasks help collect mountains of data each year. The vast majority of these data come from the ordinary processing of clients into and out of service delivery systems—in admission forms, social histories, and progress notes. Data available for unobtrusive research is also contained in the records of institutionalized persons, in the portfolios of immigrants, and in the files of persons who've enrolled in community educational presentations. Sometimes this data is kept in "hard copy" form and stored in filing cabinets, or it may be contained in the electronic memory of a computer. This data is not collected with research purposes in mind. However, collections of such data represent a wealth of research opportunities for interested social workers.

Researchers who rely upon public documents, reports, and historical data are said to be engaged in a type of unobtrusive research called **archival research** or **secondary data analysis**. This type of research involves the analysis of an existing data set that results in knowledge, interpretations, and conclusions beyond those stated in the original study (Hakim, 1982). The intent is not to find fault with another's study, but rather to test new hypotheses or explore questions not examined in the original report. While the original study may have collected data on the attitudes of a cross-section of Americans, a secondary analysis might examine only the attitudes of a minority subgroup. Secondary analysis extends or goes beyond what the initial investigators reported.

Investigators may limit themselves to a single data set or source document, or may utilize several data sets from different sponsors or agencies. For instance, George and Landerman (1984) reported on the use of seven data sets to examine the relationship between health and subjective well-being. These data sets were compiled by different organizations at different times and with sample sizes varying from 502 to 4,254 respondents. Particularly rich data sets may also be analyzed using different analysis techniques, new combinations of variables, or new scales created from the existing (original) variables.

Secondary data analysis should not be considered as a research approach to be employed only when a researcher does not want to collect his or her own data. In fact, Stewart (1984) argues that

> it is hard to conceive of a research effort that does not begin with at least some secondary research. Existing information provides a foundation for problem formulation, for the design of new research, and for the analysis and interpretation of new information. There is little point in rediscovering that which is already known. (P. 13)

A good use of secondary data is to identify trends. For example, a student once approached me with some concern because she had heard from a relative that her home county had the highest suicide rate in the state. I was somewhat skeptical about this, but when I had the opportunity, I went to the Government Documents section of the library and examined several of the Department of Health's *Vital Statistics* annual reports. I found that in the most recent year the county in question, with a population of 12,000, had 7 suicides. This gave it a rate of 52.5 suicides per 100,000 population. (This is a standard base for comparison so that urban counties can be compared with rural counties.) This was in fact one of the highest suicide rates in the state, as the overall average for the state was 14.3 suicides per 100,000 population.

However, a look at the previous year's statistics revealed no suicides. Thus, in the span of two years, the county had one of the lowest and one of the highest rates in the state. This is not uncommon when the actual number of events (such as suicides) is relatively small. Looking at the statistics for one additional year revealed that there were only 2 suicides, but that the rate for the county (15.2 per 100,000 population) again exceeded that state's average.

Table 8.1   Seven-Year Suicide Rate in One Rural County (per 100,000 population)

	Number of Suicides	**County Rate**	**State Rate**
1980	1	8.1	13.3
1981	2	15.7	12.1
1982	2	15.4	13.5
1983	4	31.0	13.2
1984	2	15.2	13.7
1985	0	0	13.2
1986	7	52.5	14.3

As you can tell by looking at table 8.1, there is a noticeable trend for the suicide rate in this rural county to exceed the state's average. In fact, in five of seven years, the county's suicide rate was higher than the average rate for the whole state.

Had the student looked at the rates for only the last two years, or just one of those two years, a mistaken impression might have been obtained. There is a certain inherent danger in misinterpreting real trends or patterns whenever one selectively draws from a study. By looking at a longer span of time, we can have greater confidence that a trend is real and well established.

Advantages and Disadvantages of Unobtrusive Approaches

Right away, some exciting advantages of unobtrusive research are apparent. First, if you discover that someone else has already collected data that you can use for a study, you can save considerable time and effort in your data collection phase. Once an interesting data base has been identified, it is often possible to move rapidly into data analysis. Secondary data sources may already be held by the library or university, or you may be able to purchase them for a nominal fee.

Second, any bias associated with the collection of the data may be generally known and accepted. It may be known, for instance, that the data tends to underestimate the true incidence of a social problem (as in the case of suicide data). Other data sets may overestimate the incidence of a problem. For example, data on psychiatric hospital admissions that combined new patients with those who had previous admissions could overestimate incidence of the most severe form of mental illness. (Incidence is the number of *new* cases or events during a given period of time.) Since all studies have some limitations, the secondary data analyst may choose to use a data set even though it has several known problems. Problems with the data set are not a reflection upon the researcher using secondary data analysis. After all, the secondary data analyst is only borrowing the data set.

Third, since you are not interviewing clients or patients or interacting with them in any way, you need not worry that your inquiries will put them at risk or have any harmful effects. If the data are in the public domain, you may not need consent or permission from institutional review boards or other research and review committees to conduct your research.

The final but best reason for conducting secondary data analysis is that it provides an opportunity to study social problems in terms of long-term change and enables comparative study. Secondary data analysts can make comparisons across localities, states, and nations (presuming, of course, that the data are available).

On the other hand, there are some disadvantages associated with relying upon secondary or archival data. Sometimes the important historical records you need have been destroyed by fire, flood, tornadoes, or rodents. Sometimes researchers, well into their projects, find gaps in the data because of changes in procedures or policies that affected the data collection. With the passage of time, conditions such as laws change, which can affect the definitions of variables. Categories can suddenly become more or less inclusive.

I once discovered that a set of child abuse archival data I wanted to explore was compartmentalized. The data were recorded in two different computers in two different formats because the data collection forms had been redesigned. There was no way to combine the data sets into one large file without going to the expense of hiring computer programmers to prepare the data in a more usable form. As a result, I did no research with that data.

If the data were reported more or less voluntarily (there was no penalty for not reporting) it may not be as reliable as when 100 percent of the units were required to report. Finally, recent data may not be available as soon as the researcher may desire it. It is not unusual for some agencies or departments to take six to twelve months (or longer) to produce their most "current" annual report of the previous year's data.

In summary, while there are many advantages associated with secondary data analysis, the researcher should be alert to changes in the way the data were collected, completeness of data, and the ease with which data can be manipulated.

State-Maintained Data Sets Are Useful for Secondary Analysis

Secondary analyses can be conducted in both private and public agencies. However, private agencies tend to be protective of their data. Even though researchers agree not to divulge personal data, private agencies often feel that any research within their agencies may endanger the privacy of individual clients. Another argument often heard from both public and private agencies is that the proposed research will require too much clerical support to locate archival records or selected cases. Unlike private agencies, public agencies and departments are often required to keep certain statistics that are viewed as public information and available to all. While public agencies are not always as cooperative as many researchers would like, they generally do provide some form of aggregated data each year in the form of annual reports.

Table 8.2 contains examples of variables or **social indicators**

Table 8.2 Examples of Variables for Secondary Research

Indicator	Source
Marriages	Department of Health
Divorces	Department of Health
Suicides	Department of Health
Live births	Department of Health
Infant deaths	Department of Health
Deaths (all ages)	Department of Health
Deaths from cirrhosis of the liver	Department of Health
Inpatient admissions	Department of Mental Health
Outpatient admissions	Department of Mental Health
General relief cases	Department of Public Welfare
Aid to dependent children	Department of Public Welfare
Motor vehicle injury accidents	Department of Highway Safety
Motor vehicle deaths	Department of Highway Safety
Motor vehicle accidents	Department of Highway Safety
Dependency and neglect cases	Department of Child Welfare
Delinquency cases	Juvenile Court Statistics
Arraignments	Supreme Court Statistics
School dropouts	Department of Education
School enrollment	Department of Education
Unemployment	Bureau of Employment
Average weekly earnings	Bureau of Employment
Retail alcohol sales	Department of Liquor Control

(they tell us something about trends within social problems) that are commonly collected by all states. Generally these data are reported by county.

These examples are only some of the variables that are routinely collected and reported each month, quarter, or year. Public and university libraries often will be designated as state depositories and will have recent reports as well as more historical reports. If the reports you need are not found in the library, contact various departments in your state capital. Eventually you will locate the appropriate department from which to collect the data. Departmental names vary across the states. For example, in some states the Department of Highway Safety is known as the Transportation Department.

Applications of Secondary Data Analysis

If information is power (Francis Bacon noted that "knowledge itself is power"), then the possibilities of being able to effect change are enormous when one has access to secondary data.

Example 1: Suppose you are a school social worker, and a number of children have been injured because there is no traffic light at a busy intersection they must cross before they can get to school. Let's further suppose that "officials" are dragging their feet, saying that a traffic light is not needed. You obtain a list of all the locations where vehicular and pedestrian-injury accidents have occurred in your city in the past year. What if the intersection that you feel needs a light was the site of more injury accidents than any other location in the city not only for the previous year, but also the past three years? Isn't that powerful information that you could use to help advocate for a traffic light?

Example 2: You are a state employee, the supervisor of a child abuse investigation team. You are painfully aware that your unit is understaffed. In talking with others, you sense that your unit may investigate more reported cases of abuse and neglect than any other unit in the state. Yet, when you talk to the agency director about this problem, he or she is not sympathetic about your need for additional staff. The director indicates that cases of abuse are increasing over the whole state—that it isn't just a problem in your county.

However, because you occasionally have the opportunity to talk to other social workers from across the state, you learn that some investigation units are adding staff, while your unit has added no new staff in three years. A research question forms in your mind. Which county has the highest incidence of child abuse/neglect cases in the state? When you look at the data you discover that while the more populous counties have significantly more cases of abuse and neglect, your county has more cases of child abuse and neglect *per thousand population* than any other county in the state. Would this information be enough to use for leverage to get some additional staff. If not, a next step might be to gather data on how many staff the other investigation units have and which units have the lowest ratio of cases to staff. If your county has the highest ratio (the most cases but fewest staff), this would be compelling objective information that could influence the decision to allocate additional staff to your unit.

This example could be carried further. If the data were available, you could examine the ratio of cases to child protective services staff in your state to those of surrounding states. This type of information might be used to influence your legislators to increase appropriations at the state level. You could also compare salaries of child protective workers in your state with those in other states. If workers in your state are paid below the average, lobby for increased pay.

Example 3: You become concerned about adolescents' use of illegal drugs in your community. You suspect that a new street drug is the cause of a rash of fatal overdoses, but you have no "hard" data to support this assumption. Since you want to conduct a drug education campaign for adolescents, you feel that local data are needed. You learn that the data are not obtainable from the state Health Department or from the police department. You find, however, that the hospital emergency room keeps this sort of data. Even if the hospital does not make these records available, you may find that the county's ambulance service keeps this data and would be happy to share it.

There is no shortage of ways that secondary data can be used. You could investigate whether the high school dropout rate has decreased within your community over the past five years. Has the dropout prevention program had an impact? Most school systems have good records on the number of dropouts. It would be relatively easy to determine if there has been a dramatic change in the dropout rate. Other uses of social indicators include examining how your state compares with other states in terms of unemployment, teen pregnancies, or some other social problem.

Additionally, you might want to formally test hypotheses, for example, that concern about AIDS will result in fewer divorces. You might want to conduct correlational studies to see if increases in unemployment are associated with increases in mental hospital admissions or if high school dropout rates are associated with juvenile delinquency rates. You could be interested in whether relations among the races are improving. (See, for example, the Roper Center for Public Opinion Research, *A Guide to the Roper Center's Resources for the Study of American Race Relations*, 1982, and Schuman's *Racial Attitudes in America: Trends and Interpretations*, 1985.)

Social indicators can also be used to make national comparisons. How does the United States compare against other industrialized countries on such indicators as infant deaths or literacy rates? Have we made advances in the last five years, or have these indicators remained at about the same level?

There is virtually no end to social indicators that may be gleaned from state and federal departments, bureaus, agencies, and offices. And, there are thousands of organizations that collect information on their membership and the services provided to members. Social service agencies across this nation have fascinating questions they would like explored—if only someone with the right combination of research skills and interest would come along.

As you have seen from these illustrations, secondary data analysis is versatile and can be used with problems that vary from those with a macro focus to those with a micro concern. One of the main strengths of secondary data analysis is that there are generally multiple sources of data relevant to the topic in which you are interested. If you cannot obtain data from one source, there is almost always another, sometimes better data set.

Secondary Analysis of Survey Data

With the advent of computer processing has come a proliferation of large-scale surveys. These surveys, often with thousands of respondents, are generally available to a broad range of researchers because of the ease with which this data can be shared via computer tape, disk, or diskette. These surveys differ in several ways from the occasional surveys conducted by social workers.

First of all, these surveys are coded so that they can be easily manipulated by computer processing. This greatly facilitates their use by researchers other than the original investigators. In fact, some of the surveys (e.g., the General Social Survey) were designed particularly for secondary analysis (Glenn, Converse, Cutler, and Hyman, 1978).

Second, these surveys tend to use large, national, cross-sectional samples. Some of these surveys (or at least portions of their questions) are repeated at regular intervals, so that trends can be observed over time.

Finally, these surveys often are indexed, and copies are made available so that the entire data set can be purchased at nominal cost.

Catalogs may also be produced so that researchers have a good idea of the data available before purchasing the data set.

Secondary analysis of survey data usually comes about in one of two ways: (1) a data base is discovered that contains information not fully reported or examined; or (2) a hypothesis is generated and then a search is conducted to find an appropriate data base. Normally, hypotheses occur before data collection; however, in the case of archival research and secondary survey analysis, the researcher needs to know beforehand that the type of data needed does exist. He or she could spend several months requesting catalogs, reviewing existing data bases, and contacting various research centers only to learn that the type of data needed is not available. Consequently, some researchers develop hypotheses *after* they come across (perhaps accidentally) a particularly exciting data base. Hyman (1987) has written, "Among investigators with *broad* interests, serendipity is a likely occurrence. By chance, they are likely to find some of what they are seeking, and also to discover fortuitously in the course of one search valuable bodies of data that are strategic for the study of other problems" (p. 83).

Secondary Survey and Additional Secondary Data Sources

The federal government conducts more than two hundred surveys and censuses every year (Turner and Martin, 1984). Perhaps the best known of these are the decennial Census of Population and Housing. The U.S. Bureau of the Census also conducts special purpose surveys that supply statistical information on social, economic, and demographic characteristics (e.g. *The Hispanic Population in the United States: March 1986 and 1987*), as well as national information on such topics as employment and unemployment, income, and adult education.

To identify recent publications of the U.S. Bureau of the Census, see the *Census Catalog and Guide* (annual) and *The American Statistics Index: A Comprehensive Guide and Index to the Statistical Publications of the United States Government* (ASI). The ASI is a comprehensive annual index that contains abstracts of publications issued by all the departments and agencies of the federal government. These publications can include such items as special surveys of health care costs and reports of AFDC demonstration projects.

The U.S. Bureau of the Census is just one source of good secondary data; there are many more. For instance, the Federal Bureau of Investigation prepares the *Uniform Crime Reports for the United States* based on crimes cleared by arrests and reported by local police departments across the country. Five-year trend data is reported in addition to the annual statistics. The U.S. Department of Education (National Center for Education Statistics) provides data on enrollment, number of teachers, sources of revenue, years of schooling completed by state, and even unemployment rates of persons sixteen and older by the number of years of school completed. Their report is entitled *Digest of Educational Statistics.*

The Department of Health and Human Services compiles such data as births by age of mother and birth order, mortality rates by age, race, sex, and cause of death for each state and the fifty largest standard metropolitan statistical areas. Its publication is entitled *Vital Statistics of the United States.* The Department of Labor produces a *Monthly Labor Review* that monitors trends such as employment in the civilian labor force, unemployment rates by age, sex, race, duration of unemployment, employment by type of industry (e.g., mining, government, retail), average weekly earnings, and consumer price indexes.

A depository for social science data collected by academic survey research organizations in this country is held by the Interuniversity Consortium for Political and Social Research (ICPSR) at the University of Michigan. The consortium's holdings can be identified through their publication *A Guide to Resources and Services.* Their holdings are voluminous and vary from census data to special surveys of health and crime to the historical voting records of all the members of Congress. Archives are held also at the Louis Harris Political Data Center at the University of North Carolina, which publishes the *Directory of Louis Harris Public Opinion Machine-Readable Data.*

The Roper Center for Public Opinion Research at the University of Connecticut is a public opinion research library. The Center's library contains complete data files and documentation for over ten thousand surveys conducted over the past sixty years. It houses collections of surveys taken by the Roper and Gallup organizations, as well as those commissioned by ABC, CBS, and NBC news and such papers as the *New York Times, Washington Post, Wall Street Journal,* and the *Los Angeles Times.* And there are other sources too numerous to mention.

The Roper Center has periodic publications to announce its holdings, and is also a depository for annual surveys known as the General Social Surveys. With just two exceptions (1979 and 1981), the National Opinion Research Center has been conducting large-scale national surveys as part of a program to collect and make available social indicator data. By the end of 1987, there were a total of

Table 8.3 Survey Data Presented in the Codebook

DECL 5
COLS. 36–39
Qs. 84C-87A

84. (Continued)

84.C. If some people in your community suggested that a book he wrote in favor of homosexuality should be taken out of your public library, would you favor removing this book, or not?

[VAR: LIBHOMO]

COL. 36

Response	Punch	Year								All
		1972–82	1982B	1983	1984	1985	1986	1987	1987B	
Favor	1	3707	153	0	552	636	0	580	159	5787
Not favor	2	4987	162	0	873	848	0	846	182	7898
Don't know	8	276	35	0	43	45	0	34	12	445
No answer	9	21	4	0	5	5	0	6	0	41
Not applicable	BK	4635	0	1599	0	0	1470	0	0	7704

85. Are you in favor of the death penalty for persons convicted of murder?

[VAR: CAPPUN2]

COL. 37

Response	Punch	Year								All
		1972–82	1982B	1983	1984	1985	1986	1987	1987B	
Yes	1	1750	0	0	0	0	0	0	0	1750
No	2	1151	0	0	0	0	0	0	0	1151
Don't know	8	200	0	0	0	0	0	0	0	200
No answer	9	16	0	0	0	0	0	0	0	16
Not applicable	BK	10509	354	1599	1473	1534	1470	1466	353	18758

86. Do you favor or oppose the death penalty for persons convicted of murder?
[VAR: CAPPUN]

| Response | Punch | Year | | | | | | | | COL. 38 |
		1972–82	1982B	1983	1984	1985	1986	1987	1987B	All
Favor	1	6933	154	1169	1029	1154	1046	1012	154	12651
Oppose	2	2936	165	354	347	297	344	354	165	4962
Don't know	8	607	32	74	86	75	76	88	33	1071
No answer	9	33	3	2	11	8	4	12	1	74
Not applicable	BK	3117	0	0	0	0	0	0	0	3117

87. How important is the death penalty issue to you—would you say it is one of the most important, important, not very important, or not important at all?
[VAR: CAPIMP]

| Response | Punch | Year | | | | | | | | COL. 39 |
		1972–82	1982B	1983	1984	1985	1986	1987	1987B	All
One of the most important	1	0	0	0	67	0	0	0	0	67
Important	2	0	0	0	261	0	0	0	0	261
Not very important	3	0	0	0	120	0	0	0	0	120
Not important at all	4	0	0	0	26	0	0	0	0	26
Don't know	8	0	0	0	6	0	0	0	0	6
No answer	9	0	0	0	4	0	0	0	0	4
Not applicable	BK	13626	354	1599	989	1534	1470	1466	353	21391

Source: J. A. Davis and T. W. Smith (1987).

21,875 completed interviews from fourteen surveys available for researchers to analyze as part of the General Social Surveys. By obtaining the latest cumulative codebook from the Roper Center, you can identify questions that have been replicated over several surveys. Permanent questions as well as rotating questions and some occasional questions occur on each survey. Data can be obtained from the Roper Center directly or through the International Survey Library Association (ISLA) in which many colleges and universities hold a membership.

Table 8.3 shows how the survey data is presented in the codebook. Because each of the surveys obtains comprehensive demographic information from the respondents, the General Social Survey questions can be analyzed in great detail. For example, you could test the hypothesis that persons over sixty are more supportive of the death penalty than younger persons. Or, you could look at responses by level of education, race, geographic region, family income, and so on. This data is useful for finding trends over time.

For information about studies conducted in countries other than the United States, the *Index to International Statistics* is a helpful resource. Also, the United Nations has a *Demographic Yearbook*, an annual publication with statistics such as estimates by country of population by age and sex, rates of population increase, birth and death rates, marriage and divorce rates, and life expectancy at birth. The United Nations' *Monthly Bulletin of Statistics* contains mid-year population estimates by country, as well as birth, death and marriage rates for selected countries, paid employment, unemployment rates, hours worked in manufacturing, production from mines, textile mills, rubber, chemical and other manufacturing, motor vehicles, electricity produced, and trade data. The *United Nations Statistical Yearbook* provides information on unemployment, housing conditions, persons per household, households with inside water, government disbursements (e.g., expenditures for social welfare and defense, and total government expenditures), hospitals, health personnel, schools, pupils, teachers, agricultural production, world trade, and tourist arrivals.

Content Analysis

Content Analysis is another unobtrusive research process that objectively examines the content of communications. This objectivity is made possible by reliance upon quantification. Accordingly, content analysis involves searching for and counting key words, phrases, or concepts in communications. These may be counted (frequencies of occurrence), measured (e.g., the size of a newspaper article in column inches or the amount of time allocated to a specific topic in a speech), or otherwise categorized in a manner that others could replicate. Content analysis can be used either retrospectively (to examine materials already in existence) or prospectively (to analyze impending events or narratives). However, the major use of content analysis is to provide a framework so that a quantitative approach can be used to analyze communications after they have been spoken or printed.

Examples of materials that can be content analyzed include: newspapers, magazines, journals, books, television programs, audio and video tapes, minutes from agency board meetings, congressional records, presidential addresses, and historical documents such as letters, diaries, and so on.

While the first dictionary definition of content analysis occurred in 1961, its intellectual roots go back considerably farther. In 1910, Max Weber proposed a large-scale content analysis of newspapers at the first meeting of the German Sociological Society. Also, around the turn of the century in this country, quantitative newspaper analyses (measuring the column inches devoted to specific subjects) were conducted because of concern that newspapers were not providing as much factual content as they were gossip, sports, and scandals (Krippendorff, 1980).

During World War II, content analysis was used to analyze propaganda. After the war, the value of content analysis as a research tool was widely recognized, and interest in it spread beyond the field of communications to the disciplines of political science, psychology, history, sociology, and literature.

Several interesting applications of content analysis have been made by social workers. Jenkins et. al. (1982) used content analysis to review 712 abstracts of social work dissertations published from 1975 to 1979. They found that 44 percent of the dissertations were focused on direct practice with individuals, families, groups, and communities; 36 percent concerned the method of social policy and administration; and 3 percent involved social work education. The history and philosophy of social work made up 3 percent of the entries, research, 5 percent, and all other topics, 3 percent. Further, when they looked at fields of specialization, they found that almost two-thirds of all the dissertation abstracts fell into five main fields. The largest, "professional issues," made up more than 19 percent of all theses. The other main specializations were: family and child welfare, 14 percent; mental health, 13 percent; personal social services, 11 percent; and aging, 8 percent.

Wilson (1982) reported on the use of computer software to conduct content analysis of debates contained in the Congressional Record specific to a policy focus, the Employment Act of 1946. Wilson was able to find that the categories of "role of organized social welfare" and "role of families and individuals" received almost no mention in the debates. In other words, social services were not seen as being instrumental in affecting employment nor was there any emphasis on the "rights, or responsibilities of families and individuals" (p. 41.)

More recently, Billups and Julia (1987) used a content analysis of position-vacancy descriptions in *Social Casework and NASW News* to find out how social work practice was represented in these position descriptions. Among their findings were that family and child welfare position vacancies decreased from 58.9 percent in 1960 to 21.3 percent in 1980, while mental health related descriptions went from 11 percent to 45 percent in 1980. The titles "clinical social worker" and "therapist" constituted less than 2 percent of the total in 1960 but about 20 percent of the titles in 1980.

Other uses of content analysis have been suggested by Allen-Mears (1984):

> to analyze the recorded interactions of social work students before and after a training program in order to evaluate the efficacy of the training: "Did students who participated in the training use more reflective listening statements after training?" Content analysis might also be used to study social work texts: "Do recent texts present gays and lesbians in a more positive context than older texts? Are blacks more likely than women or other minority groups to be presented in a negative context in social work texts?" (P. 52)

Content analysis lends itself well to other techniques employed by social workers. For instance, Barry (1988) has discussed the use of autobiographical writing with elderly adults. Content analysis could be used to show that this technique is successful in ameliorating depression, improving self-acceptance, and helping older adults to focus on the present. As a research tool, content analysis would allow social workers to measure older adults' progress by quantifying the positive themes in their writings.

Advantages and Disadvantages of Content Analysis

Like secondary data analysis, content analysis has the advantages of being (1) unobtrusive, (2) generally inexpensive to conduct, and (3) able to deal with large volumes of data. No special training or expertise is required—all that is needed is a research question or hypothesis and a set of communications or body of materials from which to begin developing categories.

One of the disadvantages of content analysis is that coding or categorizing the items can be a problem if several individuals are involved in the process. Reliability must be maintained throughout this phase of the project. If categories are vaguely defined, more mistakes will be made than if classification rules are clearly defined. However, it is not difficult to determine the reliability of the categorization process (the consistency among coders). See, for instance, Allen-Meares' (1984) description of computation for reliability.

The most common units of analysis are individual words or terms. However, if you search for selected key words, you may miss other terms that could also refer to the concept you are studying. Thus, if you instruct reviewers to search for the number of times "clinical social worker" is used in the newspaper, they might overlook references to "mental health worker." The term "mental health worker" could be an indirect reference to a clinical social worker. Reference can be made to the subject directly or indirectly. Indirect references might be discovered late in the project or not at all. This problem is more likely to occur when computers are used to conduct the content analysis without the investigator pretesting categories on a sample of source materials.

Essentials of Content Analysis

When you want to employ content analysis you start with a research question or hypothesis. Perhaps you want to know when the term "clinical social worker" evolved in social work literature. Or perhaps you have a notion that the newspaper you most frequently read has a negative opinion of social workers or some other definite bias that you want to document. You may want to test the hypothesis that fewer articles on the topic of community development have been written in the past five years than on private practice. Some question or assumption that can be tested through an examination of written or spoken communications occurs to you.

From that hypothesis or research question, you begin to think about what materials would provide the best source of communications for the content analysis. Will you use a local newspaper, the *New York Times, Social Work, Social Service Review, Social Casework*, or some combination of journals or papers? Naturally, there are pragmatic decisions to be faced. The materials should be relatively easy to obtain. It is easier to conclude your study if your library has a complete collection of the materials you need than if you have to travel out of state to examine them. Familiarity with the source materials is also needed; some journals or newsletters may be less relevant to your topic than you originally thought. Newer journals may not have the historical record in which you are interested.

Third, you will need to decide what will constitute the **units of the analysis**, or the recording units. Depending upon the amount of data to be analyzed, you may choose to examine words or terms, entire paragraphs, or the whole item itself (e.g., an entire article or speech). Most commonly, content analysis involves quantification of words or terms (counting the number of times that certain terms such as "social action" and "community organizer" appeared in social work journals during 1989).

The examination of themes and whole items can involve more complex rules for categorization. Take, for instance, the situation where newspaper editorials were analyzed for opinions of President Bush. How would such editorials be categorized? Searching for a set of specific words or phrases (e.g., "good President") may not be of much help. The editorials may not use those particular words but still be favorably impressed with Bush's performance. It is also possible that an editorial may like some of his policies but not others. A simplistic way would be to determine if the context of an editorial was basically positive (supportive) or negative (nonsupportive).

When determining units of analysis, think about what you intend to count or quantify. This generally leads to conceptualizing what categories will be needed. These categories should not be developed apart from the material being reviewed; your familiarity with the material will assist you in devising definitions and categories. As with questionnaire development, the use of a pilot test will assist you in refining the operational definitions of categories. Written rules, especially if more than one person is going to be involved in the content analysis, assist with the classifying and categorizing of data. It is important that categories be exhaustive and mutually exclusive.

Another decision that needs to be made is how much of the material to review. This issue cannot be addressed until the researcher can define the universe of items to be reviewed. This is not a problem when the universe of items is so small that all of it can be examined. However, when there are volumes of material available for examination, it is often advisable to sample those materials. (As discussed in the chapter on survey research, there are several ways to sample). With regard to content analysis, it makes the most sense to think of sampling in terms of whether it should be random or systematic.

However, there may be times when you want to have a stratified sample because magazines and journals differ in their prime audiences and in the characteristics of their subscribers. Krippendorff (1980) has also described cluster, multistage, and other forms of sampling with content analysis.

A Practical Application of Content Analysis

A serious problem for most mental health and social service agencies is public image. Bad publicity may affect agency admissions or the community's perception of the quality of care provided by an agency. What follows is a partially true (Royse and Wellons, 1988), partially fictionalized account of how content analysis has been used as a research tool to bring about needed change.

At one point in my career I was employed by a mental health system that was (so the administrators thought) too often in the local news. A local newspaper covered every board meeting, and much of the coverage had a negative slant to it. For instance, one editorial stated that the mental health system had "axed practically all hope of renewing the [mental health] levy with the construction of a $2.2 million building." Since the vote on the mental health levy was over two years away, such a statement by the newspaper seemed to indicate a stance that was not supportive of the community mental health system's need for the county's property tax levy. Our fear was that the newspaper had a powerful potential for influencing citizens of the community to vote against the renewal of the mental health levy. Since more than half of the revenue to operate the mental health system came from the tax levy, it became clear that effort should begin right away to counter negative perceptions held by the newspaper staff. Part of the strategy was to objectively demonstrate to them how the content of their articles and headlines was not balanced and could have a detrimental effect upon public opinion.

Every morning the director's secretary clipped articles from the local newspapers that referred to the mental health system. These were kept in a historical file. Clippings had been kept for about ten years and constituted an obvious source of material for a content analysis. Since reading ten years of newspaper clippings was a sizable task, we decided that reading headlines was much more manageable. A listing of all the headlines and captions above the news articles was made, and this constituted our units of analysis.

While our interest was in identifying the amount of negative coverage by the newspaper, this quickly became problematic. It was not difficult to identify those headlines we regarded as negative

("Hostility Erupts at Mental Health Board Meeting," "Mental Health Board in Dispute," "Mental Health Officials Squabble"). However, there were other headlines that we took to be negative, but that others who were not affiliated with the mental health system might not have interpreted that way. In addition, a headline might have been categorized as positive, but the article below it might have been negative. And some headlines were difficult to interpret ("Crisis Center May Resume Services" or "Judge Promises Fast Ruling") without reading the whole article. Consequently, it was decided to conduct the content analysis on selected key words.

It would not have been possible to anticipate every term or key word that indicated a negative reflection on the mental health system. Even clusters of negative words or phrases would have been very difficult to specify. Therefore, we decided to search for those key words that had something to do with the delivery of services or administrative issues.

Among our findings was that there were thirty-seven headlines, over the ten-year period, containing the key word "facility." This number of appearances was larger than that of any problem-specific key word, such as "divorce," "alcohol," "stress," "depression," "addiction," "domestic violence," "incest," "runaways," "death," and so on. It also occurred more times than population-specific terms, such as "aging," "elderly," "stepparent," "families," "teen-agers," "juveniles," "children," and "students." Clearly, the newspaper was much more concerned with administrative issues (such as building a new facility) than with service delivery issues.

The number of square inches of newspaper coverage associated with each headline was also included in the study. We found that over 40 percent of all the coverage dealt with the mental health system's administrative board. The balance of the coverage was spread over the five local mental health agencies that actually delivered services to consumers. We also found that of the three local newspapers, the one perceived to be the most negative was providing about a third more coverage on the mental health system in terms of square inches of the articles than either of the two other papers.

When the study was finished, it was nicely typed and presented during a meeting of the agency staff and the editorial staff of the most negative newspaper. When confronted with the results of the study and examples of how the public could be interpreting their coverage, the editorial staff agreed to review their policies and coverage of the mental health system. Subsequent coverage was much more balanced and presented no opposition to the renewal of the mental health levy.

Summary

This chapter has provided a small sample of the secondary data sources of interest to social workers and illustration of the way in which social workers can use unobtrusive methods for applied research. Unobtrusive methods provide a needed alternative for those situations where resources are lacking to conduct large-scale surveys or other more rigorous forms of investigation, or where the nature of the question or problem does not lend itself to first-hand data collection.

Given the considerable wealth of information available in this society, just for the asking, unobtrusive approaches ought to be considered first when research is required. Since unobtrusive methods do not require a lot of research or statistical expertise, even social workers who don't think of themselves as researchers can apply them when there is a need for research. Finally, informed social workers need to be familiar with the social indicators available in the special fields in which they work. And where there is no good source of data about the problems with which we are concerned, then we need to advocate for and help establish mechanisms to collect needed data.

QUESTIONS FOR CLASS DISCUSSION

1. On the blackboard, list the social service agencies where students have worked or been placed in a practicum. In a separate column, list the types of social problems with which these agencies deal. Next, make a list of the social indicators that could be used by social workers in these agencies to determine if their programs are having an impact on the social problems.
2. Discuss ways in which secondary data may be biased.
3. Discuss ways in which secondary data analysis could be used by social service agencies in your community.
4. Among social service agencies with which you are familiar, what local information is reported to the state capital and might be found later in an annual report?
5. Identify a local issue or controversy in your community or on your campus. How might content analysis be used to provide some insight into the controversy?
6. Discuss the relative merits and problems with conducting a content analysis using key words as the unit of analysis.
7. What are the advantages and disadvantages associated with a content analysis that would categorize entire items such as editorials or speeches?

MINI-PROJECTS FOR EXPERIENCING RESEARCH FIRSTHAND

1. Think about the information collected by a social service agency with which you are familiar. List the different types of information that are available. Develop two hypotheses that could be tested using archival records from the agency.
2. Are higher rates of suicide found in rural counties or urban counties? Develop a hypothesis and test it using actual state data. (Hint: you will need to operationally define rural and urban counties by their population size). How would you explain your findings?
3. Read all the past month's editorials in one daily newspaper. What consistent patterns or themes emerge? If this effort constituted a pilot study for a content analysis, what hypothesis could you develop? What kinds of categories or decision rules would you need to develop?
4. Skim through advertisements in a popular magazine such as *Newsweek, U.S. News & World Report,* or *Time.* What strikes you about the products being advertised or the way these products are presented? Develop a hypothesis to test using the last three issues of one magazine. What did you learn from this content analysis of magazine advertisements?
5. Using the *United Nations Statistical Yearbook,* develop a hypothesis about government defense and social welfare expenditures in Third World Countries. (For example: do South American countries tend to spend a greater percentage of their budget on defense or in social welfare? Do African countries spend more on social welfare than South American countries?) Test your hypothesis by looking at clusters of countries grouped by continent (e.g., Africa, South America, Europe).
6. Locate the book *Unobtrusive Measures: Nonreactive Research in the Social Sciences.* Note that the authors discuss physical traces (such as controlled erosion and accretion measures) and other topics. Modifying one of their examples, devise a method of unobtrusively measuring some phenomena of interest to social workers.

RESOURCES AND REFERENCES

Allen-Mears, P. (1984). Content analysis: It does have a place in social work research. *Journal of Social Service Research,* 7 (4), 51–68.
Barry, Joan. (1988). Autobiographical writing: An effective tool for practice with the oldest old. *Social Work,* 33 (5), 449–451.

Billups, J.O. and Julia, M.C. (1987). Changing profile of social work practice: A content analysis. *Social Work Research and Abstracts*, 23 (4), 18–22.

Colby, A. (1982). The use of secondary analysis in the study of women and social change. *Journal of Social Issues*, 38 (1), 119–23.

Davis, J.A. and Smith T.W. (1987). *General Social Surveys, 1972–1987.* (Machine-readable data file). Principal Investigator, James A. Davis; Senior Study Director, Tom W. Smith; NORC ed.; National Opinion Research Center, Chicago, producer; The Roper Center for Public Opinion Research, University of Connecticut, Storrs, CT; distributor.

George, L.K. and Landerman, R. (1984). Health and subjective well-being: A replicated secondary data analysis. *International Journal of Aging and Human Development*, 19(2), 133–156.

Glenn, N., Converse, P.E., Cutler, S.J., and Hyman, H.H. (1978). The general social surveys. *Contemporary Sociology*, 7 (5), 532–549.

Hakim, C. (1982). *Secondary Analysis in Social Research: Guide to Data Sources and Methods with Examples.* London: Allen & Unwin.

Harris, L. (1987). *Inside America: Public Opinion Expert Louis Harris Looks at Who We Are, What We Think, Where We're Headed.* New York: Vintage Books.

Hyman, H.H. (1987). *Secondary Analysis of Sample Surveys.* Middletown, CT: Wesleyan Press.

Jenkins, S., Sainz, R.A., Cherry, A., Nishimoto, R., Alvelo, J. and Ockert, D. (1982). Abstracts as data: dissertation trends 1975–1979. *Social Work Research & Abstracts*, 18 (1), 29–34.

Kielcolt, K.J. and Nathan, L.E. (1985). *Secondary Analysis of Survey Data.* Beverly Hills, CA: Sage.

Kulka, R.A. and Colten, M.E. (1982) Secondary analysis of a longitudinal survey of educated women: A social psychological perspective. *Journal of Social Issues*, 38 (1), 73–87.

Krippendorff, K. (1980). *Content Analysis: An Introduction to Its Methodolgy.* Beverly Hills, CA: Sage.

Myers, D.E. and Rockwell, R.C. (1984). Large-scale data bases: Who produces them, how to obtain them, what they contain. *New Directions for Program Evaluation*, 22, 5–25.

Royse, D. (1988). Voter support for human services: A case study. *Arete*, 13 (2), 26–34.

Royse, D. (1986). Newspaper coverage of a community mental health system: A descriptive study. *Journal of Marketing for Mental Health*, 1 (1), 113–125.

Royse, D. and Wellons, K.W. (1988). Mental health coverage in newspaper headlines: A content analysis. *Journal of Marketing for Mental Health,*1 (2), 113–124.

Schuman, H. (1985). *Racial Attitudes in America: Trends and Interpretations.* Cambridge, MA: Harvard University Press.

Stewart, D.W. (1984). *Secondary Research: Information Sources and Methods.* Beverly Hills, CA: Sage.

Turner, C.F. and Martin, E. (Eds.) (1984). *Surveys of Subjective Phenomena.* Vol. 1. New York: Russell Sage Foundation.

Webb, E.J., Campbell, D.T., Schwartz, R.D., and Sechrest, L. (1966). *Unobtrusive Measures: Nonreactive Research in the Social Sciences.* Chicago: Rand McNally.

Wilson, S.M. (1982). Objective analysis of values in a social policy debate. *Social Work Research & Abstracts,* 18 (1), 35–41.

Nine

Preparing and Analyzing Data

Most researchers enjoy data analysis. It is in this stage where the data begin to "come alive." Patterns emerge, trends are detected, and support either is or is not found for our pet hypotheses. We may come away with the smug feeling that we were right in our predictions all along (and we now have the data to prove it!). Or, perhaps we did not learn as much as we had hoped (but ideas and questions were produced that can be tested in the next project).

The purpose of data analysis is to take the **raw data** (the completed survey forms or questionnaires) produced in the data collection stage and condense, distill, or summarize it. In a sense, the researcher is involved in a translation process. From a pile of raw data, which may seem bewildering and without any order to the untrained eye, the researcher hopes to wring something meaningful—patterns, trends, or relationships.

Analysis goes beyond displaying all the responses that were given. Simply reporting the individual responses that seventy-five people gave to a specific question or questionnaire is not analysis. The researcher seeks order within the data and tests hypotheses that have "driven" the research.

There is no single way to go about analyzing a data set. The way you analyze your data will depend upon what you want to know. However, there are some basic techniques that are frequently used by all researchers. These techniques will not only introduce you to the topic of data analysis but also assist you in understanding your data.

Before data analysis can begin, you need to examine the raw data for errors and completeness. Whenever there is a large collection of data, there will be questionnaires containing missed or inadvertently skipped items. When interviewers merely failed to record responses, they can be asked to review their notes and supply the missing items. In other instances, respondents can be recontacted and encouraged to complete vital information. When all the data have been reviewed and made as complete as possible, you are ready to code the data for computer processing.

The Use of Computers for Data Processing

The reason for using computers for data analysis will become clear to you when you consider the problems of keeping in mind the individual responses of as few as thirty different respondents. While the results of small surveys can be manually tabulated, it is almost impossible to manually tabulate large-scale surveys. Tabulating by hand even small surveys or projects can be very time-consuming if you want to know something other than how many responded one way or another. Consider how difficult it would be to tabulate the results of a survey of 525 persons when you want to know if there were differences in the responses of low-income and middle-income persons or between young and old adults. Computers can analyze data a lot faster than you can, and they can conduct statistical tests more accurately than a person using a formula and a hand calculator. Computers are such powerful tools that analysis without computer assistance makes absolutely no sense except for the smallest of surveys.

Computers are increasingly available to practitioners and researchers alike. Finn (1988) found that almost half of a group of human service agencies in North Carolina were using microcomputers. Of the agencies without microcomputers, 54 percent indicated that they planned to purchase one within the next three to five years.

Computers come in various sizes and capabilities. In addition to micro or personal computers are the "mainframe" computers, which can process multiple jobs and communicate with many users simultaneously. While mainframe computers are not commonly found in social service agencies, it is often possible to obtain a computer account and purchase processing time from a university. Personal computers can do just about everything that the mainframe computers can do except process extremely large data sets.

The collection of electronic components that make up the computer equipment are known as the "hardware." But it is not enough to have the hardware; you also need programs that instruct the computer how to perform the needed functions. Computer programs are referred to as "software."

There is no shortage of computer software that will assist the researcher in constructing charts, graphs, and tables and in conducting statistical analyses. So much software is available that it is not possible to provide detailed descriptions here. Hundreds, possibly thousands, of computer programs vary not only in the tasks they can perform, but also the computers in which they operate. For instance, programs designed for IBM personal computers will not operate in Apple computers. Before purchasing software, be sure of the functions you want the software to perform on *your* computer.

Most universities provide many choices of programs for mainframe computers. The Statistical Package for the Social Sciences (SPSS-X) and the Statistical Analysis System (SAS) are two of the more popular programs used by social scientists. Either of these programs can be expected to meet most users' needs for processing statistical data. Manuals for operating these programs are generally available at university bookstores. These programs can be used for such functions as listing the number and percentage of those responding to each questionnaire item, constructing tables, and conducting more sophisticated analyses (e.g., multiple regressions).

Coding Data for the Computer

When you plan a questionnaire or data collection instrument, design it for processing by a computer. Anticipate computer coding problems, and rectify them in the design phase rather than try to make sense out of raw data where response choices have overlapped or where inadequate instructions resulted in inconsistent and ambiguous data. For instance, inexperience might lead one to use the open-ended question, "What is your marital status?" instead of a close-ended one with response choices. This could present a problem if a respondent answered "Single," which the interviewer took to mean never married, when the respondent meant that she was presently single having been divorced recently.

Coding is a process of taking data from the data collection instrument and putting it into a form that can be digested by a computer. Coding translates a verbal or written response into a numerical value. Table 9.1 contains examples of three demographic variables and two items from a larger survey instrument and shows how the data might be coded.

Notice that in the last two items, CHILD ABUSE AS A COMMUNITY PROBLEM and STRICTER PROSECUTION NEEDED, the coding scheme did not start with 1 as it did with MARITAL STATUS. There is no rule requiring that you start coding with 1. Sometimes it is logical to code the responses so that a high value represents the seriousness of a problem or those who have the most of a given trait.

Accordingly, if we devised a scale to measure the use of corporal punishment in disciplining children, it would be logical to code the

Table 9.1 Transforming Data for coding

Variable	Code
Q1 Marital Status	
Never married	1
Married	2
Separated	3
Divorced	4
Widowed	5
Q2 Gender	
Female	1
Male	2
Q3 Age	[Actual age]
Q4 Child Abuse as a Community Problem	
Very serious problem	4
Somewhat serious problem	3
Not very serious problem	2
Not a problem at all	1
Don't know	8
Q5 Stricter Prosecution Needed	
Strongly agree	5
Agree	4
Undecided	3
Disagree	2
Strongly disagree	1

data so that those who made the most use of corporal punishment receive scores with the highest numerical values. If our scale had 20 questions with a 5 point Likert response scale, a respondent who "Always" used corporal punishment could attain a possible score of 100 (5 points times 20 questions) while the lowest possible score ("Never" uses corporal punishment) would be 20 (1 point times 20 questions).

You will make fewer mistakes in coding data if you follow a handful of simple rules. First of all, be consistent. You will find that it is much easier to remember a rule as "yes is always coded 1" than to try to remember exceptions to this rule. If you start coding "yes" as 1 on question 15, don't change the rule later on when you are on item 37 or 45. With such a rule, it would follow that "no" would always be coded as 0—"no" indicates the absence of a trait, behavior, or attitude and "yes" indicates its presence.

Second, use one value (such as 9) for missing data. Thus, if a respondent did not indicate his or her marital status, a 9 could be used to communicate this to the computer. Similarly, if a respondent did not provide his or her age, 99 might be used to indicate the missing age. (While it is possible that a 99-year-old could be a respondent, it is unlikely. If you are interviewing older adults and have a 99-year-old as a respondent, provide a value for missing information that is not within the range of your respondents' ages, such as 00).

Third, anticipate the maximum number of response codes needed for each variable, so that you don't find that a one-column variable should have been coded with two columns after you have coded a stack of survey forms. In order to avoid this problem, "test" the coding scheme by randomly choosing several completed surveys and coding them before developing a final version of your **codebook**.

A codebook is a reference sheet or guide for coding. It tells coders what numerical values to use in transforming data to a machine readable format and indicates the location in which the computer should record this information. You'll understand this when you think about computer cards. The 7 1/4" long by 3 1/4" wide cards were designed with an 80-column format. Computers "understand" information punched onto these cards based upon the location of the holes punched in them. Even though these cards are no longer widely used by researchers (having been replaced by electronic storage of data on silicon chips), information that is going to be computer processed using statistical programs must still utilize an 80-column format. Table 9.2 is an example of how the codebook indicates both location and coding instructions. Notice that the respondent's marital status is coded only in column 4. Also note that the variable of age, unlike the others, requires two columns. If the respondent is 35, a 3 would be placed in column 6 and a 5 would be placed in column 7. If the respondent is 9 years old, a zero would be placed in column 6 and a 9 in column 7.

Figure 9.1 provides an illustration of a portion of coded data obtained from persons 9, 24, and 35 years old as they would be coded on Fortran paper.

Special paper facilitates coding for the computer. Fortran coding paper contains 80 columns and 24 rows. Think of each row as a separate case or respondent and the 80 columns as 80 separate pieces of information (or responses to questions) that you can feed into the computer for analysis. Actually, information about a respondent is not limited to 80 columns; two, three, or more rows of information could refer to a single respondent. And some responses, as in the example of age, require more than one column.

While coding data onto Fortran sheets is usually necessary for

177

computer processing, these sheets are also helpful when question-naires are manually tabulated. It is easier and more accurate to check data on Fortran sheets than it is to use tally marks. Just run a straight-edge alongside the column representing the variable you are tabulat-ing and look for values that are misplaced. Note, for instance, in fig-ure 9.1 the variable of gender. Our codebook suggests that the values should be 1 or 2 (respondents are either males or females). The 3 ap-pearing in the gender column is an error.

Note, however, that some universities have computers that can optically scan specially designed answer sheets. If the responses to your questions fit into this format (e.g., a multiple choice format of the type used by standardized tests), it may not be necessary to manu-ally code your data for the computer. (This is another reason to con-sult an experienced researcher before beginning to collect data.)

Table 9.2   Portion of a Codebook

Variable	Code	Column
Respondent Number		1-3
Q1 Marital Status		4
Never married	1	
Married	2	
Separated	3	
Divorced	4	
Widowed	5	
Q2 Gender		5
Female	1	
Male	2	
Q3 Age		6-7
Q4 Child Abuse as a Community Problem		8
Very serious problem	4	
Somewhat serious problem	3	
Not very serious problem	2	
Not a problem at all	1	
Don't know	8	
Q5 Stricter Prosecution Needed		9
Strongly agree	5	
Agree	4	
Undecided	3	
Disagree	2	
Strongly disagree	1	

Figure 9.1 A Partially Coded Data Sheet

PROGRAM																																	

| COMM | STATEMENT NUMBER | | | | CONT | | | | | | | | | | | | | | | | | | | | | | | | | | | | | |

PROGRAMMER	DATE

1	2	3	4	5	6	7	8	9	10	11	12	13	14	15	16	17	18	19	20	21	22	23	24	25	26	27	28	29	30	31	32	33	34
0	0	0	1	1	0	9	4	3																									
0	0	2	3	2	2	4	3	2																									
0	0	3	2	3	3	5	2	4																									

So far this discussion of coding covers only closed-ended questions. If you employed several open-ended questions and want to code the results, it may not be immediately obvious how you should proceed. At some point you will need to create categories for the responses you have obtained. Rather than establish the first category according to the first response you read, study twenty-five or so of the responses to the open-ended questions to see if there are similarities in the way respondents replied. Take, for example, the question asking why respondents dropped out of school; all of the following responses might be similar enough to fit into the category "Financial reasons": "I had no more money"; "couldn't borrow any more money"; "parents could no longer afford to send me."

When coding open-ended data, you may not know how many categories are needed to adequately reflect the responses. As a rule of thumb, too many categories (ten or more) make analysis just as difficult as too few categories. Let your choice of the number of categories be influenced by what you want to learn from the data. Draft a preliminary table with fictitious data in order to help you visualize your results. Even after data have been grouped into categories, some categories can be merged with others. This is useful when less than 10 percent of the responses are found in a category. (In table 9.3, for example, "Strongly disagree" might be merged with "Disagree.")

Univariate Analysis

After the coded data have been entered into the computer, look over a printout of the raw data for data entry errors before proceeding with analysis. Examine each variable (such as gender) to see if there are any unusual values that do not belong. This process is sometimes referred to as "cleaning" the data. If no correction is needed, the next step is preparing **frequency distributions**.

Frequency distributions present the responses obtained for each item. Data are generally displayed in ascending values. Table 9.3 provides an illustration of a frequency distribution for two items from a survey. This table displays how each response choice was coded and gives the number and percentage of respondents for each response choice. The last column provides adjusted percentages after deleting the missing data (those for whom no response was recorded) from the total respondents available. Because of the large sample size, the deletion of four respondents on item Q15 had little effect upon the figures reported under the adjusted percentages. A much greater effect would have been noticed had the sample been considerably smaller. As a rule, it is better to use the adjusted percentages, because these percentages are based on actual responses. A major difference in the relative and adjusted percentages indicates a large block of missing responses. The researcher should then consider whether too much missing data renders the item useless.

Looking at the data one variable at a time constitutes **univariate**

Table 9.3 Example of a Frequency Distribution

Q15		"I am well informed about AIDS."		
Category Label	Code	Absolute Frequency	Relative Frequency (Percent)	Adjusted Frequency (Percent)
Strongly disagree	1	18	2.4	2.4
Disagree	2	228	30.6	30.7
Undecided	3	36	4.8	4.9
Agree	4	386	51.7	52.0
Strongly agree	5	74	9.9	10.0
No answer/refused	9	4	0.5	Missing data
Total		746	100.0	100.0
Q45		Gender of Respondent		
Female	1	477	63.9	63.9
Male	2	269	36.1	36.1
Total		746	100.0	100.0

analysis. From the frequency distribution in table 8.3 we can tell (by adding together the "Strongly agrees" and the "Agrees" and adding the "Strongly disagrees" to the "Disagrees") that two-thirds of the respondents (62 percent) believe that they are well informed about AIDS. One-third of the sample disagree with the statement (they do not feel well-informed about AIDS).

The computer programs that produce frequency distributions commonly produce other information, such as measures of central tendency (the mean, median, and mode) for each variable. Such information is much more meaningful when discussing the averages of some variables (such as age, income, and years of education) than learning that the mean of Q45, "Gender," in table 9.3 was a nonsensical 1.3.

Variables such as gender, occupation, political party, race and marital status are **nominal variables**; their primary feature is that they allow for some categorization by name. It is not possible to average nominal variables or perform many other statistical operations with them. The measure of central tendency that is used with nominal variable is the **mode**, the largest category or the most common response. In table 9.3 "Female" is the mode for the nominal variable of gender.

Variable Q15 (the statement "I am well-informed about AIDS") has response choices that are not nominal but **ordinal**. Ordinal variables represent a scale where ranking is important. Thus, "Strongly agree" represents a higher level of knowledge about AIDS than an "Agree" response, which represents more knowledge about AIDS than either "Disagree" or "Strongly disagree." The mode can be used as a measure of central tendency for ordinal variables, but the **median** is more appropriate. The median is the category that includes the next respondent past 50 percent of the data. With regard to the "I am well-informed about AIDS" item, the second category, "Agree," would represent the median value.

Frequency distributions lend themselves to graphic, or visual, portrayal of the data. Graphs, pie charts, histograms, and polygrams can be prepared either manually or with a computer. Figure 9.2 and 9.3 provide two examples of ways a computer program can present data from frequency distributions in the form of bar and pie charts.

Bivariate Analysis of Data

After the data have been examined one item at a time, researchers often begin to look at the relationship among variables taken two at a time. A researcher may, for example, have the hypothesis that women are more knowledgeable about AIDS than men. Testing this would re-

Figure 9.2 "I am well-informed about AIDS"

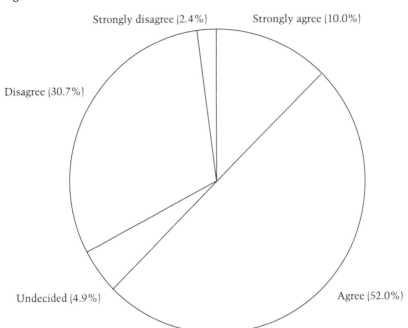

Strongly disagree (2.4%)   Strongly agree (10.0%)

Disagree (30.7%)

Undecided (4.9%)   Agree (52.0%)

quire using the variable of gender to analyze the responses obtained to Q15 ("I am well-informed about AIDS"). Researchers find it helpful to construct tables that allow them to examine two variables at a time. These tables may be prepared manually or by the computer; the computer version is sometimes called a **crosstabulation**, or crosstabs. Though it is not easy to determine by looking at the raw numbers, we can tell by looking at the column percentages in table 9.4 that there is virtually no difference in respondents' knowledge about AIDS by gender. Almost two-thirds of both the men and women indicated either agreement or strong agreement with the statement that they were well-informed about AIDS. Displaying the data in this way allows researchers to easily detect patterns or relationships.

Had the results been different—had women been significantly more informed than men—further research might be required to explain this. It might then be hypothesized that women are more health conscious than men or that they more frequently read newspapers, the major source of information about AIDS. Thus, additional research might show an association between newspaper readership and knowledge about AIDS.

Sometimes it is difficult to tell whether or not there is any statistical association between two variables just by looking at percentages (visual inspection). Look again at the raw data in table 9.4, and avoid looking at the percentages. Unless you are very good at doing math in your head, you probably would not recognize that the males and females in this sample would be so similar in their responses. A statistical procedure may be needed to find out if there is a statistical difference between the two groups. The most common statistic used to test differences among categories in crosstabulations is the **chi square** (X^2) (DiLeonardi and Curtis, 1988). This is a popular test because it is widely understood; it can be easily calculated by hand or by computer, and it requires only nominal level data. These features make it particularly well-suited for a number of social work research applications (Weinbach and Grinnell, 1987). If we were to use SPSS-X on the mainframe computer, we would learn that the computed chi square for the variables represented in table 9.4 is less than 1 and the probability level is .84. This means that there is no statistically significant difference between males and females in their perceptions of how well informed they are about AIDS.

Had there been an association between the variables, the chi square would have been much larger, and statistically significant. Findings of statistical significance are represented in the following

Figure 9.3 "I am well-informed about AIDS"

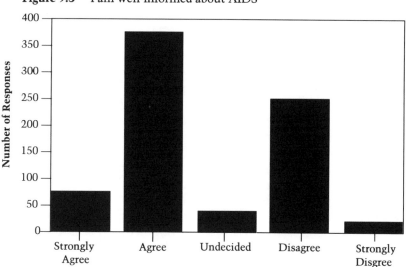

Table 9.4   Crosstabulation of Knowledge about AIDS by Gender ("I am well-informed about AIDS")

	Female	**Male**
Strongly agree/Agree	291 (66%)	169 (65%)
Strongly disagree/Disagree	153 (34%)	93 (35%)
Column totals	444	262

format: $p < .05$. A probability (p) level of .05 means that chance alone might have produced the same pattern of results 5 times in 100. Another way of saying this is that there are 5 chances in 100 that the hypothesis will be rejected unintentionally; in other words, males and females would have had very different opinions regarding their level of knowledge.

As useful as chi square is, it can also be misleading in those situations where there are a large number of cells with an expected frequency of fewer than five respondents or subjects. (Cells are the little boxes formed by the computer, shown in table 9.4.) Some computer programs (e.g., SPSS-X) will monitor this potential problem for you and tell you the number and percentage of cells having an expected frequency of 5 or under. These expected frequencies are generated in the process of calculating chi square. If you use some other program that does not report the number of cells with an expected frequency of 5 or fewer, be very cautious if you have a large number of blank cells. If more than 20 percent of your cells have an expected frequency of less than 5, then the produced chi square can be invalid. The procedure in such circumstances is to combine, or collapse, categories so that there are fewer cells with more respondents in them. (In table 9.4, the "Strongly agree" and "Agree" categories have been combined, as have "Strongly disagree" and "Disagree," in order to facilitate the presentation of the data.)

Another crosstabulation is presented in table 9.5. In this example, a trend can be seen. Rural respondents rate themselves lower on knowledge of AIDS than small town or urban dwellers. When chi square is computed on this data, a value of 13.2 is obtained with a probability level less than .001 ($p < .001$). This means that there are differences in responding patterns and that these differences are real and not likely to be due to chance. A probability level of less than .001 means that chance could have distributed these two variables in this way 1 (or fewer) time in 1,000.

Table 9.5 Knowledge of AIDS by Community Type ("I am well-informed about AIDS")

Category	Rural	Small Town	City/Suburb
Strongly agree/Agree	121	164	174
	(57%)	(65%)	(73%)
Strongly disagree/Disagree	93	88	65
	(43%)	(35%)	(27%)
Column totals	214	252	239

Most social scientists seek a probability level of at least $p < .05$ when reviewing the results of their statistical tests. This provides them with a reasonable amount of confidence that there are statistically significant differences between or among groups they are examining. A probability level of $p < .01$ is desirable when researchers want to be even more confident in their findings. Since most social science research does not involve life or death decisions (unlike, for instance, medical products research), it is rare to find social scientists rejecting a hypothesis because the probability that the groups were significantly different was greater than .001. Occasionally, a probability of .001 or even .0001 will be obtained, but these are not encountered as often in the literature as the .05 or the .01 probability levels.

In addition to the tabular display of data and chi square, other procedures establish differences between or among groups. Another procedure is useful with interval and ratio data. Suppose you have the hypothesis that medical students are more homophobic than social work students. You have devised a homophobia scale that provides you with **interval level data**. Interval data are variables that are continuous and have intervals of equal length, like I.Q. scores or age. It is assumed that the scales we develop using Likert-type response choices provide interval level data (Mitchell and Jolley, 1988). Another type of scale, called a **ratio scale**, has a true zero. Temperature is a ratio-level variable because measurements below zero can be made. For most purposes in data analysis, it is not important to distinguish between interval and ratio level variables. In the social sciences, there are hardly any measurements that produce ratio-level data (Weinbach and Grinnell, 1987).

Know your variables' level of measurement because statistical procedures that test hypotheses are largely determined by the level at which the data were measured. While a chi square can be performed when both variables are nominal, it would be inappropriate to use chi square if the dependent variable were continuous or interval. When

Figure 9.4 Computer Printout of a T-Test

Variable	N	Mean	t value	Probability
Homophobia				
Med Students	63	6.8	2.67	.009
SW Students	60	5.7		

you have a normally distributed dependent variable measured at the interval level, and nominal level independent variables, you can test for statistical differences between two groups with the **t-test**. The t-test compares the mean scores from two groups and provides you with a t value and a probability statement. The t-test is appropriate even with small samples of about thirty individuals.

Practical Application of Statistics

Suppose you are conducting an AIDS educational program for medical and social work students. As part of that program you have them complete a questionnaire that measures their homophobia. Later you perform a t-test to find out if their scores are statistically different. The computer might provide information that looks something like figure 9.4.

The beauty of statistical tests is that you don't have to go out on a limb and guess whether the differences in the means are substantially different. The computer will tell you if the groups are statistically different in their levels of homophobia. In this example, the medical students have a higher level of homophobia than social work students, and the probability of these findings occurring by chance would be 9 times in 1,000—which makes the differences highly statistically significant. The SPSS-X generated printout will provide a two-tailed test of significance. This is used whenever the direction of the outcome cannot be predicted in advance as when a null hypothesis has been stated. The null hypothesis is rejected whenever the difference between the means of the two groups is so large that the probability of its occurring by chance is greater than the established level of significance (for example, .05).

Assume that we do some additional research; we attempt to measure fear of AIDS among various health professionals. Since we are interested in surveying more than two groups (we want to interview medical, dental, social work, and nursing students), we would have to use a different statistical procedure. This procedure, which is almost identical to the t-test, is called the **one-way analysis of vari-**

ance (sometimes referred to as **ANOVA**). Interpretation of the one-way analysis of variance is straightforward and similar to the t-test, but, instead of a t value, it provides an F ratio. A computer printout of fear of AIDS by students pursuing degrees in various health careers might look like figure 9.5.

Information from this one-way analysis of variance informs us that the levels of fear of AIDS among these four groups is not similar. If we were testing a null hypothesis, this ANOVA would tell us that all the means from the four groups were not equal—there were differences among these four groups of students in their fear of AIDS. This F ratio and the associated probability does not prove that the difference between the group with the most fear and the group with the least fear is statistically significant. To test such a hypothesis, we would have to use a t-test with those two groups. The ANOVA merely indicates that among the groups being examined, there were some statistically significant differences in the pattern of responding.

Even though fear of AIDS was examined in four different career groups, only two variables were used—type of health career student and fear of AIDS. If the data from figure 9.5 were made into a table, it might have the caption "Fear of AIDS by Health Career Orientation."

Another way to analyze bivariate data is to use a **correlation coefficient** to summarize the relationship. This statistic is often produced by the same program that produced the crosstabulation. As discussed in chapter 2, a correlation coefficient is a statistic, or a numerical value, that ranges between -1.00 and $+1.00$. The closer the correlation coefficient is to one end or the other of the range, the stronger the relationship between the two variables. (This does not mean, however, that one variable was the cause of the other variable. A high correlation between the amount of street crime in a city and the number of social workers does not mean that the social workers caused the street crime.) A correlation coefficient hovering around .00 indicates no relationship between the two variables, while a coef-

Figure 9.5 Computer Printout of a One-way Analysis of Variance

Variable	N	Mean	F-Ratio	Probability
Fear of AIDS				
Dental Students	38	14.3		
Social Work Students	83	12.9	5.7	.001
Medical Students	79	15.2		
Nursing Students	62	13.3		
Total	262	13.9		

ficient of .14 indicates a very weak relationship. By squaring the correlation coefficient (multiplying it by itself), it is possible to determine the strength of the relationship between two variables. This tells us how much of the variance in the two variables is shared or explained. We are able to determine, then, that a coefficient of .14 explains about 2 percent of the variance, while a coefficient of .88 explains 77 percent of the variance between two variables. A coefficient of .31 would explain less than 10 percent of the variance. Correlations as high as .70 are rarely found in social science research, and the average of all correlations reported in the literature is thought to be less than .40 (Nunnally, 1978).

In the above examples, the plus sign is understood. A plus sign indicates a positive direction—as one variable goes, so goes the other variable. If one variable tends to increase, so does the other. A negative sign in front of a correlation coefficient indicates an inverse relationship—the variables go in opposite directions. As one variable increases, the other decreases.

In table 9.6, empathy for AIDS victims has an inverse relationship with fear of AIDS (-.55). In other words, individuals with greater levels of fear will tend to have less empathy for AIDS victims and individuals with the least amount of fear will tend to have the most empathy for persons with AIDS.

Finally, keep in mind that a correlation may be statistically significant (meaning that it is likely that it did not occur by chance) but explains very little variation in the data. A correlation coefficient of .18 may be statistically significant at $p < .05$, but this isn't meaningful when you consider that only 3 percent of the variation in the data is explained. A high level of statistical significance does not automatically confer value or meaning in the sense of being clinically or practically useful to the practitioner (Schulman, Kupst and Suran, 1976). You might be less tempted to put too much emphasis on finding a statistically significant correlation coefficient once you realize that, often, simply gathering additional respondents can produce significance. In fact, Schulman, Kupst, and Suran (1976) note that there is even a statistical test to find out how many additional subjects are necessary to get a significant difference once some preliminary data have been gathered.

A correlation matrix is presented in table 9.6. This matrix resulted from correlating four scales, Homophobia, Empathy, Fear of AIDS, and Desired Social Distance from AIDS Victims, with each other. It produces some perfect correlations (when a scale is correlated with itself) as well as some positive and negative correlations. As

Table 9.6   A Correlation Matrix with Four Scales

	Homophobia Scale	Empathy Scale	Fear Scale	Social Distance Scale
Homophobia Scale	1.00	− .63	.60	.66
Empathy Scale	− .63	1.00	− .55	− .68
Fear Scale	.60	− .55	1.00	.67
Social Distance Scale	.66	− .68	.67	1.00

you look at these correlations, do you understand why some have a negative sign in front of them while others do not?

Multivariate Analysis of Data

The most common meaning of the term **multivariate analysis** is an analysis that involves one or more independent variables and two or more dependent variables (Glisson and Fischer, 1982). Typically, a computer is needed to perform statistical computations such as partial correlations, factor analysis, multiple regressions, and such. The appearance of these sophisticated statistical procedures in social work journals is increasing. However, at least one study has revealed numerous incidences in which multivariate statistics should have been used but were not. The authors of that study describe the problem of underuse of multivariate procedures as "severe" (Glisson and Fischer, 1982).

Such procedures as multivariate analysis of variance and covariance, canonical analysis, and discriminant analysis are beyond the scope of this chapter. However, it is possible to begin to understand multivariate analysis by constructing a table that will allow us to examine three variables at one time. Table 9.7 provides an illustration of this.

Table 9.7 provides us with a more detailed view of the pattern of data we first viewed in table 9.5. The trend shown in table 9.5 still holds: city dwellers rate their knowledge of AIDS higher than rural dwellers. However, now we observe that the difference in male urban dwellers and male rural dwellers is much more dramatic than the difference between female urban and female rural dwellers. By introducing the third variable (gender) to table 9.5, we are better able to explain the relationship between knowledge of AIDS and community of residence. With the use of statistical multivariate analysis it is possible to determine which of your variables makes the better predictor.

Table 9.7 Knowledge of Aids by Community Type and Gender ("I am well-informed about AIDS")

	Female respondents			Male respondents		
	Rural	Small town	City/ Suburb	Rural	Small town	City/ Suburb
Strongly agree/Agree	73	105	112	48	59	60
	(59%)	(65%)	(71%)	(53%)	(65%)	(76%)
Strongly disagree/Disagree	51	56	45	42	32	19
	(41%)	(35%)	(29%)	(47%)	(35%)	(24%)
Totals	124	161	157	90	91	79

Using this example, we could determine whether gender or type of community is the better predictor of knowledge about AIDS.

Final Thoughts

This chapter has provided an overview of the processes researchers use to analyze their data. (This is not to suggest, however, that this chapter contains all that you need to know about the use of statistics. A reading of this chapter is not a substitute for a course in applied statistics.) As you become more involved with research, you will want to know more about statistical applications.

If you are comfortable with your knowledge of statistics, test your recognition of the following statistical symbols:

1. SD, S   5. F
2. $\bar{X}$ 6. t
3. r   7. X^2
4. p < .05   8. df

Several articles have been written on social workers' knowledge of statistics. Weed and Greenwald (1973) reported in a small study that less than half of the social workers they surveyed knew any of six commonly used statistical symbols. Witkin, Edleson, and Lindsey (1980), using a larger sample, corroborated the earlier findings of Weed and Greenwald. More than a decade has passed since this last study. Are social workers now any more knowledgeable of statistics? How many of the statistical symbols did you recognize?

Answers: (1) standard deviation; (2) mean (or average); (3) correlation coefficient; (4) probability of happening by chance is less than 5 times in 100; (5) an F value (from an F ratio or F-test, as with one-way analysis of variance); (6) a t value (from a t-test); (7) the symbol for chi square; (8) degrees of freedom.

QUESTIONS FOR CLASS DISCUSSION

1. A student who had not been attentive during a lecture on coding data for the computer used two columns to code the variable for gender. This student coded males in column 4 and females in column 5. Why won't this approach work?
2. Explain how the computer "knows" that in a frequency distribution from a recent survey a "1" under MARITAL STATUS indicates "never married," while a "1" under "GENDER" indicates "female."
3. Do you notice any pattern in the correlations presented in table 9.6?
4. What does the correlation between the Social Distance and Fear scales indicate in table 9.6?
5. What are some limitations associated with correlation research?
6. While charts or graphs can simplify complex findings, what limitations are associated with trying to understand a study solely from its charts or graphs?

MINI-PROJECTS FOR EXPERIENCING RESEARCH FIRSTHAND

1. Using the "Attitudes about Research Courses" contained in the Appendix, develop a complete codebook, and code fifteen cases of fictitious data on Fortran paper.
2. Skim through several issues of a professional journal until you find an example of statistical analysis of data. How does the author interpret these statistics in terms of the theoretical or practical significance and the statistical significance of the relationships?
3. Find a frequency distribution reported in a magazine, newspaper, or journal, and prepare a bar or pie chart to display the data.
4. Read the articles by Weed and Greenwald and by Witkin et al. Design a small project to determine if social workers (or social work students) are now more knowledgeable about statistical symbols than reported in these articles. (Note that the sym-

bols are contained on the second page of the questionnaire "Attitudes about Research Courses" found in the Appendix.)

5. Find a program evaluation reported in a journal. Summarize what you learned about the success or failure of the program by reviewing what the author reports in statistics and tables. How were the data analyzed? What didn't you understand? Be sure to give a full citation for the article so that it can be found by others.

RESOURCES AND REFERENCES

Benbenishty, R. and Ben-Zaken, A. (1988). Computer-aided process of monitoring task-centered family interventions. *Social Work Research and Abstracts*, 24 (1), 7–9.

Clark, C.F. (1988). Computer applications in social work. *Social Work Research and Abstracts*, 24 (1), 15–19.

DiLeonardi, J.W. and Curtis, P.A. (1988). *What to Do When the Numbers Are In*. Chicago: Nelson-Hall.

Finn, J. (1988). Microcomputers in private, nonprofit agencies: A survey of trends and training requirements. *Social Work Research and Abstracts*, 24 (1), 10–14.

Glisson, C. and Fischer, J. (1982). Research notes: Use and nonuse of multivariate statistics. *Social Work Research and Abstracts*, 18 (1), 42–44.

Lindsey, D. (1977). General-purpose computer packages in the social sciences. *Social Work Research and Abstracts*, 13 (4), 38–42.

Mitchell, M. and Jolley, J. (1988). *Research Design Explained*. New York: Holt, Rinehart and Winston.

Nunnally, J.M. (1978). *Psychometric Theory*. New York: McGraw-Hill.

Royse, D. and Birge, B. (1987). Homophobia and attitudes towards AIDS among medical, nursing, and paramedical students. *Psychological Reports*, 61, 867–870.

Royse, D., Dhooper, S. and Hatch, L.R. (1987). Undergraduate and graduate students' attitudes towards AIDS. *Psychological Reports*, 60, 1185–1186.

Schulman, J.L., Kupst, M.J., and Suran, B.G. (1976). The worship of "p": Significant yet meaningless research results. *Bulletin of the Menninger Clinic*, 40(2), 134–143.

Weed, P. and Greenwald, S.R. (1973). Brief notes: The Mystics of statistics. *Social Work*, 18, 113–115.

Weinbach, R.W. and Grinnell. (1987). *Statistics for Social Workers*. New York: Longman.

Witkin, S.L. Edleson, J.L., and Lindsey, D. (1980). Social workers and statistics: Preparation, attitudes, and knowledge. *Journal of Social Service Research*, 3(3), 313–322.

Ten

Program Evaluation

The mission of program evaluation is to provide information that can be used to improve social programs (Tripodi, 1987). Unlike strictly theoretical research, program evaluation is synonymous with applied research. Most often, program evaluation starts with a specific problem or question to be answered, such as: "Is our outpatient treatment program as effective as inpatient treatment?" Or, "Are we as successful with our group counseling program as with our individual counseling?" Administrators, board members, and others may want to know if the program is a "good" program. If they decide that the program is not "good," then corrective action may be taken or funding may be cut off. Program evaluation, then, is an aid to program managers. It can improve program effectiveness and aid in decision-making.

Program evaluation attempts to answer such general questions as:

1. Are clients being helped?
2. Is there a better (cheaper, faster) way of doing this?
3. How does this effort or level of activity compare with what was produced or accomplished last year? (Did we achieve our objectives?)
4. How does our success rate compare with those of other agencies?
5. Should this program be continued?
6. How can we improve our program?

Why do we need to conduct program evaluation? The best argument for evaluating social service programs comes from an analogy: conducting a program without evaluating it is like driving a car blindfolded. You certainly are going places, but you don't know where you are or who you've endangered along the way. Program evaluation provides accountability. It can be used to assure the public, funders of programs and even the clients themselves that a particular program works and that it deserves further financial support. Program evaluation can be used to insure that certain expectations are met, that efforts are appropriately applied to the identified needs, and that the community is better off because the program is having a positive effect. There are many other reasons for conducting program evaluation. In addition to accountability, Posavac and Carey (1985) list: fulfillment of accreditation requirements; answering requests for information; making administrative decisions; assisting staff in program development; and learning about unintended effects of programs. Ultimately, program evaluation benefits clients. It tells us whether clients are being helped or not, and it can indicate how we can better assist clients.

Program evaluation fits into the program development cycle outlined by Lewis and Lewis (1983) and others. Briefly (and perhaps ideally), the program development process starts with a needs assessment being conducted before a program is funded. The documentation of unmet needs in the community results in funds being allocated for a new program. As the new program is planned, attention is given to ways the program can be evaluated. After the program has been implemented, conscientious managers ask: Is there a better way to provide this program? What have we accomplished? Are we having an impact on the community's needs? And, is this a good program? Funding sources may ask, "Should we continue this program next year?"

Starting to Think about Conducting a Program Evaluation

Think about a social service program with which you have been associated. Perhaps it was in an agency where you were employed or where you had a field practicum. Suppose the agency director asked to see you one day and said, "I've got to convince our principal funding source that we run a good program. And, I don't have the slightest idea how to go about it. They aren't interested in our opinions about the program. I get the impression that they want some objective data. Since you are taking classes at the university, I'm sure that planning a program evaluation won't be difficult for you. After all, we know we have a good program, we just have to demonstrate it. Take a couple of days to sketch out an evaluation plan, and let's go over it at our administrative team meeting on Friday. We'll want to have the evaluation completed in about sixty days."

What would you do if you found yourself in this situation? What information would you need to have? How would you demonstrate that any program was "good"?

Beginning a Program Evaluation

Once you understand (1) the purpose of the evaluation (including important questions to be answered or hypotheses to be tested), (2) the audience (those who will be reading the evaluation report), (3) the time frame, and (4) the funds that can be expended, you are in a position to start thinking about designing an evaluation process.

On the most basic level, you can begin to gather some descriptive data (e.g., the number of clients who used the program in the past six or twelve months). And, you can obtain information on the proportion of these clients who are minorities, elderly, children, and low income, or who are referred by specific sources. However, this **client utilization** or **patterns of use data** can tell you something about only those clients who have expressed a need for the program (by their appearing on your agency's doorstep). It will tell you nothing about those who *could* have benefited from your program but who did not request services. Table 10.1 displays some client utilization data from a fictitious agency.

As demonstrated in table 10.1, descriptive data do not allow us to conclude that programs are "good," effective, or efficient. While the data informs us about the number of clients served and allows us to establish who the recipients of our services were, they tell us nothing about the quality of care clients were provided. We can reach no conclusion about whether the clients were better off as a result of being served by one of the agency's three programs. Even though many social service agencies report descriptive client utilization data in their annual reports, such information by itself does not constitute an evaluation of the agencies' activities or programs.

Patterns of use data are best used for indicating pockets of clients who are within the agency's target group for services but who are not being served. Once we start thinking about this problem, it is apparent that table 10.1 would be much more meaningful if census data were included so that we could determine which groups were not being served in proportion to their representation in the population. For instance, if you knew that 15 percent of the community's residents were minorities, then it would be easy to determine that all three of the programs presented in table 10.1 are underserving minorities. Data presented in this way are useful for **program monitoring**.

Program monitoring is described by Rossi and Freeman (1985)

Table 10.1 The Reasonably Healthy Minds Agency: Annual Report of Client Data

	Program A	Program B	Program C
Number of clients served this fiscal year	523	750	297
Female clients	45%	69%	57%
Minority admissions	5%	9%	10%
Clients under 21	98%	5%	0%
Clients 21–55	2%	91%	8%
Clients 56 and older	0%	4%	92%
Clients on public assistance	13%	94%	24%
Prior mental health service	20%	40%	50%
Self-referrals	60%	25%	15%

as measuring the extent to which a program reaches its intended target population and whether the service being provided matches what was intended to be delivered. Despite the best intentions, programs sometimes slowly change or drift away from their original mission.

I once observed this firsthand with an agency that had drifted away from its primary mission of serving the whole community. At the time I encountered the agency, the vast majority of its clientele were white middle-class persons who were young, fairly articulate, and motivated to work on their problems. This public agency had chosen to serve a select group of clients, the bulk of whom could have obtained assistance from private practitioners. Since there were no other agencies in that area to serve low income families, these families simply were not being served. This situation came about because there was no program monitoring being done. Program managers ought to monitor who is being served and who is not. When done regularly and routinely, program monitoring can be considered a basic form of program evaluation. While it may not answer many questions, it does provide a foundation upon which to start a program evaluation.

Types of Program Evaluation

If your principal funding sources are impressed with the kind of data presented in table 10.1, then your program evaluation need go no further. If their expectations are greater (for the reasons we've already discussed), then it may be necessary to consider another type of program evaluation.

Because social workers are employed in so many diverse fields of practice (e.g., health, aging, schools, mental health, substance abuse), choosing an evaluation design or model is sometimes problematic. No one model fits all situations and circumstances. Lipsey (1988) observed, "We can now distinguish quantitative and qualitative evaluation, experimental and naturalistic evaluation, outcome and process evaluation, summative and formative evaluation, and a host of other such variants" (p. 5). Dush and Cassileth (1985) have noted, "There are as many evaluative strategies as evaluation questions" (p. 61).While this may be an exaggeration, there are quite a few evaluation models or strategies. Patton listed one hundred different types of evaluation in his 1981 book and thirty-three others in 1982. Let's take his word for it and not double-check his arithmetic. With so many different evaluation designs to choose from, it is not as important that you memorize every possible variation of a design as it is that you be able to *conceptualize* ways to evaluate programs.

In addition to program monitoring, another type of program evaluation is **formative evaluation**. Formation evaluation is not specifically concerned with the "worth" of a program. Instead, it focuses on improving programs.

Formative evaluations are used to modify or shape programs that are still in development (i.e., model programs). Formative evaluations vary with regard to sophistication. On some occasions they may involve an "evaluator" who is an "expert" employed by another agency that operates a program similar to the model program. This evaluator may visit clients and staff, tour the facility, and perhaps observe some of the programming. Ultimately, he or she produces a report that contains some constructive information about how the program could be improved. These evaluations are sometimes referred to as *process evaluations* and tend to be more qualitative in approach than quantitative. Process evaluations look at how a product or outcome was produced rather than at the product itself (Patton, 1980).

Formative evaluations usually rely upon participant observation and informal interviews. They tend to be descriptive and not to rely upon statistics or analysis of numerical data. However, one can use qualitative methods to evaluate any program. Like formative evaluations, qualitative evaluations usually do not produce conclusions about whether the program is successful or not; rather, they describe how participants (staff and clients) experience the program (Schuerman, 1983). Such qualitative evaluations are sometimes called goal-free evaluations. The qualitative description of a program at a particular point in time may be useful in helping to explain later findings of outcome evaluations that determine the degree of success of the program.

Another type of program evaluation could be called **outcome, effectiveness, or impact evaluation**. This program evaluation effort involves quantitative-comparative techniques and has the best chance of providing information about treatment effectiveness. It may use experimental or quasi-experimental designs and aims to gather "hard" evidence that could be used to demonstrate the worth of a program.

In the remainder of this chapter we will be primarily concerned with evaluating program outcome. We will examine several general purpose evaluation designs that can be used in a variety of settings. These designs are not experimental nor could they always be considered quasi-experimental. Each has its own name and perspective on program evaluation.

Think of evaluation designs as blueprints or guides for the evaluative process. They do not in themselves provide any guarantee that the results will be noteworthy or that every expectation of the evaluation will be met. They describe the key features and procedures to be followed in conducting an evaluation. A design is a plan that "dictates when and from whom measurements will be gathered during the course of an evaluation" (Fitz-Gibbon and Morris, 1987, 9). Your evaluation is valuable to the audience reading your evaluation report because it provides answers to the questions they asked. Your choice of a particular design needs to follow from the questions or concerns about a program.

Experimental and Quasi-Experimental Designs

If, in thinking about how you might plan an agency evaluation, you consider the experimental and quasi-experimental designs of chapter 5, you are on the right track. The classical experimental design would certainly be the traditional scholarly approach to determining if a program were effective. And it would be a good choice if you could randomly assign clients to a control group and if pretesting, posttesting, and intervention could be accomplished within the sixty days allocated for the program evaluation in our hypothetical example. (See, for example, Valasquez and McCubbin, 1980, for a report of a program evaluation of community-based residential treatment that used an experimental design with a pretest-posttest comparison group procedure.) In situations where randomization and the use of control groups are not possible, you need to be able to conceptualize other ways of evaluating programs.

The Discrepancy Model

The Discrepancy Model can be attributed to Malcolm Provus (1971), although it has been discussed and refined by others in the field of educational evaluation. In its simplest form, a discrepancy approach to evaluating a program entails a comparison of a program's performance against some standard(s). Variances are identified according to where the program "ought to be" and where it actually "is."

Three different types of sources provide these standards. First, an evaluator could turn to accrediting bodies or national organizations and examine the standards they have produced. For instance, some of the standards published by the Child Welfare League of America include: *Standards for Organizations and Administration for All Child Welfare Services; Standards for Child Protective Service; Standards for Day Care Service; Standards for Foster Family Service; and Standards for Residential Centers for Children.* The American Correctional Association has published standards for: *Juvenile Community Residential Facilities; Juvenile Probation and Aftercare Services; and Juvenile Detention Facilities and Juvenile Training Schools.* Among the many standards prepared by the Joint Commission on the Accreditation of Hospitals are the *Hospice Standards Manual* and the *Ambulatory Health Care Standards.* The National League for Nursing has prepared standards for home health care in *Accreditation Criteria, Standards and Substantiating Evidences.*

This is just a small sampling of a wide range of standards that already exist for certain programs. Within your area, various state departments may have developed standards for certain programs. Standards contained in these documents may provide guidelines for directing a local program. Sometimes, however, these standards are vague, minimal, or so general that much is left open for interpretation. Some standards may specify that the program have a written policy and procedures manual, but they do not specify what should be in it. Other standards may be very specific about limitations on staff caseload or the amount of time within which certain types of services must be provided. If you are attempting to provide a formative evaluation, you may find such standards helpful. They will not be as helpful for evaluations where outcomes or impact data are needed.

A second source of standards is journal articles or studies that have been conducted on programs similar to the one you are interested in evaluating. Carter (1983) located information on client outcomes in a number of different program areas; he reported that with regard to a delinquency program, between 27 percent and 52 percent of all males will be rearrested within twelve months after release, but between 16 percent and 30 percent of the females will be rearrested within twelve months. Between 24 percent and 49 percent of foster care cases achieved a permanent placement within six months; and in child protective services, between 17 percent and 33 percent of substantiated abuse or neglect cases will reabuse or reneglect. In marital counseling, about two-thirds of clients and counselors reported improvement in the presenting problem.

Clearly, if your agency has a delinquency program (or foster care, protective services, or marital counseling program) and experiences higher rates of recidivism or dissatisfaction than those cited in the literature, then there is a discrepancy between what was expected and actual performance. On the other hand, your program may perform better than these rates, and you would have some basis for concluding that your program is a "good" program.

These first two sources of standards of evaluation rely on finding *available* literature or standards. Formal standards that have been prepared by an accrediting body or professional organization may be readily available or already known to the evaluator. It may be more difficult for the evaluator to identify relevant studies in the literature that would provide standards against which his or her program can be measured.

Because of differences in the way programs evolve, the availability of resources, and the mix of clients and staff, there is great variability in the way even similar programs are structured. One divorce support group may meet twice a week for six weeks with both male and female co-leaders, while another may run for twelve weeks, meeting only once a week and utilizing only a female therapist. Are these programs similar? Probably not. You are likely to be disappointed if you expect to find useful comparative data for a program exactly like yours. While there may be programs similar to yours that have conducted evaluations, the reports of these evaluations may not have made it into the professional literature. An alternative is to approach agencies that you know have similar programs and request client outcome data for comparison with your program.

A third way to find standards for your program's performance is to look within your agency. Most programs have concrete, measurable objectives that were developed earlier (perhaps prior to the start of the program or at the beginning of the program year). These objectives may be stated as:

1. To make an eligibility determination of 100 percent of ADC applications within forty-five days.

2. To place 225 new job trainees in full-time paid positions by January 1, 1992.
3. To increase admissions from minority clients by 20 percent over the number served last year.
4. To reduce the number of clients who recidivate by 25 percent during the first six months of the calendar year.
5. To have 75 percent of the program participants attain a G.E.D. prior to release.

Notice that these objectives have in common several characteristics: (1) they are specific—they state a desired result; (2) they are measurable (easily verified); and (3) they indicate when the result can be expected. Contrast these objectives with the following goals:

1. To eliminate poverty.
2. To reduce the incidence of child abuse.
3. To promote happier, healthier families.

Goals provide direction; they help us to recognize if some activity may not be appropriate given a chosen goal. However, note that there is a certain ambiguousness associated with goals. At an agency or program level, goals may never be achieved. While all hunger may never be eliminated from the state of Texas, the goal can still be a most worthwhile one to work toward. The problem comes when agencies confuse goals with objectives. Often, the first actions of the evaluator are to help the program administrator and staff to develop measurable program objectives.

Once you establish program objectives, you can use the discrepancy model to determine whether the objectives were met. This approach could also be described simply as program monitoring. That is, the evaluator is trying to determine if the program is going to meet the objectives that it set for itself. If the objectives are met, the evaluator could conclude that the program is doing what it ought to do. If the objectives are not being met, then perhaps they were unrealistic or unmeasurable, or there may have been mitigating circumstances that could explain the discrepancy.

The problem with reliance upon the program's own objectives to determine how the program is doing is that whoever developed the objectives may have made them so easy to accomplish that they are essentially worthless. For instance, if a program objective stated that 2,200 new clients would be served within the year, but for the past two years the agency has been serving almost 2,500 new clients, the objective will have been met—there was no discrepancy—but we would still have no idea about how "good" or effective the program was. Ideally, a program should have to stretch a bit in order to meet its objectives. Objectives should be obtainable, but not be so easy to reach that no special effort is required.

The Hammond Model

A completely different evaluation model has been proposed by Robert Hammond (1975). The Hammond Model is a systematic approach that is useful for conceptualizing alternatives for program evaluation. For instance, a population (those individuals involved in or influenced by the program) can be conceptualized as consisting of three elements: clients, staff, and administration. A program operates in an environment defined by its intents (the purposes, goals, or objectives established for it), its methods (whatever intervention is employed), and its resources (the people, money, space, materials, and equipment used to implement the methods).

Once these program elements have been identified, the evaluator can organize questions into two groups: those that relate to areas of opinion (judgments and beliefs) and those that relate to behavioral performance.

With this model the evaluator has a number of choices. He or she can decide to be very comprehensive and cover all of the population and environmental elements with regard to opinions and performance. Or, the evaluator may select some of the elements under each heading. In our initial example, in which we have only sixty days to conduct a program evaluation, we might choose to interview *staff* (a population element) concerning their *opinions* of *clients' performance* after a certain intervention (behavior elements).

We might also choose to survey clients from a particular program about their opinions of staff performance (were they satisfied with the services they received?). We could ask clients if they were satisfied with the program objectives or the resources available to the program. We might examine clients' outcomes (performance) as a result of receiving a specific intervention. The strength of the Hammond Model is that it suggests a variety of elements for evaluators to consider in planning an evaluation.

The Judicial Model

Another evaluation model has been described by Wolf (1975), Levine et al. (1978), Smith (1985), and others. The Judicial or Adversarial Model relies upon testimony and a judge or jury to weigh the evi-

Table 10.2 The Hammond Model

Population	Environment	Behavior
Clients	Intents	Performance
Staff	Methods	Opinion
Administration	Resources	

dence. Being a litigious society, we understand the judicial process. We derive a certain amount of satisfaction from being able to present our best arguments and evidence as to why a program is "good" and worthy of being continued. (Where there is no natural adversary to argue against a program, staff can be given the assignment to serve as the adversary).

Several strengths are associated with the use of a Judicial Model. The jury or hearing panel can be formed with experts, consumers of services, board members, representatives from the funding source, ordinary citizens, or some combination of these. If, in the presentation of data, a particular point is not understood, the hearing officer or the jury panel can request additional information and clarification on the spot. Perhaps the greatest strength of this approach is that it encourages a wide variety of perspectives and alternative interpretations of evidence, allowing program administrators to get a better (more balanced) view of their programs.

Wolf (1975) indicates that this approach is dependent upon having clearly communicated hearing rules and procedures dealing with such items as cross-examination, criteria for determining the admissibility of evidence, instructions for the hearing panel, and so forth. While he reports that six months of planning took place before a two-day hearing, I believe this process could be simplified and utilized with much less planning. Many United Ways across the country appear to use a much less formal version of this approach when they have citizen committees make recommendations regarding continued funding for new programs.

Client Satisfaction Approaches

When asked to plan a program evaluation, many students have a tendency to think only of client feedback or client satisfaction surveys. While clients' input should certainly not be denigrated or excluded from a comprehensive program evaluation, client feedback data alone will not necessarily provide information about the worth or benefit of a program. The vast majority of published consumer satisfaction studies show that clients almost invariably report high levels of satisfaction (Royse, 1985).

What constitutes high levels of satisfaction? Lebow (1982) reviewed twenty-six studies examining satisfaction with mental health treatment and found half of the studies reported satisfaction in the range of 80-100 percent. More than three-quarters of the studies had satisfaction rates higher than 70 percent in spite of the surveys being conducted of totally different programs in dissimilar settings and using various counseling approaches and assessment methods. As Lebow (1982) has noted, these high satisfaction rates come from clients who "have little choice of facility, type of treatment, or practitioner" (p. 250).

Positive client evaluations are not proof of a "good" program. In fact, Rocheleau and Mackesey (1980) suggest that a problem may be indicated if a program receives satisfaction rates *less* than 70-75 percent. If only two-thirds of your clients are pleased with your services, then your program may warrant closer inspection.

There can be many reasons why consumer satisfaction studies tend to reveal positive findings. First of all, client feedback instruments are often "homemade," and nothing is known about their reliability or validity. Your program could receive very high marks on an instrument of your making, which could later be found to be lacking reliability or validity. (Remember our discussion of these topics in chapter 2.) Another reason is that persons who are dissatisfied with services tend to drop out early. If you are conducting a study of those who have completed services, you may not be capturing a representational sample of all the clients who came into your agency for assistance.

Third, the methodology for distributing the survey instrument may present some difficulties. Clients may move frequently and not leave forwarding addresses. If a high percentage of clients have low educational levels, they will not be as responsive to mailed questionnaires as those with higher levels of education. Finally, since you can estimate that only about 30 percent will respond to a mailed questionnaire, what do you conclude about the 70 percent who chose not to respond? Did they tend to be satisfied or dissatisfied? The results of a survey with only a 30 percent response rate are virtually meaningless.

On the other hand, clients receiving their consumer satisfaction questionnaires in the social worker's office may be more likely to respond, but these clients may feel that their anonymity is threatened. Clients may also have concerns about receiving future services if they report any dissatisfaction.

There are several reasons for conducting client satisfaction studies: (1) they tend to be relatively inexpensive; (2) they can be implemented with a minimal amount of prior planning; and (3) they require very little research or statistical expertise (the results tend to be obvious). Sometimes because of time constraints, cost, or inadequate planning for other types of program evaluation, a client satisfaction approach is the only type of program evaluation that can be implemented. Here are a few recommendations for getting data:

1. Use a scale that has good reliability and has been used successfully in other studies. An example of this would be the Client Satisfaction Questionnaire developed by Larsen and his colleagues (1979). The use of a standard scale will eliminate many of the problems found in hastily designed questionnaires.
2. This instrument should be used to monitor satisfaction over time so that there is a baseline from which to observe departures. If client satisfaction studies are conducted regularly and routinely, then data can be compared periodically with results from prior efforts. One way to get data regularly that is not as biased as mailing to those who completed services is the "ballot box" approach. For one week every quarter, each client coming into the agency (both new and old) is given a brief questionnaire and asked to complete it. (If a significant proportion of the agency's clients are illiterate, procedures have to be developed for those who cannot read.)
3. At least one or two open-ended questions should be employed— given the opportunity, consumers may inform you about problems you didn't suspect and couldn't anticipate (e.g., the receptionist is extremely rude to consumers but not to staff). Ask, "How could our program be improved?" or, "Can you think of any ways the agency's services can be improved?"

Other Models

No discussion about evaluation models would be complete without at least a mention of cost-analytic models. These models are sometimes discussed in terms of benefit-cost analysis, cost-benefit analysis, or cost-effectiveness studies; they can be very complicated. A number of misconceptions are associated with them (Roid, 1982). First, cost-benefit analysis and cost-effectiveness studies are not the same thing. Cost-benefit analysis involves estimating intangible benefits. For example, how do you arrive at a monetary value for a feeling of security? What is the value of the aesthetic benefit of a park or green space created within a city?

However, it is possible to demonstrate that some social service programs are cost-effective. Decker, Starrett, and Redhorse (1986) did this rather convincingly when they showed that the implementation of an Employee Assistance Program reduced the number of absences and saved a company $26,314. In some instances, program evaluations are able to demonstrate tangible cost-savings. Much more could be said about cost-analytic models than space allows. For further information on these approaches, see Thompson, 1980; Levin, 1983; and Rossi and Freeman, 1985 (especially pages 321-56).

A good many models have originated from the field of education, for instance, Stufflebeam's CIPP Model. CIPP is an acronym made up of the first letters of Context, Input, Process, and Product. According to Stufflebeam, these represent four types of evaluation. Context evaluation is similar to needs assessment. Input evaluation is a means of identifying and assessing competing plans. Process evaluation assesses and guides the implementation of plans. Product evaluation assesses outcomes (Stufflebeam, 1983). The CIPP Model is seen as presenting a system view and does not so much guide a specific evaluation as provide an outline for ongoing evaluation of a program. The CIPP Model can be used with either a formative evaluation or a **summative evaluation** (where a conclusive statement is rendered regarding the worth of a program).

This chapter has presented an overview aimed to simplify what can be a complex subject. I have not discussed in any depth the topic of needs assessment (an evaluation conducted before a new program is begun to identify the need for the program) or evaluability assessment (an effort directed toward assessing the feasibility of various evaluation methods that might be used), although both of these can be considered types of evaluation. Nor have I discussed a type of evaluation known as meta-evaluation (which can be thought of as an evaluation of previous evaluations). Meta-evaluations aggregate pertinent research findings across prior studies in order to obtain a better understanding of developments in an area of interest. Gibbs (1989), for instance, constructed an instrument to help practitioners "synthesize" or make practical sense out of multiple evaluations—as when trying to determine what is the most effective treatment when there are numerous competing approaches. Other examples of meta-evaluations in the literature include: Hogarty (1989); Videka-Sherman (1988); Miller and Hester (1986); Wilner, Freeman, Surber, and Goldstein (1985); Rubin (1985); Nurius (1984); and Reid and Hanrahan (1982).

I have tried to remove some of the complexity associated with program evaluation without limiting the focus to the topics of effort, effectiveness, or efficiency. What should be apparent to you by now is that there is probably an infinite number of approaches available to the program evaluator. The designs presented in this chapter are illustrative of the variety available for your use. You are free to take any one of these or to combine elements from several designs to fit the requirements of an actual situation.

Practical Considerations

When you have finished reading this chapter you will have some ideas about how you might go about conducting a program evaluation. While the conceptualization of the evaluation design may be the most difficult part of a program evaluation, any number of factors can influence the choice of a design, such as political considerations within the agency as well as pragmatic considerations.

All evaluation is inherently threatening. Most of us feel a little uncomfortable when we know we are being evaluated—especially when the evaluator is unknown to us. We are even more threatened when that person is not perceived as being our advocate. Therefore, you need to be sensitive to the feelings of those who may be affected by the findings of your program evaluation. Try not to create anxiety within the staff. Communicate frequently with involved personnel about what will be happening. Avoid surprises. If at all possible, involve staff in the planning of the evaluation. Remember that evaluations take place within an agency's political arena. Someone may have a vested interest in making one program look good at the expense of another program. Some managers may hope to use the program evaluation to justify firing staff or to justify past expenditures.

Second, obstacles to program evaluation may arise from unexpected quarters. Staff members may have strongly held opinions that what they do is too complex or too intangible to measure. Or, they may feel that any problems they have could be eliminated if only the program had a larger budget. Other professionals who make referrals to a program may not be completely candid if asked to evaluate a program. They may feel that criticism will jeopardize future referrals being accepted or that the program could be cut out altogether—a serious problem if there are no other similar services for their clients. Additional issues and obstacles to conducting program evaluation are addressed in Palumbo (1987).

Third, develop a contract with the organization you are doing the evaluation for (even if you are a staff member there) that clearly sets down their expectations about the evaluation. This agreement should cover such items as:

1. The *purpose* of the evaluation (alternatively, list questions to be answered or hypotheses to be tested).
2. The *audience* for whom you will be writing the evaluation report. (Will this report go only to the program director, to the whole staff, the board of directors, the agency administrator? Will it be made available to the public?)
3. The *amount of time* you have to conduct the evaluation. (When is the final report expected?)
4. The terms of your *reimbursement* or statement regarding your release from other duties in order to allow you to conduct the evaluation. Also, specify any funds that you may require for the conduct of the evaluation (e.g., postage; the purchase of standardized instruments or computer processing).

Program evaluations often require a lot of negotiation, and you should feel free to negotiate any areas that may present a problem. For instance, will you be free to utilize the evaluation design of your choosing? Is a certain methodology specified by the agency? To what extent will you have (or do you need) cooperation of the staff? Who will "own" the data, and can it be used for publication? Finally, don't take on too much at one time. When you conduct your first program evaluation, don't attempt to evaluate a comprehensive service delivery agency—start with one program.

Reading Program Evaluation Reports

Even if you don't think you will ever be interested in conducting a program evaluation, at some point in your social work career you will come across a program evaluation report. It may be an evaluation of your program that has been conducted by some "outsider" or consultant. You may be asked to read an evaluation of a program in order to determine if that program should be adopted by your agency. As a board member, administrator, or policymaker, you may attend a program evaluation presentation so that decisions can be made about whether a program should be continued, curtailed, or expanded. Some evaluations will be poorly done and have little merit; others will be thoughtfully conceptualized and well executed, providing substantive evaluative information for decision-making. What are some of the criteria to help you distinguish the better from the poorer evaluations?

Blythe (1983), in analyzing outcome evaluations of child abuse treatment programs, found that these studies tended to have problems in several areas. We can draw from her findings to discuss elements that are essential to good evaluation reports. Whether you are reading an evaluation report or preparing one yourself, the report should contain enough information on the topics listed below so that others can fully comprehend what was done and to whom.

1. *Target populations.* The population should be clearly described. Even if all the sample cases involve child abuse, it is important to know such details as whether the perpetrators were first offenders or repeat offenders, if the abuse was physical or sexual, and the severity of the abuse. Is the intervention group homogeneous with regard to these traits? It is conceivable that an intervention designed for parents who had abused their children could have worked differently with a sample of college graduates, persons on welfare, or persons who were severely abused themselves as children. How was the sample selected? Was random sampling used? Before you compare the results from your intervention with results from another intervention program, you need to know if the populations are similar. To what extent do the clients in the intervention group resemble those with whom you are familiar?

2. *Evaluation design.* Random assignment to a control or intervention group is a very strong evaluation design. If no control group is used, how do you know that the intervention was responsible for the changes in clients' behavior? (Remember the discussion of threats to internal validity in chapter 4). It is also important to look at the posttest or follow-up data. Ideally, evaluators should allow enough time to pass after intervention for problem behavior to recur. Two or three weeks after an intervention for child abuse is an inadequate period of time to allow for a follow-up if one wants to conclude that the intervention is instrumental in reducing child abuse. Six, nine, or even better, twelve months after the intervention is a more creditable length of time. (Guidance on the choice of the time frame should follow from the review of the literature.)

3. *Measurement of variables.* When reading an evaluation of an intervention, we must fully understand what was provided in the treatment. Did the treatment result from interventions described in the literature, or was it totally new—a locally designed intervention? The evaluation report should give the length, duration, and frequency of interventive sessions. It

should describe the staff (e.g., their professional training) and tell whether the same staff provided all the treatment or if some responsibilities were shared (e.g., with volunteers).

More credibility will be given to those studies that use scales for which there is information about reliability and validity. If an instrument has no reliability, then even "conclusive" or "definitive" differences between the control and intervention groups should be viewed with skepticism.

When you study social problems such as child abuse, official reports of abuse and behavioral measures may be the preferred dependent variable, instead of "change of attitude" or "increase of knowledge about parenting." As a rule, dependent variables should be clearly defined, objective, and verifiable. Do not rely upon abusive parents to inform you of the number of incidents of emotional or physical child abuse in their home during past six months. They may fail to remember or have an unequivocal interest in minimizing the incidents, and the number of incidents are not easily verified. While there is no rule requiring more than one dependent variable, two or more nonredundant estimates of a treatment's effectiveness provide greater confidence in the results (LeCroy, 1985).

4. *Results and interpretation of the data.* Do the authors present their data so that it can be understood? Are there analyses involving the dependent variable(s)? Are all of the hypotheses or research questions addressed? Is there baseline data? Are the sample sizes adequate? Do the authors attempt to overgeneralize? Can the results be generalized across time, geography, and environment? Are differences between groups statistically significant? Are limitations of the evaluation discussed? Finally, based upon the presented data, would any intelligent, rational person come to the same conclusions as the author of the evaluation report?

Final Comments

How important is it for social workers to know about program evaluation? Miller and Hester (1986) informally polled two dozen local alcoholism treatment programs about their cost and effectiveness. Slightly fewer than half of the programs were able to quote percentages of treatment success. Upon further inquiry, none of these programs were able to provide data to substantiate their claims of success. When you make referrals to treatment programs, aren't you interested in how successful their interventions are? Don't clients have a right to know this information?

While sometimes we perform program evaluations because they are mandated, the best reason for conducting them is to demonstrate that we are helping our clients. How do we know that we aren't in fact hurting them? How do we improve our programs without some kind of evaluative feedback?

The editors-in-chief of *Social Work* and *Social Work Research and Abstracts* recently contributed another reason why social workers should engage in program evaluation.

> When social work fails to use research effectively, other professionals gain more public credibility in what we have considered "our" traditional areas (such as psychologists' and nurses' work in the area of child abuse). These professionals are able to show funding agencies evaluative research that demonstrates the effectiveness of their interventions. (Hopps and Gambrill, 1988, p. 387)

Given the increasing research prowess of other human service professionals, social workers cannot shy away from those areas where research is required. We cannot continue to rely upon others to demonstrate that our clients benefit from our services.

QUESTIONS FOR CLASS DISCUSSION

The following could be called "Exemplars of Poor Evaluation Designs." What is wrong with each of the following plans for evaluating programs?

1. The agency is a halfway house run by the Department of Corrections. Residents are all young men (under thirty) who have been in prison for the first time and are now on parole in a pre-release program. In this program evaluation, three new residents who have outward signs of depression will be selected and compared with two other residents who are not depressed. The Zung Self-Rating Depression Inventory will be the instrument used to determine if a caring attitude by the program staff and conjugal visits can help with adjustment from prison to the larger community. A pretest-posttest design will be employed.

2. A school is planning to develop a latchkey program for students in kindergarten through the sixth grade. This program

will be open to parents who can pay $45.00 per week per child for enrollment. A quasi-experimental design (nonequivalent control group) will be used to compare students enrolled in the latchkey program with students not enrolled in the program but whose teachers suspect are in need of a latchkey program. Comparisons between the two groups of students will be made at the beginning and end of the school year in terms of their academic achievement levels and the number of incidents with the police.

3. A special intensive services unit was devised by a social service agency for families who had been referred because of child abuse. With this demonstration program, each social worker had no more than five families at a time. Each worker in this program selected the families to be initially involved with intensive services. After the first wave of families completed the intervention, random assignment of additional families was then employed. The control group consisted of families who were also referred for child abuse but who received only a regular caseworker. Each family received intensive services for no more than eight weeks. Fourteen months after the opening of each case a graduate assistant called the family to learn if the victim of the abuse was still in the home. It is hypothesized that those families that received the intensive services will have a higher proportion of children still in the home.

4. After phone calls were made to the families described in number 3 above, it was found that only twenty-four of the thirty families that were served by the intensive services staff could be located by phone. However, three-quarters of these families still had their children at home with them. In contrast thirty-five of the fifty families in the control group could be located by phone, but only 66 percent of these families retained their children. Can the graduate assistant conclude that the program is a success because 75 percent of the families receiving intensive services retained their children compared with 66 percent of those families that received regular casework services?

5. What is wrong with the following objectives? How could they be reworded to make them better?
   a. Maintain and improve community forensic services.
   b. Expand the hospital volunteer services program.
   c. Develop needed community residential facilities.
   d. Provide psychiatric services to inmates of the county jail.

   e. Increase the openness in communications between adolescents and their parents.
6. A social work student working in her practicum was asked to evaluate a program designed to prevent adolescent pregnancies among high school students. The developers of the program had four expectations for the students participating in the ten-week education program: (a) students will become more knowledgeable about reproduction; (b) students will become more knowledgeable about contraception; (c) parent/adolescent communications about sexuality will become less strained and more open; (d) there will be fewer pregnancies among females who complete the program than among those who were not able to participate because of the scheduling of required classes.
   Which of these expectations will be the easiest to measure? What would be the best evidence for success of this program?
7. Look back at table 10.1. What additional information would you need in order to determine whether any of those three programs were "good," effective, or efficient?
8. What political and pragmatic considerations could influence program evaluations to be conducted in the social service agencies with which you are familiar?

MINI-PROJECTS FOR EXPERIENCING RESEARCH FIRSTHAND

1. Locate an example of client utilization data from a social service agency. (Sometimes this information is printed in annual reports.) Examine this data to see if you can determine what groups the agency is primarily serving. Then, obtain census data for the same geographic region. Compare rates of key variables. For instance, if the percentage of older adults in the larger population is 10 percent, what percentage of older adults is the agency serving? How do the rates of minorities in the community and those being served compare? What other comparisons would be important to make?
2. Design a program evaluation to demonstrate that the Reasonably Healthy Minds Agency runs a "good" outpatient counseling program for families with children. Address the following:
   a. What questions do you want to investigate?
   b. Define your dependent and independent variables.
   c. Which design or methodological approach will you use?
   d. How will you collect your data?

213

  e. How will you analyze your data?

  f. What limitations will your study have?

3. Think of a social service program. Briefly describe it. How would you go about showing that this program ultimately had a favorable impact within the community? Could you design a program evaluation to show taxpayers that the program saved more money than it cost to operate it? Describe the approach you would use.

4. Choose a human service program with which you are familiar, and then do the following:

  a. Briefly describe it.

  b. Write at least one program goal.

  c. Write three specific program objectives.

RESOURCES AND REFERENCES

Austin, M. and Associates. (1982). *Evaluating Your Agency's Programs.* Beverly Hills, CA: Sage.

Blythe, B. J. (1983). A critique of outcome evaluation in child abuse treatment. *Child Welfare* 62 (4), 325–335.

Carter, R. K. (1983). *The Accountable Agency.* Beverly Hills, CA: Sage.

Decker, J. T., Starrett, R., and Redhorse, J. (1986). Evaluating the cost-effectiveness of employee assistance programs. *Social Work* 31 (5), 391–393.

Dush, D. M. and Cassileth, B. R. (1985). Program evaluation in terminal care. *Hospice Journal* 1 (1), 55–72.

Fitz-Gibbon, C. T. and Morris, L. L. (1987). *How to Design a Program Evaluation.* Beverly Hills, CA: Sage.

Gibbs, L. E. (1989). Quality of study rating form: An instrument for synthesizing evaluation studies. *Journal of Social Work Education* 25 (1), 55–67.

Hammond, R. L. (1975). Establishing priorities for information and design specifications for evaluating community education programs. *Community Education Journal,* March/April, 1975.

Hogarty, G. E. (1989). Meta-analysis of the effects of practice with the chronically mentally ill: A critique and reappraisal of the literature. *Social Work* 34 (4), 363–373.

Hopps, J. G. and Gambrill, E. (1988). Who's Losing? *Social Work* 33 (5), 387–388.

Hornick, J. P. and Burrows, B. (1988). Program evaluation. In R. M. Grinnell, Jr. (Ed.), *Social Work Research and Evaluation.* Itasca, IL: Peacock.

Kushler, M. G. and Davidson, W. S. (1979). Using experimental designs to evaluate social programs. *Social Work Research and Abstracts* 15 (1), 27–32.

Larsen, D. L., Attkisson, C. C., Hargreaves, W. A., and Nguyen, T. D. (1979). Assessment of client/patient satisfaction: development of a general scale. *Evaluation and Program Planning* 2, 197–207.

Lebow, J. (1982). Consumer satisfaction with mental health treatment. *Psychological Bulletin* 91 (2), 244–59.

LeCroy, C. W. (1985). Methodological issues in the evaluation of social work practice. *Social Service Review* 59 (3), 345–357.

Levin, H. M. (1983). *Cost-effectiveness: A Primer.* Beverly Hills, CA: Sage.

Levine, M., Brown, E., Fitzgerald, C., Goplerud, E., Gordon, M. E., Jayne-Lazarus, C., Rosenberg, N., and Slater, J. (1978). Adapting the jury trial for program evaluation: A report of an experience. *Evaluation and Program Planning* 1, 177–186.

Lewis, J. A. and Lewis, M. D. (1983). *Management of Human Service Programs.* Monterey, CA: Brooks/Cole.

Lipsey, M. W. (1988). Practice and malpractice in evaluation research. *Evaluation Practice* 9 (4), 5–24.

McMahon, P. M. (1987). Shifts in intervention procedures: A problem in evaluating human service interventions. *Social Work Research and Abstracts* 23 (4), 13–16.

Miller, W. and Hestor, R. (1986). Inpatient alcoholism treatment: Who benefits? *American Psychologist* 41 (7), 794–805.

Nurius, P. S. (1984). Utility of data synthesis for social work. *Social Work Research and Abstracts* 20 (3), 23–32.

Palumbo, D. J. (1987). *The Politics of Program Evaluation.* Beverly Hills, CA: Sage.

Patton, M. Q. (1981). *Creative Evaluation.* Beverly Hills, CA: Sage.

Patton, M. Q. (1982). *Practical Evaluation.* Beverly Hills, CA: Sage.

Patton, M. Q. (1980). *Qualitative Evaluation Methods.* Beverly Hills, CA: Sage.

Posavac, E. J. and Carey, R. G. (1985). *Program Evaluation: Methods and Case Studies.* Englewood Cliffs, NJ: Prentice-Hall.

Provus, M. (1971). *Discrepancy Evaluation for Educational Program Improvement and Assessment.* Berkeley, CA: McCutchan.

Reid, W. J. and Hanrahan, P. (1982). Recent Evaluations of Social Work: Grounds for Optimism. *Social Work* 27 (4), 328–340.

Roberts, A. R. (1988). A strategy for making decisions and evaluating alternative juvenile offender treatment programs. *Evaluation and Program Planning* 11, 115–122.

Roberts, A. R. (1988). Wilderness programs for juvenile offenders: A challenging alternative. *Juvenile and Family Court Journal* 39 (1), 1–12.

Roid, G. H. (1982). Cost-effectiveness analysis in mental health policy research. *American Psychologist* 37 (1), 94–95.

Rocheleau, B. and Mackesey, T. (1980). What, consumer feedback surveys again? *Evaluation and the Health Professions* 3 (4), 405–419.

Rossi, P. H. and Freeman, H. E. (1985). *Evaluation: A Systematic Approach.* Beverly Hills, CA: Sage.

Royse, D. (1985). Client satisfaction with the helping process: a review for the pastoral counselor. *Journal of Pastoral Care* 39 (1), 3–11.

Rubin, A. (1985). Practice effectiveness: More grounds for optimism. *Social Work* 30 (6), 469–476.

Schuerman, J. R. (1983). *Research and Evaluation in the Human Services.* New York: Free Press.

Smith. N. (1985). Adversary and committee hearings as evaluation methods. *Evaluation Review* 9 (6), 735–750.

Stufflebeam, D. (1983). In George F. Madaus, Michael S. Scriven, and Daniel L. Stufflebeam (eds.), *Evaluation Models: Viewpoints on Educational and Human Services Evaluation.* Boston: Kluwer-Nijhoff.

Thompson, M. S. (1980). *Benefit-cost Analysis for Program Evaluation.* Beverly Hills, CA: Sage.

Tripodi, T. (1987). Program evaluation. In Sumner M. Rosen, David Fanshel and Marey E. Lutz, (eds.), *Encyclopedia of Social Work.* Silver Spring, MD: National Association of Social Workers.

Velasquex, J. S. and McCubbin, H. I. (1980). Towards establishing the effectiveness of community-based residential treatment: Program evaluation by experimental research. *Journal of Social Service Research* 3 (4), 337–359.

Videka-Sherman, L. (1988). Meta-analysis of research on social work practice in mental health. *Social Work* 33 (4), 325–338.

Wilner, D. M., Freeman, H. E., Surber, M., and Goldstein, M. S. (1985). Success in mental health treatment interventions: A review of 211 random assignment studies. *Journal of Social Service Review* 8 (4), 1–21.

Wolf, R. L. (1975). Trial by jury: A new evaluation method. *Phi Delta Kappan* 57, 185–187.

Eleven

Qualitative Research

Have you ever wondered what it would be like to be an older adult? Do you know what it feels like to be eighty-five years old and frail? If you were eighty-five, do you think people would look out for you, or would they tend to ignore and overlook you? What is it like to reside in a nursing home or a mental hospital? What is it like to have to use food stamps or to be physically handicapped? How do you think drug addicts and prostitutes experience the world? These questions illustrate the kinds of topics that cannot be measured with standardized instruments and scales and for which randomization, sample sizes, and control groups are not relevant. Such questions as these beg to be investigated by qualitative research methods.

Qualitative researchers seek to understand lifestyles and social phenomena firsthand. They try to describe subgroups or cultures (e.g., the world of drug addicts, the chronically mentally ill, illegal immigrants) from the point of view of the persons being studied. A goal of understanding is emphasized rather than prediction regarding some dependent variable.

Social workers often discover that their clients use special terms and vocabularies different from their own. A fine example of this has been provided by Rosenstiel (1980) in his study of black heroin addicts. He discovered that "punks" are men who do not defend themselves and who are used sexually by other men (in institutional settings) with the consequence that they are not respected and have a low status. According to Rosenstiel, one informant was a punk who, in nine months of group and personal therapy, never discussed this problem. While most of his fellow addicts knew of his status, none of the staff at a residential treatment center knew. The informant was "promoted to a therapy group leader, but was powerless in his group. No one from the streets listens to a 'punk' " (p. 230). It is important to understand the language and values of these clients in order to be effective as an agent of change.

Qualitative approaches provide detail and add richness and depth to our understanding of any phenomenon being investigated and are similar to the "case studies" so familiar to social workers. Let's take the question, "What is it like to live in a nursing home?" Using a quantitative approach, we would begin by identifying some problem or by stating a testable hypothesis, for example, "The majority of nursing home residents would rather live somewhere else," or, "Nursing home residents are more lonely or depressed than older adults who do not live in nursing homes." Even if we surveyed a large sample of older adults and gathered sufficient data, we still would have only a limited perspective on what life is like in a nursing home; the quality of the day-to-day life in the home would escape us.

In contrast, a qualitative research approach to this problem might involve an investigator living in the nursing home in order to talk informally with the residents, to observe what happens in their social world, and to experience the kinds of interactions that they have with staff and with each other.

A story told to me by a former student provides an illustration of how one incident can tell much about the quality of life in a particular nursing home. In talking with a resident about what it was like living in the home, the student heard the following account: One day, several residents were in the back wing of the building watching television when two fellows, who didn't look like they belonged there, appeared. They announced that they were television repairmen and proceeded to cart away the television, which had been working perfectly. Being somewhat suspicious, one resident slipped away to her room and pressed her call button, which rang at the nurses' station. Meanwhile, the men loaded the television into a truck and left. Twenty minutes later, one of the staff strolled back to the resident's room to see why the call button had been used.

This incident raises several questions. First, why did it take the staff so long to answer the call button? What would have happened if there had been a true emergency, such as a nursing home resident choking on a piece of food or falling out of bed? How good is the security in the facility—do residents fear that they will be robbed or their personal possessions stolen? If we were to informally interview other residents from this nursing home, we might find other equally alarming accounts. Such accounts provide a richer image of the quality of life in the nursing home than any objective scale that quantitatively measures such dimensions as the residents' satisfaction with life, or their loneliness and depression.

Qualitative research is different from the type of research that has been discussed so far. In quantitative research, the investigator relies on counting, measuring, and analyzing numbers. In qualitative research, there is little or no use made of statistics. While counting may be employed, it is not the major emphasis. The qualitative researcher seeks to understand social relationships and patterns of interaction. Anecdotal accounts are used to describe the world of the persons being investigated.

Qualitative researchers are flexible; their research goals or questions may be altered even while data are being collected. While they usually have a methodology in mind prior to starting their project, they do not require that the research design and methodology be rigidly and unalterably stated before they begin to collect data. There is nothing "wrong" with this fluidity, since many researchers feel that the purpose of qualitative research is to generate hypotheses for later testing. In this sense, qualitative research is commonly regarded as being exploratory.

Among social scientists, cultural anthropologists are best known for their use of qualitative research methods. Sometimes these approaches are known as **ethnography** (folk description). One prominent ethnographer describes ethnography as follows: "Such work requires an intensive personal involvement, an abandonment of traditional scientific control, an improvisational style to meet situations not of the researcher's making, and an ability to learn from a long series of mistakes" (Agar, 1986, p. 12).

Methods of Qualitative Research

Qualitative research (also known as field research) uses procedures that produce descriptive data: personal observations and people's spoken or written words. Qualitative research allows investigators to know their subjects personally and to understand their struggles and explanations of their world (Bogdan and Taylor, 1975). It involves participant observation and in-depth interviewing, although analysis of personal documents (such as letters and diaries) is also done.

Participant observation involves immersion in the world of those being investigated. If you are investigating a nursing home, this may require that you live in the home where you are awakened from a sound sleep at 6:30 A.M. so that vital signs can be checked, where you experience the frustration of being ignored by staff, and where twenty-four hours a day you are surrounded with the same sights, sounds, and smells. Eating a meal there once or twice may not be quite the same as eating all of your meals there for an extended period. (Some qualitative researchers feel that at least one year in residence is required in order to fully understand another culture.)

As a participant observer, you experience the world of those who are being observed by living alongside them and sharing their activities. You do what your subjects do (without violating personal or professional ethics, of course).

There are several ways to approach participant observation. You could stress the observer role and place less emphasis on the participant role. For instance, you could go directly to your subjects or to your informant and begin interviewing. Steffensmeier (1986) uses this approach to learn about the world of the fence (a dealer in stolen goods). Steffensmeier was a participant only in the sense that he interviewed, at some length, a fence and observed the fence at work. He did not fence goods himself. He also interviewed thieves, the fence's customers and friends, other fences, and the police. One's degree of involvement as participant or observer depends on the nature of the subjects being studied.

Another approach is to become an active participant in addition to being an observer. Because Estroff (1981) felt it essential to establish her position in the polarized staff-client social system, she informed long-term psychiatric patients in a community treatment program that she was not staff. She says that she did not masquerade as a client, but she admits to looking too much like a staff member on the first day, and subsequently she dressed more inconspicuously. Estroff's approach was to participate as if she were a client. She attended recreational and treatment-related activities, visited clients in their apartments, sought out clients in the street, ate at a lunch counter frequented by clients, sometimes took clients shopping or went bar hopping with them, and so forth. In order to more fully understand the everyday world of the psychiatric patient, Estroff even took a potent antipsychotic medication (Prolixin) for six weeks.

Participant observation can also involve a greater level of masquerade. For example, in the book *Disguised*, Moore (1985) describes her experiences while masquerading as an eighty-five-year-old woman. It took her up to four hours to apply special latex foam make-up to give her face the folds and wrinkles of an elderly woman. Conover (1987) describes his experiences with illegal Mexican aliens. There are numerous examples, some occurring over forty years ago, of investigators using disguised observation in order to learn first-hand about life in institutions. (See, for example, Caudill, Redlich, Gilmore, and Brody, 1952; Deane, 1961; Ishiyama, Batman, and Hewitt, 1967; Goldman, Bohr, and Steinberg, 1970; Rosenhan, 1973.)

Participant observers make use of notes (often called "field notes") to help recall important events, conversations, and persons. Field notes are brief condensations of conversations or observations that are developed later when the investigator is away from the field. Unlike those investigators who are more interested in quantification, qualitative researchers record feelings and interpretations in these field notes.

Sometimes when a criminal subgroup (e.g., drug dealers, prostitutes, gang members) is being studied, the investigator may need to acquire a special vocabulary used by the group. Qualitative researchers ask questions that allow the subjects to talk about themselves and their world so that special experiences, ways of viewing the world, or vocabulary can be learned. In qualitative research, few questions are developed ahead of time. The majority of questions flow from the investigator's interactions with subjects and his or her desire to understand various aspects of their world.

Steps in Doing Qualitative Research

The first step in qualitative research is identifying a topic (or group of people) of interest. Generally, you will have an initial question or set of questions about the topic or group that you want answered. Let's say that you are interested in poverty and how impoverished people survive and cope under adverse conditions. Since poverty is a broad topic, you may want to narrow the focus and concentrate on impoverished families in Appalachian coal-mining communities or on impoverished tenant farmers in the southern part of the United States.

Generally, it is a good idea to become familiar with any literature relevant to your topic. However, with qualitative research, there is no requirement that the literature review come before data collection. Bogdan and Taylor (1975) have written, "After and perhaps during the intensive observation stage of the research, the observer consults the professional literature" (p. 84). These researchers seem to feel that the purpose of the literature review is to enable the investigator to look for unanswered questions that the present study might address and to compare findings. Agar (1980) sees literature review as "clouding" the researcher's mind with misconceptions and the mistakes of others. Early in his career he found that a thorough literature review "introduced a lot of unnecessary noise into my mind as I tried to learn about being a heroin addict from 'patients' in the institution" (p. 25).

The argument for diminishing the importance of the literature review is based on the belief that the ethnographer's role is "to give some sense of different lifestyles to people who either do not know about them, or who are so bogged down in their own stereotypes that they do not understand them" (Agar, 1980, 26–27). Agar recommends that the investigator become familiar with the topic by talking with people who have worked with the group of interest, by reading novels that produce a "feel" for the lifestyle of the group, and by viewing existing literature with a skeptic's eye.

The third step in conducting qualitative research requires locating one or more informants. These are the insiders or group members who are "native speakers" and teachers for the investigator (Spradley, 1979). Informants are the "insider" experts on the culture or group who relay their information to the researcher (who can be thought of as a student or apprentice). They are willing to share their everyday experiences and serve as translators—helping the ethnographer to acquire the necessary vocabulary to maneuver within the culture.

Once informants have been located and rapport established, the qualitative researcher begins to interview them. Interviews may involve predetermined questions or no prior planning. Whyte (1984) and perhaps a majority of qualitative researchers tend to make greater use of the "nondirective" interview. These informal interviews occur in the workplace, in homes, on the street, or wherever the respondents may be. Because the qualitative researcher is a learner, he or she does a lot of listening and spends time establishing rapport. Ethnographers tend to develop long-term relationships; over time, they are able to see the various sides of their respondents as revealed in various situations.

It is much easier to stress the importance of establishing rapport than it is to actually accomplish good rapport. Every culture or subculture is different. Rapport can be difficult to establish if the researcher is insensitive to local practices and patterns of communication. For instance, Thompson (1989), in writing about her experiences in Islamic countries, noted that indirect methods of communication and action are socially preferable to direct methods.

> If a person wants to raise an issue with another, he or she will visit the other, have tea, talk a great deal about generalities, and only at the end of the visit mention his or her real purpose in an offhanded way. . . . They couch negative responses in carefully selected terms so as not to offend or disappoint others. (P. 40)

The way one would go about building rapport with an informant in an Islamic country is very different from the approach one would use on the streets of New York.

Questions about the culture or subgroup arise from observation of informants in different situations as they engage in various activities as well as from the need to confirm or consolidate newly acquired knowledge. Agar (1980) expressed his interest in predetermined questions this way:

> It's not necessarily that ethnographers don't want to test hypotheses. It's just that if they do, the variables and operationalizations and sample specifications must grow from an understanding of the group rather than from being hammered on top of it no matter how poor the fit. (Pp. 69–70)

Recording the data is the next step. When you record (whether on the site or later, when you are at home) and how you record (tape-recorder or written notes) are up to you. Even with guarantees of anonymity, respondents often will not talk freely in the presence of a tape recorder or other such devices. While informants may not be as threatened by note-taking, this will depend upon what they are saying and where they are at the time. In addition to interesting incidents, record the setting, the participants involved, and key words in conversations (if you are unable to record conversations verbatim). It is not crucial to have a perfect reproduction of what was said. Approximate wording and paraphrasing are acceptable. However, it is important to capture the meaning of any remarks. If you make sketchy notes in the field, expand them as soon afterwards as possible so that the details of important observations and incidents are not forgotten.

The last step in qualitative research is analyzing the data and writing a report. As with quantitative methods, the investigator is looking for patterns. In order to find these patterns, transcriptions of interviews may be sorted or catalogued. Computer software exists to assist the researcher in finding selected key words from pages of text (Uriarte-Gaston, 1987). Gigun and Connor (1989), in studying how perpetrators view child sexual abuse, analyzed life history interviews of fourteen male perpetrators using the computer program *Ethnograph*.

Lofland and Lofland (1984) suggest that at least half of the final report should be devoted to accounts of incidents, events, exchanges, remarks, conversations, actions, and so forth. From this data, the investigator should discuss commonly held meanings and norms of behavior in that setting and implications of the findings. From insights garnered, field investigators are then in a position to make recommendations about how social workers can better direct their efforts to the special population that was observed.

Qualitative researchers sometimes employ standardized scales or instruments; they may sample from available respondents or attempt in other ways to provide some confirmation that their findings are reliable. Agar (1980) discusses the use of a small survey as well as simulated and hypothetical situations to confirm his understanding of the heroin addict's world. He feels that the qualitative researcher's findings have good reliability because "something learned in a conversation becomes a hypothesis to check in further conversations or observations" (p. 171). In this way, the meaning of a new term or the significance of some observation can be verified on various occasions and with different respondents within the same culture.

Qualitative researchers seek to establish reliability in other ways. Sometimes they have those who were being studied read the report in order to ferret out inaccuracies or misrepresentations. Information can also be confirmed through public records or by officials (police and legal officials read and commented on parts of Steffensmeier's manuscript).

How strong are the findings produced by qualitative research? To paraphrase Van Maanen (1983), the strength of qualitative research derives from its reliance upon multiple sources of data—it is not committed to one source alone. Babbie (1986) refers to the "superior validity" of field research as compared with surveys and experiments. This stems from the qualitative researcher "being there" and, as a result of those experiences, being able to furnish detailed and extensive illustrations of the phenomenon being studied. This contrasts markedly with the more objective social survey approach of learning about something by asking a series of prepared (sometimes abstract and hypothetical) questions in a standard Likert-type format.

The Great Debate

Because of the enormous differences in the way that the research is conducted, quantitatively minded researchers are often suspicious of the findings of qualitative researchers. In the 1950s and 1960s, a debate began in professional journals regarding the relative virtues of quantitative and qualitative methodology (Bryman, 1984). A continuation of this debate over appropriate research methods for social work has vigorously reappeared in recent social work journals. Peile (1988) has provided a brief overview of some of the major protagonists and their arguments. The debate appears to have surfaced once again because social work researchers are making greater use of the quantitative, empirical, scientific (sometimes known as the logical positivist) approach (Tripodi, 1984). Advocates for the use of quantitative methods (such as Hudson, 1982, 1983, 1986, and Fischer, 1981 and 1984) believe that qualitative methods will not produce the knowledge needed to document effectiveness and to guide practice.

On the other hand, those who advocate for greater use of qualitative approaches (such as Heineman, 1981, 1982; Heineman-Pieper, 1982, 1985, 1986, and Ruckdeschel and Farris, 1982) argue that the trend toward empiricism results in research that is too restrictive and superficial, because of the tendency to investigate only those aspects that can be operationally defined and measured and for which data can be collected. Instead of looking at the whole situation, empiricists fragment a situation and focus on what they can easily count. In the empiricists' quest for "objectivity," important interactions between participants or other details are often overlooked.

Which viewpoint is right? What is the most appropriate research method for social work? Actually, both sides are right. There are limitations associated with both quantitative and qualitative approaches to learning about a phenomenon. As researchers-in-training, you should learn how to use both approaches. Both methodologies can be used profitably by social workers in their practice. Each approach can be used to enrich the findings of the other.

Madey (1982) has addressed the benefits of integrating qualitative and quantitative methods in program evaluation. Some of the ways each approach enriches the other are as follows: Qualitative approaches can assist with the selection of survey items to be used in instrument construction. They can provide external validation of empirically generated constructs. From the field notes of qualitative researchers come real-life examples that can be used to help illustrate the findings of a quantitative study. Quantitative procedures benefit the qualitative researcher by: indentifying representative and unrepresentative (overlooked) informants/cases; providing leads for later interviews and observations; correcting "elite bias" (the tendency to interview primarily the elite or gatekeepers in a social system) in the collection of data; and verifying the findings of a qualitative study by systematically collecting data on a larger scale.

A number of other writers have called for qualitative and quantitative approaches to be used together. Kidder and Judd (1986), for instance, note that participant observation can involve quantitative measures. They cite a qualitative study of parole officers in which the investigator used a quantitative approach to investigate a hypothesis dealing with the amount of paperwork performed by each parole officer. The investigator analyzed the number of copies made by each parole officer on the office's photocopying machine as a quantitative (and unobtrusive) measure of parole violations.

Patton (1980) and Jick (1983) discuss a methodological mix of both quantitative and qualitative strategies in an effort called "triangulation." The name is a reference to navigation and surveying, which uses multiple reference points to locate an exact position. Thus, multiple methods (methodological triangulation) could be used to study a single problem or phenomenon.

Finally, a noted qualitative researcher, William Foote Whyte (1984), said this about the integration of qualitative and quantitative methods:

> Reliance upon a single research method is bound to impede the progress of science. If we use the survey alone, we may gather highly quantitative data measuring the subjective states of respondents, in relation to certain demographic characteristics. . . . Some apparently objective questions may yield answers of doubtful validity. . . . In any case, the survey yields a snapshot of responses at a particular time. We can fill in this dimension partially with a resurvey, but this by itself only provides evidence of the direction and magnitude of change. Without the use of other methods, we can only speculate on the dynamics of change. (P. 149)

Final Thoughts on the Quantitative-Qualitative Controversy

Sometimes it seems easy to divide all the world into two parts. Under such a schema, we may identify those who think like we do and those who are "wrong" or "out of it." For example, you may be sympathetic to the qualitative perspective, while your best friend may recognize only research that uses quantitative procedures. Like disagreements over politics and religion, you may become frustrated if you try to convert your friend to your viewpoint. In my opinion, it is more important to recognize the strengths and advantages that each perspective brings to the understanding of a problem or phenomenon than it is to insist upon the superiority of one approach over another.

The findings of qualitative research can be rich and comprehensive, providing insight into poorly understood behaviors or cultures through the use of accounts of actual dialogue and graphic descriptions. Qualitative research vividly brings out perspectives that may be quite different from those with which we started. Ruckdeschel (1985) noted, "The researcher thus discovers no single, universal truth, but rather, different perspectives that reflect how different groups with different interests view the same situation" (p. 19).

Some will feel attracted to qualitative approaches because of the flexibility in determining research designs (and ease of modifying them once data collection has begun) and data collection techniques. This "freedom" becomes abundantly clear in the following humorous account of graduate student folklore from Agar (1980):

> A graduate student, at the end of her first year, was given a few hundred dollars by the department and told to go and study an Indian group during the summer. Not only had no one told her how to do ethnography; neither had anyone bothered to describe the location of the tribe. With trembling heart and sweaty palms, she approached the door of Kroeber himself [one of the founding fathers of American anthropology] for some advice. After several passes by the open door, she entered and nervously cleared her throat. Kroeber was typing (naturally) and did not look up for a minute or so. When he did, the student explained her dilemma and asked for advice. "Well," said Kroeber, returning to his typing, "I suggest you buy a notebook and pencil." (P. 2)

While this account may or may not be true, it serves to illustrate the point that qualitative researchers do not need extensive planning, nor do they need to be too concerned about instruments, sampling, computers, or statistical procedures. You want to know something about a group that is poorly understood. An informant is found. Questions are asked. More questions are asked. The focus might even shift from the original one. Qualitative research can be relatively inexpensive to do if you choose subjects or a culture close by. But, if you must travel quite a distance and have no means to support yourself in that setting, the research could be quite expensive.

It could be said that a qualitative researcher is always prepared when an interesting topic comes across his or her path. No scrambling to find a control group or representative sample is necessary, and there is no need to spend hours in the library trying to find the most psychometrically sound instrument(s) to measure the dependent variables. Most quantitatively oriented researchers could not begin their work so easily.

One criticism of qualitative research is that the results are not objective—that they reflect the perspective of one investigator whose view is colored by his or her biases. A related problem is that there is potential for biased sampling of respondents and perhaps even a tendency to overgeneralize. However, qualitative researchers are interested in objectivity—if this means that others would be likely to obtain the same results providing that they were able to follow the same procedures with the same group (Kirk and Miller, 1986).

Qualitative approaches can use procedures to minimize the

likelihood that findings are the product of a single misguided observer. A large number of informants and a variety of sources can be used to confirm observations. Since researchers devote an extended period of time to observing and studying the group, there are multiple occasions to "check-out" new insights. Open-ended questions may be asked in order to understand other points of view without predetermining them through prior selection of questionnaire items (Patton, 1980). Then, other participant observers can be brought in to verify findings. The qualitative researcher can even use small-group or informal surveys to test hypotheses.

For these and other reasons, I believe that it is short-sighted to dismiss qualitative research or to insist that it is less valuable than quantitative research. The contributions of both the quantitative and qualitative approaches have been highlighted by Madey (1982) in a quote from Willems and Raush (1969):

> The methods are analogous to zooming in and zooming out with a lens. To the extent that they are reproduced objectively, wide-angle, telephoto, and microscopic views must be simultaneously valid, and zooming from different directions merely focuses attention on different facets of the same phenomenon. . . . There are no grounds, logical or otherwise, for calling any view simple. We can start anywhere and zoom in to infinite detail or zoom out to indefinite scope. (Pp. 82–83).

Both approaches attempt to explain the world around us. There are times when one approach will have an advantage over the other or will provide information that the other cannot. Choosing a qualitative or quantitative approach might be likened to interviewing clients. There are times when social workers ask open-ended questions and times when they need to probe for specific detail and obtain precise responses. Seldom would they find that they could conduct their interventions using just open-ended questions or closed-ended ones.

As social workers, we are trained in the use of ethnographic techniques (although they are not usually presented under that label). We acquire these techniques in the process of becoming a social worker, and they remain a part of us. Rompf (1989) made this point in her ethnographic case study of large-scale economic change in a rural community:

> My social work background provided a solid foundation for using ethnographic techniques. I was taught how to be a good listener and a keen observer, especially of nonverbal communication. I learned how to interview people and analyze the dynamics of

228

group work. I was taught how to record interviews and group meetings. I was encouraged to be self-aware, to recognize my biases, and to strive to overcome them. (Pp. 47–48)

Qualitative research methods are valuable tools to use in trying to better understand our clients and the world in which they live.

QUESTIONS FOR CLASS DISCUSSION

1. Suppose you want to know what it is like to live in poverty, so you interview an impoverished person in-depth one Saturday afternoon. Compare and contrast a lengthy interview with an ethnographic study of impoverished persons. In what ways would they be similar? How would they differ?
2. Which research approach has the greatest potential for advancing social work practice? (List arguments for and against qualitative and quantitative approaches.)
3. What are the pros and cons associated with not doing a thorough literature search before beginning an ethnographic study?
4. Discuss any books, movies, or plays that recently may have helped you to better understand the life of a unique group of persons.
5. Share your life experiences that have given you insight into other cultures. What special world views or vocabularies were discovered?
6. Into what situations or settings would you like to go in disguise? What would you learn that you couldn't learn without disguise?
7. Discuss how, qualitative research is different from research employing a single system design.

MINI-PROJECTS FOR EXPERIENCING RESEARCH FIRSTHAND

1. Spend no less that eight hours observing (it can be on separate occasions) one of the following persons. Try to discover what problems they encounter, their coping or survival strategies, and any special terms or vocabulary that they use. Write a report summarizing what you learned.
   a. An impoverished person
   b. An elderly person
   c. A person with physical handicaps
   d. A social worker with a child-abuse protection team

2. Arrange to spend the night in a shelter for homeless persons. Keep a notebook with you and record your impressions and significant events. Share your observations with the class. If more than one person in your class engages in this activity, what patterns or themes emerge from the observations?

3. Consider a problem common to many persons who receive some form of welfare payment or food stamps. Since the amount of support is inadequate to their needs, they run out of food toward the end of the month. How do they survive? Do they borrow money to buy groceries? Do they go without food? Do they pool their supplies with neighbors or other family members? Do they go to soup kitchens? Draft a design for an ethnographic study of impoverished families that could provide some answers to these questions. Assume that you have received a grant that will allow you to take up to six months to live with or observe these families. Where would you go to begin your study? How would you find informants? What kinds of questions would you start with? How would you insure that your findings weren't fabrications of your observed family or a product of your own presuppositions about poverty?

4. Interview in-depth a recent immigrant to this country. Obtain a life history or autobiography. Try to capture the experiences that would assist your fellow classmates in understanding both the quality of life in the home culture and the experiences the immigrant has had in adjusting to the new culture.

RESOURCES AND REFERENCES

Agar, M. (1986). *Speaking of Ethnography.* Beverly Hills, CA: Sage.

Agar, M. (1980). *The Professional Stranger: An Informal Introduction to Ethnography.* New York: Academic Press.

Babbie, E. (1986). *The Practice of Social Research.* Belmont, CA: Wadsworth.

Becker, D.G., Blumenfield, S., and Gordon, N. (1984). Voices from the eighties and beyond: Reminiscences of nursing home residents. *Journal of Gerontological Social Work,* 8 (1,2), 83–100.

Bernard, H.R. and Pedraza, J.S. (1989). *Native Ethnography: A Mexican Indian Describes His Culture.* Beverly Hills, CA: Sage.

Bogdan, R. and Taylor, S.J. (1975). *Introduction to Qualitative Research Methods.* New York: Wiley.

Bryman, A. (1984). The debate about quantitative and qualitative research: A question of method or epistemology? *British Journal of Sociology,* 35 (1), 75–92.

Caudill, W., Redlich, F.C., Gilmore, H.R. and Brody, E.B. (1952). Social structure and interaction processes on a psychiatric ward. *American Journal of Orthopsychiatry*, 22, 314–334.

Conover, T. (1987). *Coyotes: A Journey Through the Secret World of America's Illegal Aliens.* New York: Random House.

Deane, W.N. (1961). The reactions of a nonpatient to a stay on a mental hospital ward. *Psychiatry*, 24, 61–68.

Estroff, S. (1981). *Making It Crazy: An Ethnography of Psychiatric Clients in an American Community.* Berkeley, CA: University of California Press.

Fetterman, D. M. (1989). *Ethnography: Step by Step.* Beverly Hills, CA: Sage.

Fischer, J. (1984). Revolution, schmevolution: Is social work changing or not? *Social Work*, 29 (1), 71–74.

Fischer, J. (1981). The social work revolution. *Social Work*, 26 (3), 199–207.

Gilgun, J.F. and Connor, T.M. (1989). How perpetrators view child sexual abuse. *Social Work*, 34 (3), 249–251.

Goldman, A.R., Bohr, R.H., and Steinberg, T.A. (1970). On posing as mental patients: Reminiscences and recommendations. *Professional Psychology*, 1 (5), 427–434.

Heineman, M.B. (1981). The obsolete scientific imperative in social work research and practice. *Social Service Review*, 55, 371–397.

Heineman, M.B. (1982). Author's reply. *Social Service Review*, 56, 146–148.

Heineman-Pieper, M. (1982). Author's reply. *Social Service Review*, 56, 312.

Heineman-Pieper, M. (1985). The future of social work research. *Social Work Research and Abstracts*, 21 (4), 3–11.

Heineman-Pieper, M. (1986). The author replies. *Social Work Research and Abstracts*, 22 (2), p. 2.

Hudson, W.H. (1982). Scientific imperatives in social work research and practice. *Social Service Review*, 56, 242–258.

Hudson, W.H. (1983). Author's reply. *Social Service Review*, 57, 340–341.

Ishiyama, T., Batman, R., and Hewitt, E. (1967). Let's be patients. *American Journal of Nursing*, 67, 569–571.

Jacobsen, G.M. (1988). Rural social work: A case for qualitative methods. *Human Services in the Rural Environment*, 11 (3), 22–28.

Jick, T.D. (1983). Mixing qualitative and quantitative methods: Triangulation in action. In John Van Maanen (ed.), *Qualitative methodology.* Beverly Hills, CA: Sage.

Kidder, L.H. and Judd, C.M. (1986). *Research Methods in Social Relations.* New York: Holt, Rinehart and Winston.

Kirk, J. and Miller, M.L. (1986). *Reliability and Validity in Qualitative Research.* Beverly Hills, CA: Sage.

Lofland, J. and Lofland, L.H. (1984). *Analyzing Social Settings.* Belmont, CA: Wadsworth.

Madey, D.L. (1982). Some benefits of integrating qualitative and quantitative methods in program evaluation, with illustrations. *Educational Evaluation*, 4 (2), 223–236.

Marshall, C. and Rossman, G.B. (1989). *Designing Qualitative Research.* Beverly Hills, CA: Sage.

Moore, P. and Conn, P. (1985). *Disguised.* Waco, TX: Word Books.

Patton, M.Q. (1980). *Qualitative Evaluation Methods.* Beverly Hills, CA: Sage.

Peile, C. (1988). Research paradigms in social work: From stalemate to creative synthesis. *Social Service Review,* 62, 1–18.

Rompf, B.L. (1989). The local dynamics of educational planning: Acting on Toyota's arrival in rural Kentucky. Doctoral dissertation, University of Kentucky.

Rosenhan, D.L. (1973). Being sane in insane places. *Science,* 179 (4070), 250–258.

Rosenstiel, C.R. (1980). That fast life: An emic ethnography of the black heroin addict hustler. Doctoral dissertation, University of Kentucky.

Rousseau, A.M. (1981). *Shopping Bag Ladies: Homeless Women Speak about Their Lives.* New York: Pilgrim Press.

Ruckdeschel, R.A. (1985). Qualitative research as a perspective. *Social Work Research and Abstracts,* 21 (2), 17–21.

Ruckdeschel, R.A. and Farris, B.E. (1982). Science: Critical faith or dogmatic ritual: A rebuttal. *Social Casework,* 63, 272–275.

Steffensmeier, D.J. (1986). *The Fence: In the Shadow of Two Worlds.* Totowa, NJ: Rowman & Littlefield.

Spradley, J.P. (1979). *The Ethnographic Interview.* New York: Holt, Rinehart and Winston.

Thompson, R.J. (1989). Evaluator as power broker: Issues in the Maghreb. International Innovations in Evaluation Methodology. *New Directions for Program Evaluation,* 42 (Summer), 39–48.

Tripodi, T. (1984). Trends in research publication: A study of social work journals from 1956 to 1980. *Social Work,* 29 (4), 353–359.

Uriarte-Gaston, M. (1987). Computer analysis of qualitative data. *Social Work Research and Abstracts,* 23 (4), 9–12.

Van Maanen, J. (1983). Epilogue: Qualitative methods reclaimed. In John Van Maanen (Ed.), *Qualitative Methodology.* Beverly Hills, CA: Sage.

Whyte, W.F. (1984). *Learning from the Field: A Guide from Experience.* Beverly Hills, CA: Sage.

Willems, E.P. and Raush, H.L. (1969). *Naturalistic Viewpoints in Psychological Research.* New York: Holt, Rinehart and Winston.

Twelve

Ethical Thinking and Research

Would it ever be right to intentionally deceive in the interest of research? Was Moore wrong to disguise herself as an eighty-five-year-old woman in order to learn firsthand the way society interacts with older adults? If no harm came to anyone she observed, did she do anything unethical as a researcher? (The only risk, it seems, was to her. Once, while in disguise, she was mugged.) Would she have gathered useful information if she informed those around her that she wasn't really eighty-five years old but that they should act as if she were?

In his book, Conover (1987) describes how his participant observation almost got him into trouble with governmental authorities because he drove a car containing (and therefore assisted) illegal immigrants traveling in America. Do you think that driving in a car with illegal immigrants in order to learn about their problems and experiences is unethical? What is the difference between illegal and unethical behaviors?

As social workers, we learn about the powerful "expectancy" effects that labeling can have. Persons who are expected to act in a certain way ("mentally retarded," "behavioral problem," "delinquent") often find it difficult to perform outside of expectations. Is this a legitimate area for social workers to study? If you agree, then one way to study expectancy effects might be to give false information to a group (e.g., workshop supervisors of persons with mental retardation) and to indicate that some of the trainees could be expected to "blossom" in intelligence and workshop performance as shown by their scores on a fictitious "Latent Capabilities Scale." Unlike studies that focus on negative expectations and labels, Wellons (1973) created positive expectations. At the end of one month he found that the experimental group of adult trainees not only had a higher level of productivity, but also showed gains in intelligence tests. There were no changes of this sort for the control group. The subjects were not harmed; instead, they benefitted from the experiment. Was this research unethical?

Almost all of the social workers I have known have struck me as being ethical individuals. They (for the most part) seem to be concerned with such issues as protecting clients' confidentiality and privacy. This being the case, why do we need a chapter on ethics? Simply because ethical behavior involves much more than protecting anonymity and confidentiality. Even social workers who know the National Association of Social Work's Code of Ethics can become involved in unethical research practices.

Because the Code of Ethics is based on values that are difficult to operationalize, it may also be difficult to determine if a specific situation is a violation of the Code. For example, try to operationalize "integrity" or the following principle from the Code of Ethics: "The social worker should maintain high standards of personal conduct in the capacity or identity as social worker." It is hard to anticipate every way in which a social worker might violate "high standards of personal conduct" or fail to demonstrate integrity. Codes of ethics provide guidelines that, because they are so general, are often open to individual interpretation. We see this in the next example.

I once was asked to evaluate a counseling agency and its director. While this agency had its own board of directors, it was also accountable to a funding agency, with another board of directors. The directors of the funding agency had reason to believe that the counseling agency could do a better job. They believed that the director of the counseling agency spent an excessive amount of time playing tennis during business hours and was generally not conscientious as an agency manager.

I went about the evaluation by contacting key professionals in the community who either had been or who should have been making referrals to the agency. I obtained a mixed bag of comments. While it was evident that the agency could have done better in some areas, it also did some things reasonably well. I knew that the way the results were presented could affect whether or not the director continued in that position. Since the instructions to me had been vague, I chose to present the findings in a formative manner rather than in a summative style. I attempted to make a balanced presentation, and in so far as possible, to let the data speak for itself. I did not feel comfortable concluding what the policymakers should do in this situation. Had they been kindly disposed toward the agency director, some of the findings from the evaluation would have been seen as providing constructive suggestions for change. Other statements would have provided positive strokes for the agency and its staff. However, there were political shenanigans going on.

The director of the counseling agency felt that the evaluation of the agency was an undeserved and unwarranted affront and soon resigned. At the funding agency, the individual who had been the strongest critic of the outgoing director, the one who pushed the hardest for an evaluation of the agency, applied for the director's position and was subsequently hired.

I came away with a firm sense of having been used to oust the former agency director. The new agency director (the individual who had advocated for an evaluation of the outgoing director) had a masters degree in social work and would have been incensed if anyone suggested that something "unethical" had been done. What do you think? Is the act of causing an evaluation to be conducted unethical? At what point was something unethical done?

Heated controversies occasionally arise because of disagreements over what constitutes an unethical act. My final example involves a researcher who submitted a fabricated study of the benefits of temporarily separating asthmatic children from their parents to 146 journals in social work and related fields (Coughlin, 1988). One version of the article claimed that social work intervention benefitted the children. A second version indicated that the intervention had no effect. Upon acceptance or rejection of the manuscript, the study's investigator notified the journal of the real purpose of his study—to collect data on whether there was a tendency among journals to accept articles that confirm the value of social work intervention.

The controversy arose when an editor of the *Social Service Review* lodged a formal complaint against the author with the National Association of Social Workers. The author's position is that the review procedures of journals ought to be investigated because of their potential influence in determining what will be printed in professional journals. Some argue that the author should not have initiated such a large-scale deception of journals, but how does one investigate the hypothesis that professional journals have a bias that constitutes "prior censorship" without using a little deception? In many instances of unethical research, some harm results. Who was harmed in this example?

Historical Context

Guidelines to protect the subjects of research originated with the Nuremberg trials after World War II, which, among other areas of concern, examined the Nazis' medical experiments upon involuntary prisoners. Nazi physicians conducted cruel and harmful experiments on human subjects. Some of their experiments, for example, were designed to determine how long it was possible for human subjects to live in ice water. Prisoners were subjected to conditions that literally froze them. Female prisoners were ordered to warm the frozen subjects with their naked bodies in order to determine if more subjects lived with slow thawing than with quick thawing.

Other prisoners (including children) were injected with diseases such as typhus, malaria, and epidemic jaundice in order to test vaccines. To test antibiotics, human beings were wounded and had limbs amputated. Grass, dirt, gangrene cultures, and other debris were rubbed into the wounds so that the injuries would simulate those received on the battlefield. To simulate the problems of high altitude flying, test chambers were created where oxygen was removed and the effect of oxygen starvation on humans studied. Other prisoners of the Nazis were given intravenous injections of gasoline or various forms of poison to study how long it would take them to die. These involuntary subjects experienced extreme pain, and of those few who lived, most suffered permanent injury or mutilation (Conot, 1983; Faden and Beauchamp, 1986; Grundner, 1986).

These and other atrocities resulted in what became known as the Nuremberg Code—a set of ethical standards by which research with human subjects can be judged. Organizations such as the World Medical Association subsequently developed their own guidelines (The Declaration of Helsinki) for distinguishing ethical from unethical clinical research. The American Medical Association and other groups endorsed the Declaration or developed similar guidelines.

Despite awareness of the Nazi atrocities and the development of ethical guidelines for research by a number of organizations and professional associations, there have been unfortunate incidents in this country in which subjects were experimented upon without their permission. In the 1960s in New York, a physician injected cancer cells into twenty-two geriatric patients. Some were informed orally that they were involved in an experiment, but were not told that they were being given injections of cancer cells. No written consent was acquired, and some patients were incompetent to give informed consent. Later it was learned that the study had not been presented to the hospital's research committee and that several physicians directly responsible for the care of the patients involved in the study had not been consulted (Faden and Beauchamp, 1986).

Another notorious case involved a sample of men with syphilis. In 1932 four hundred mostly poor and illiterate black males with tertiary stage syphilis were informed that they would receive free treatment for their "bad blood." In actuality, these men received no treatment for syphilis. They received free physical exams, periodic blood testing, hot meals on examination days, free treatment for minor disorders, and a modest burial fee for cooperating with the investigators. The researchers (supported by the Public Health Service) were interested only in tracing the pathological evolution of syphilis. Although the study was reviewed several times by Public Health Service officials and was reported in thirteen articles in prestigious medical and public health journals, it continued uninterrupted until 1972, when a reporter exposed the study in the *New York Times.* The survivors were given treatment for their disease only after this publicity. After the story broke, the Department of Health, Education and Welfare appointed an advisory panel to review the study. Not until 1975 did the government extend treatment to subjects' wives who had contracted syphilis and their children with congenital syphilis (Jones, 1981).

These and other abuses led Congress in 1974 to pass the National Research Act (Public Law 93–348), which requires any organization involved in the conduct of biomedical or behavioral research involving human subjects to establish an Institutional Review Board (IRB) to review the research to be conducted or sponsored. This act also created the National Commission for the Protection of Human Subjects of Biomedical and Behavioral Research. In October 1978, this commission produced recommendations for public comment. The Department of Health, Education and Welfare (HEW) refined the recommendations and, in 1981, issued them as regulations for research being conducted with its funds. In 1983, specific regulations protecting children were incorporated.

The impact of these standards was that colleges, universities, hospitals, and other organizations engaging in research and receiving federal funds from HEW (now the Department of Health and Human Services) and selected other departments established institutional review boards (sometimes called human subjects committees) to review and oversee research conducted by investigators affiliated with their organizations. Under some circumstances, the IRBs review students' proposed research as well. These review boards have the authority to approve, disapprove, or modify research activities covered by the regulations, to conduct a continuing review of research involving human subjects, to insure that there is an informed consent process, and to suspend or terminate the approval of any research.

Institutional Review Boards

Institutional review boards are now firmly established as our society's "watch dogs" protecting human subjects from risky or harmful research. This does not mean that IRBs prevent all unethical research practices. They cannot monitor research that is covert or not brought to their attention. However, there is much greater monitoring of research today than there was twenty or so years ago. Currently, federal agencies are adopting a common set of regulations that will apply to all research involving human subjects conducted, supported, or subject to regulation by twenty-two federal departments or agencies. This uniform policy will provide even greater protection of the rights and welfare of human subjects involved in research. Most universities and medical settings have required for some years that all proposed human subject research be approved by the local institutional review board regardless of whether federal or outside funding is supporting it.

Under the new federal regulations, each institutional review board must provide written assurance that it complies with the regulations supported by the federal department funding the research. In addition to these regulations, universities and other institutions where research is commonly done often have their own policies and procedures. Generally speaking, any investigator proposing research involving human subjects must prepare a description of the proposed research and submit this to the IRB. These descriptions vary in length and format depending upon the planned research and the procedures established by the local IRB. There are several levels of review, from the most cursory (the exempt status) to full review. Federal regulations allow for some kinds of research to be exempted from a full review by the IRB. Those activities most applicable to social work are:

1. Research conducted in established or commonly accepted educational settings, such as research on normal educational practices involving instructional strategies or research on the effectiveness of instructional techniques, curricula, or classroom management methods.
2. Research involving the use of educational tests (cognitive, diagnostic, aptitude, achievement) if information taken from these sources is recorded in such a manner that subjects cannot be identified, directly or through identifiers linked to the subjects, and if any disclosure of the human subjects' responses outside the research would not place the subjects at risk of criminal or civil liability or be damaging to the subjects' financial standing, employability, or reputation.

3. Research involving survey or interview procedures and observation of public behavior is exempted when meeting the conditions specified in (2) above.

4. Research involving the collection or study of existing data, documents, or records if these sources are publicly available or if the information is recorded by the investigator in such a manner that subjects cannot be identified directly or through identifiers linked to the subjects.

5. Research and demonstration projects conducted or subject to the approval of federal department or agency heads that examine or evaluate public benefit or service programs or procedures for obtaining benefits or services under those programs, including possible changes to programs or procedures.

6. Research involving survey or interview procedures and educational tests when the respondents are elected or appointed public officials or candidates for public office or where federal statutes require, without exception, the confidentiality of the personally identifiable information will be maintained through the research and thereafter.

Exemptions may not always be available from IRBs. In such an instance, the researcher may complete a lengthier application and may be required to appear before the IRB to make a presentation or to respond to questions. Presently, most IRBs will not grant exemptions to research involving certain vulnerable populations (children, prisoners, the mentally disabled, and economically or educationally disadvantaged persons), or when there is deception of subjects or use of techniques that expose the subject to discomfort or harassment beyond levels normally encountered in daily life. Further, exemption is not usually available when the information obtained from medical records is recorded in such a way that subjects can be identified directly or through identifiers linked to the subjects. However, some local IRBs may be more lenient than others in exemptions granted.

Under the exemption certificate, the researcher provides such information as the title of the project, the research objectives, the subject population, plans for the recruitment of the subjects, the research procedures to be followed, and potential psychological, physical, social, or legal risks.

Generally speaking, students are not required to seek approval from institutional review boards when their research projects are primarily for educational purposes (e.g., an assignment to interview a small sample of people in order to learn about interviewing, recording data, or other aspects of the research). However, if the project involves living human subjects and is likely to contribute to generalizable knowledge (that is, research that is likely to be of publishable quality), students ought to seek IRB approval. Normally, student projects with the greatest potential for generating generalizable knowledge are doctoral dissertations and some master theses.

General Guidelines for Ethical Research

Social workers do not, as a rule, get involved in biomedical or other research where physical harm to subjects is likely to occur. Research conducted by social workers involves surveys and interviews which require a certain amount of cooperation from the participants in the study. The risks to the subjects of social work research derive from the possibility that a third party will use the research data and cause the subject physical, psychological, social, or economic harm. The risk of identification is particularly acute for those subjects engaged in or with past histories of illegal acts (Murray, Donovan, Kail, and Medvene, 1980).

When questionnaires are used or interviews are conducted with adults who are not in a vulnerable population, the principle of "implied consent" is applied. The act of participation is seen as giving informed consent. In these instances, IRBs do not require written documentation that subjects gave their consent. A problem arises when potential subjects feel that they cannot refuse to participate. If potential subjects are clients (e.g., persons on probation or parole, or recipients of some form of public assistance), they may not feel free to refuse without putting themselves in some jeopardy. This is when consultation with an institutional review board can come in handy. They may suggest alternative ways to collect data or to reduce any implied coercion by informing potential subjects of their rights in writing. (A written consent form is often required that specifies clearly that the potential subject has the right to refuse participation without any penalty or loss of service.) Social workers must be alert to the possibility that encouraging their clients to participate in research could be perceived as coercion. Since social workers are often "gatekeepers" of services, clients could feel pressured into participating in order to gain access to or continue receiving services.

Not every social worker is employed by an organization or university that has an institutional review board to consult about problems associated with conducting applied research. With this in mind, the following set of guidelines has been developed. However, guidelines and codes of ethics are limited—they will not fit every situation. This is why so many are written in very general language—they must be written in such a manner to cover various types of research and situations, from large-scale program evaluations to participant observation studies. Finally, these guidelines are based on the assumption that the proposed research is worth doing—that it is not trivial. Good research in the social sciences should improve the quality of life by increasing our understanding of social problems or by providing information about how to make our interventions more effective.

Guideline 1: Research subjects must be volunteers

Social work research is not something imposed upon involuntary subjects. All of those participating in a research effort should freely decide to participate. No coercion of any kind should be used to secure participants for a study.

All subjects must be competent enough to understand their choice. If they are not able to fully comprehend (e.g., individuals under the age of majority), then their legal caretakers must give permission, and the subjects also must assent. Even if parents give permission for their children to participate in a research project, the children may still refuse to participate. The subject's right to self-determination is respected, and any research subject is free to withdraw from a study at any time.

The use of written consent forms helps assure that research subjects know that they are volunteers. These forms provide brief, general information about the nature of the research, the procedures to be followed, and any foreseeable risks, discomforts, or benefits, and they indicate that the research subject is free to withdraw consent and to discontinue participation in the project at any time without penalty or loss of benefits. Consent forms generally contain the name of someone to contact should there be questions about the research or the subject's rights.

Guideline 2: Potential research subjects should be given sufficient information about the study to determine any possible risks or discomforts as well as benefits

"Sufficient information" includes an explanation of the purpose of the research, the expected duration of the subject's participation, the procedures to be followed, and the identification of those procedures that might be experimental. The exact hypothesis does not have to be given away; it can be stated generally. However, the researcher must be specific about procedures that will involve the research subjects. If there are potential risks, these must be identified. Subjects should be given the opportunity to raise and have answered any questions about the study or procedures that will be used. Subjects must also be allowed to inquire at any time about procedures and have their questions answered.

Benefits expected from participation in a study can be described in a general fashion. For example, Maloney (1984), in a study of former residents of Boys Town, used the following in a consent form: "I understand the potential benefits of the studies are that they will help future boys experience programs that are most likely to help them after they leave Boys Town. It also will permit distribution of Boys Town methods around the world" (p. 135). If a consent form is used, it should be written at a level of readability that the potential subjects can understand. Several methods can be used to estimate the grade level equivalence of the consent form. Flesch (1948) has devised a formula that counts the number of syllables in 100-word samples. Fry's (1968) method also allows one to estimate grade level equivalences.

Guideline 3: No harm shall result as a consequence of participation in the research

Social work researchers are not likely to propose research that would result in evident harm to their subjects. But one's perspective on harmful effects should not be limited to the active participants in a study. Punch (1986) related a dilemma that he faced. A group of female students wanted to study the reactions of policemen to reports of rape. In order to conduct this study they would have had to fabricate stories. While policemen might have been quite insensitive in their dealings with rape victims, Punch objected to the study on several grounds. First, there could have been legal repercussions for filing false police reports. Second, subsequent disclosure might have made the police distrustful of researchers. But most important, it might have led police to be skeptical of legitimate claims of sexually assaulted women. The benefits did not seem to outweigh the risks and the potential harm to others that could result.

Researchers have a responsibility to identify and to minimize harm or risk of harm that might befall the research subjects. And researchers should constantly monitor the subjects for harmful effects of the research. Subjects should not go away from a study with a feeling of lowered self-esteem or sense of self-worth, or that they possess undesirable traits. Often, "debriefings" are used to inform subjects and to neutralize negative feelings once participation in a project has concluded.

Guideline 4: Sensitive information shall be protected

This guideline suggests that no harm to research subjects should result from improper handling of information. The privacy of research subjects may be protected in several ways: (1) Allow the subject to respond anonymously. (2) If the research design cannot accommodate anonymity, provide protection by separating identifying information from the research data through the use of numeric or other special codes. Where complete anonymity is not possible (e.g., because pretest and posttest scores have to be matched for each subject), it may be necessary to use special codes (such as the first four letters of a subject's mother's maiden name and the last four digits of his or her social security number) to help guard against unauthorized persons accidentally recognizing or identifying your research subject.

The confidentiality of research subjects can be maintained by not reporting personal information (such as names, addresses, phone numbers, and personal descriptors like "Mayor, Lexington, Ky.") that would result in subjects being identified by persons other than the study's investigators. Another technique is to keep sensitive data (including master lists of codes, completed questionnaires, and transcripts of interviews) in locked cabinets or files until they are no longer needed and then destroying the raw data.

As a rule, research findings are reported in the aggregate; that is, you report a group's average score or amount of improvement. It would be unethical to report the results in this fashion: "In our study the mayor and head of the personnel department showed the least improvement, while the police chief improved the most." Under no circumstances should data be reported in any fashion that would result in the identification of persons who agreed to participate on the condition that their responses would be confidential. When it is necessary to report on a "typical" research subject or to use vignettes or anecdotes, pseudonyms should be used.

A problem may arise when an "outside" researcher makes a request of a social service agency to interview clients or to collect information beyond what may be available from agency files. When former or present clients must be contacted to supply additional information for research purposes, their right to privacy must be safeguarded. Clients' privacy is protected when the agency obtains permission from clients to share personally identifying information (e.g., names, addresses, and phone numbers) with the researcher, who could then contact clients interested in assisting with the research.

Potential Ethical Problems in Research

Deception

One of the thorniest ethical problems facing researchers in the social sciences has to do with deception. Our guidelines suggest that deception ought not be employed, because the research participants would not be in a position to be fully informed about the intent of the research. But, some research could not be conducted if deception were not allowed. The *IRB Guidebook* (1982) seems to acknowledge this:

> Deception or incomplete disclosure may be the only valid approach for certain research. An example of such research would be a study designed to determine the effect of group pressure (responses of others) on a subject's estimate of the length of a series of lines. In some groups, pseudo-subjects would be told in advance to give incorrect answers to questions about the length of lines in order to determine the effect of misinformation on the real subjects' responses. Obviously, if the subjects were told all about the research design and its purpose in advance, it would not be possible to do the research. (P. 4–A3)

When Moore (1985) disguised herself as an eighty-five-year-old woman, there was very little, if any, risk of harm to those around her. People who came in contact with her were unlikely to act other than normally. It could be argued that there was no harm associated with their being unwitting participants. Certainly no one was degraded, and there was no emotional or psychological harm. This is quite a different situation from falsely reporting a criminal act in order to study police reactions.

Conover's (1987) observation of illegal immigrants seemed to result in no harm and may have been of help when a group of immigrants were being interrogated by the Mexican police. However, Conover's project could have resulted in his being arrested for assisting the illegal immigrants. Since Conover's level of masquerade was much less than that used by Moore, it seems less likely that anyone would be concerned about potential unethical behavior associated with his use of deception. In this instance, Conover was more at risk for engaging in *illegal* than in unethical behavior. Although there was some deception in both of these examples, in neither case did harm to the research subjects/participants seem to result.

We should also consider Haywood's (1977) contention that we could be guilty of unethical conduct if we fail to conduct important and needed research. If we reflect upon the Conover and Moore examples as well as those mentioned in chapter 11 (e.g., the qualitative researchers who admitted themselves to mental institutions to learn about the treatment of patients), we realize that we probably have a better understanding of the problems of old age, migrant workers, and the institutional treatment of mentally ill persons as a result of these studies. Other studies that have involved deception in order to investigate discrimination or racism have helped bring about needed institutional and social change.

Although there has been little evidence of direct physical or mental harm to participants in deception experiments (Korchin and Cowan, 1982), the social work researcher must weigh the potential harmful effects of deception against the possible benefits. Where deception is employed, subjects should not come away with a feeling of having been degraded or exploited. Debriefing the subjects after an experiment is often required by IRBs as a mechanism to counter potentially adverse effects caused by the use of deception.

The decision to use deception should not be made without consultation with friends and coworkers. As part of this process, alternative methodologies for studying the problem of interest should be examined. Since it is unlikely that an institutional review board would not approve of blatant deception (excluding research in controlled laboratory settings), social workers engaging in such deception run a risk of being labeled "unethical." Possible adverse effects on the researcher's professional and private life must be considered against the possible benefits of engaging in the study.

Denial of Treatment

Another problem for social workers who contemplate research is that use of a control group may be unethical because some clients would be denied services. It would indeed be unethical to deliberately deny beneficial services to a client for the purposes of research.

But there are ways to obtain control groups without being unethical. For instance, if we wanted to evaluate a new program or intervention, we could compare clients receiving the new or experimental intervention with those who receive the typical set of services. In this scenario, there would be no denial of services. Some clients would get a slightly different intervention or set of services from those clients normally receive. This could be to their advantage.

In those agencies or programs where there is a long waiting list, researchers might consider as a control group those clients who are at the end of the list. For instance, if a wait of six weeks or longer is inevitable before those on the waiting list could begin receiving services, there is no denial of benefits. In fact, clients on a waiting list might appreciate a periodic contact with an agency representative (even if it is limited to the administration of a pretest and posttest), because it would constitute evidence that they have not been forgotten by the agency and that they are still actively queued for services. If these clients had similar problems (e.g., alcoholism), it might be possible to distribute educational pamphlets or materials to them while they were waiting for service. This group of clients could be considered to be receiving an educational intervention. While it may be a weaker or milder intervention than they would later receive, it would be better than nothing at all and may help the researcher feel better about gathering data from them. Comparisons could be made to the waiting-list clients (the control group) and those who received the new intervention (the experimental group).

Another way to obtain a control group would be to compare your program participants with the clientele of a similar program or agency. While the groups would not be equivalent (since random assignment wasn't possible), at least you would have beginning evaluative data. Still another "natural" control group could be found in that group of clients who keep one or two appointments, then drop out of treatment. This group could be compared with those individuals who complete the intervention.

These are only some of the ways in which control groups can be identified without denying treatment.

Should Some Research Questions Not Be Investigated?

Living in an open society as we do, the suggestion that we should not investigate some research questions sounds strange indeed. However, remember that research results can be used for purposes other than those for which they were intended. Research could be conducted to support stereotypes or prejudices. For example, one research question that should not be investigated is: "Are there racial differences in intelligence?" (Sieber and Stanley, 1988). While it is conceivable that some interest groups could make funds or grants available for the conduct of such research, the ethical social work researcher has a responsibility to not engage in research that could be used to denigrate or harm a group of individuals.

Compensation

Is paying respondents or research subjects unethical? While reimbursing subjects for costs incurred (e.g., baby-sitting, time away from work, transportation) seems reasonable and is not offensive to most, questions are raised when there is a large financial incentive for participation. Yelaja (1982) suggests that researchers are ethically required to insure that the incentive is not so great that it is excessive or constitutes "undue inducement." When large financial rewards are offered for research subjects, there is a risk that some individuals may fabricate information in order to become eligible for the money.

Final Thoughts

It might be argued that going through an institutional review board is a waste of time for the knowledgeable and ethical researcher who will not be doing any harm with a simple survey. However, to by-pass review boards entails a certain risk—even if no harm is done to the participants. A recent article noted the case of a university-based investigator who did not get approval for a controversial questionnaire administered within a school district. To avoid hostile parental reaction and a possible lawsuit, a school official shredded several hundred already completed questionnaires (Schilling, Schinke, Kirkham, Meltzer, and Norelius, 1988). You can imagine how much time was lost—to say nothing about the likely fate of that research project. Consulting with a review board and having a general demeanor of openness about research is better than going it alone. Ultimately, however, it is the researcher who is responsible for the ethics of the research effort. Even with the approval of an institutional review board or other advisory group, the researcher must constantly be vigilant and correct or stop any research project in which harmful effects may be occurring.

In order to help clarify the ethical and unethical dimensions of research, some of the unfortunate consequences of unbridled research have been presented. What "should" or "ought" to be done has been emphasized. However, I do not want to leave you with a sense of burden or responsibility so great that you would never consider doing research because of fear of doing something unethical. Most researchers have little fear of doing any real "harm" to their subjects, because their interviews, surveys, or questionnaires are so innocuous. When their research proposal has been reviewed by an institutional review board or other advisory group and proper safeguards are taken to protect access to confidential information, most researchers can relax and focus their energies on their project with little fear of being "unethical."

Being a research subject can have positive effects. In clinical interventions, subjects may gain from new therapeutic procedures. Even if that doesn't occur, subjects may feel that the research is important and that they have made a contribution that will be of help to others.

Participants may experience an increase in self-worth because they feel honored to have been selected to participate in "research." Sometimes participants receive some form of remuneration, and they appreciate it—even if it is inconsequential. Another consideration is that some research projects are interesting. Participants don't mind giving their opinions or sharing their insights. These are just some of the benefits to research participants noted by Korchin and Cowan (1982).

Finally, as social work students, you should be familiar with (or at least know where you can find a copy of) the National Association of Social Work's Code of Ethics. A portion of the Code directly pertains to the profession's concern for ethical research. It is reproduced here for your use:

> **E. Scholarship and Research.** The social worker engaged in study and research should be guided by the conventions of scholarly inquiry.
> 1. The social worker engaged in research should consider carefully its possible consequences for human beings.
> 2. The social worker engaged in research should ascertain that the consent of participants in the research is voluntary and informed, without any implied deprivation or penalty for refusal to participate, and with due regard for participants' privacy and dignity.
> 3. The social worker engaged in research should protect participants from unwarranted physical or mental discomfort, distress, harm, danger, or deprivation.
> 4. The social worker who engages in the evaluation of services or cases should discuss them only for professional purposes and only with persons directly and professionally concerned with them.
> 5. Information obtained about participants in research should be treated as confidential.
> 6. The social worker should take credit only for work actually done in connection with scholarly and research endeavors and credit contributions made by others.

QUESTIONS FOR CLASS DISCUSSION

1. Discuss the institutional review board at your college or university.
2. Make lists of situations in which it would be acceptable and not acceptable to involve people in research without their knowledge.

3. A researcher wants to interview children in families where there has been a hospitalization for mental illness within the past three years. Discuss the potential ethical issues that will have to be addressed.

4. A researcher is interested in interviewing family functioning in families that have experienced a recent suicide. What precautions would the researcher need to take to insure that no psychological or emotional harm resulted from the interviews?

5. A doctoral student studying the terminally ill participating in a hospice program finds that 15 percent of the subjects are contemplating suicide. What should be done with this information?

6. A researcher wants to investigate the emotional consequences associated with abortion. Because of the difficulty in getting access to the names and addresses of women who have had abortions, the researcher proposes a snowball sampling design. What are the ethical issues involved in the use of this design? Are the problems with this design insurmountable?

MINI-PROJECTS FOR EXPERIENCING RESEARCH FIRSTHAND

1. In the late 1950s, a series of experiments were conducted to confirm the usefulness of gamma globulin to immunize against hepatitis. The researchers went to a residential school, the Willowbrook State School, where a hepatitis epidemic was in progress. Researchers obtained the consent of the parents and divided the children into experimental and control groups that received hepatitis virus at various levels of infectiousness and gamma globulin inoculations at various strengths. Some of the gamma globulin was given below the strength known to be effective. When the results were published in the professional literature, they produced a storm of controversy (Harris, 1986). Why? Because all of the children in the Willowbrook State School were children with mental retardation. Even though all the children who contracted the disease recovered, and the researchers argued that valuable medical knowledge was gained from the experiments, do you believe that this research should have been allowed? Try to find some of the arguments for and against this research and write a paper defending your position. The original articles reporting the experiment were: Ward, R., Krugman, S., Giles, J.P., Jacobs,

A.M., and Bodansky, O. (1958), "Infectious hepatitis: Studies of its natural history and prevention," *New England Journal of Medicine*, 258 (9) (Feb. 27), 407–416; and Krugman, S., Ward, R., Giles, J.P., Bodansky, O., and Jacobs, A.M. (1959), "Infectious hepatitis: Detection of the virus during the incubation period and clinically inapparent infection," *New England Journal of Medicine*, 261 (15) (Oct. 8), 729–734.

2. In the late 1960s, a sociologist, Laud Humphreys, reported his study of homosexual activity occurring in "tearooms" or public restrooms. He volunteered to be a "watchqueen"—that is, to serve as a lookout for the individuals engaged in this form of sexual activity. In order to obtain additional demographic information about homosexual men, Humphreys recorded the license numbers of their cars and traced the men to their homes. A year later, he posed as a health service interviewer and collected personal information from them. It could be argued that his research was important for its contributions to our understanding of this type of behavior. He found, for instance, that only a small percentage of his subjects were members of the gay community. Many were married men. Humphreys certainly was guilty of deception and invading the private lives of the subjects. Do you feel that the benefits of such research outweigh the methods that he used? Read Laud Humphreys' *Tearoom Trade* (1970) and other commentaries on his book, and write a paper defending your position.

3. Stanley Milgram, a social psychologist at Yale University, began a series of studies on obedience in the 1960s. His experiments involved an elaborate deception. He led subjects to believe that they were giving a dangerous level of electrical shocks to other subjects who had not learned a list of words. Those who thought they were administering the shocks believed that the study was of the effects of punishment on learning (therefore justifying the electrical shock). The "learner" did not actually receive any electrical shock, but was instructed to feign discomfort upon receipt of the shock. In actuality, Milgram was interested in the extent to which subjects obeyed authority and would administer apparently dangerous levels of electricity to other participants in the research. It could be argued that Milgram's experiments constitute important findings on how ordinary people can be led to engage in the inhuman treatment of others. Milgram's report of his findings was met with much controversy. Do you feel that the benefits of such research outweigh any potentially

unethical practices involved in the use of deception? He did, after all, debrief his subjects so that they knew no electrical shock had really been administered. Read Stanley Milgram's *Obedience to Authority*, (New York: Harper & Row, 1974) in order to write a paper defending your position.

4. Obtain a copy of the exemption certification form used by the institutional review board at your college or university. Think of some research that you would like to conduct. Develop this idea, sketch out a research design, and then complete the exemption form. Bring these to class, and exchange forms with a fellow student. Critique each other's effort.

RESOURCES AND REFERENCES

Baumrind, D. (1985). Research using intentional deception: Ethical issues revisited. *American Psychologist, 40* (2), 165–174.

Conot, R.E. (1983). *Justice at Nuremberg.* New York: Harper & Row.

Conover, T. (1987). Coyotes: *A Journey Through the Secret World of America's Illegal Aliens.* New York: Random House.

Coughlin, E.K. (1988). Scholar who submitted bogus article to journals may be disciplined. *Chronicle of Higher Education,* Nov. 2, p. A7.

Faden, R.R. and Beauchamp, T.L. (1986). *A History and Theory of Informed Consent.* New York: Oxford Unversity Press.

Flesch, R. (1948). A new readability yardstick. *Journal of Applied Psychology, 32* (3), 221–233.

Fry, E. (1968). A readability formula that saves time. *Journal of Reading,* 11, 513–516, 575–578.

Gray, B.H. (1975). *Human Subjects in Medical Experimentations.* New York: Wiley.

Grundner, T.M. (1986). *Informed Consent: A Tutorial.* Owings Mill, MD: Rynd Communications.

Harris, E.E. Jr. (1986). *Applying Moral Theories.* Belmont, CA: Wadsworth.

Haywood, H. C. (1977). The ethics of doing research . . . and of not doing it. *American Journal of Mental Deficiency,* 81 (4), 311–317.

IRB Guidebook. (1982). Bethesda, MD: President's Commission for the Study of Ethical Problems in Medicine and Biomedical and Behavioral Research.

Jones, J.H. (1981). *Bad Blood: The Tuskegee Syphilis Experiment.* New York: Free Press.

Kimmel, A.J. (1988). *Ethics and Values in Applied Social Research.* Beverly Hills, CA: Sage.

Korchin, S.J. and Cowan, P.A. (1982). Ethical perspectives in clinical research. In P.C. Kendall and J.N. Butcher (Eds.), *Handbook of Research Methods in Clinical Psychology.* New York: Wiley.

La Pierre, R.T. (1935). Attitudes vs. actions. *Social Forces,* 13, 230–37.

Maloney, D.M. (1984). *Protection of Human Research Subjects: A Practical Guide to Federal Laws and Regulations.* New York: Plenum Press.

Marshall, G.D. and Zimbardo, P.G. (1979). Affective consequences of inadequately explained physiological arousal. *Journal of Personality and Social Psychology,* 37, 970–988.

Milgram, S. (1977). Ethical issues in the study of obedience. In S. Milgram (Ed.), *The Individual in a Social World.* Reading, MA: Addison-Wesley.

Mitscherlich, A. and Mielke, F. (1949). *Doctors of Infamy: The Story of the Nazi Medical Crimes.* New York: Henry Schuman.

Moore, P. and Conn, P. (1985). *Disguised.* Waco, TX: Word Books.

Murray, L., Donovan, R., Kail, B.L., and Medvene, L.J. (1980). Protecting human subjects during social work research: Researchers' opinions. *Social Work Research and Abstracts,* 16 (2), 25–30.

Punch, M. (1986). *The Politics and Ethics of Fieldwork.* Beverly Hills, CA: Sage.

Schilling, R.F., Schinke, S.P., Kirkham, M.A., Meltzer, N.J., and Norelius, K.L. (1988). Social work research in social service agencies: Issues and guidelines. *Journal of Social Service Research,* 11 (4), 75–87.

Sieber, J.E. and Stanley, B. (1988). Ethical and professional dimensions of socially sensitive research. *American Psychologist,* 43 (1), 49–55.

Wellons, K. (1973). The expectancy component in mental retardation. Doctoral dissertation, Unversity of California, Berkeley.

Yelaja, S.A. (1982). *Ethical Issues in Social Work.* Springfield, IL: C.C. Thomas.

Zimbardo, P.G., Andersen, S.M., and Kabat, L.G. (1981). Induced hearing deficit generates experimental paranoia. *Science,* 212 (June), 1529–1531.

Thirteen

Writing Research Reports and Journal Articles

You have conducted some exciting research and now you want to (or have been asked to) communicate your findings in writing. You might be prompted to write about your research because it was funded through a grant and you are obligated to report your findings to the sponsoring organization. If the research was conducted for your thesis or dissertation, the findings must be "packaged" in a certain way for your professors. The same research results might also be used to prepare an article for a professional journal. Similarities occur in all research reports. The purpose of this chapter is to help you prepare a report of your research findings for a sponsoring organization, university faculty, or reviewers for a professional journal.

Publication as a Practice Goal

Williams and Hopps (1987) note that while few social workers "achieve comfort or familiarity with publishing," one of the hallmarks of a mature profession is that verifiable knowledge derived from practice is used to increase the quality, effectiveness, and efficiency of all practice. Where does verifiable knowledge come from? It does not flow automatically from the conduct of research, but is dependent upon reporting or communication of the research. All too often, good applied social work research is never "written up," but remains in file folders or on someone's desk until it becomes outdated or is thrown away. For the results of research to guide practice, the findings must be disseminated to colleagues and other professionals.

Meyer (1983) notes that "a profession is known by what it does. The chief way in which professional colleagues and the public get to know what social work does is through publication of its efforts" (p. 3). Writing about the successes and failures of interventions and about the problems of clients is clearly a responsibility of professional social workers. Indeed, the following passage is found in the National Association of Social Workers' Code of Ethics under "Development of Knowledge":

> The social worker should contribute to the knowledge base of social work and share research knowledge and practice wisdom with colleagues.

Writing for professional audiences can also provide a great deal of personal satisfaction as well as recognition.

The basic structure and key elements needed to report research findings are the same whether one is writing a thesis, an evaluation report, or a journal article. Of course, there are some observable differences when we compare these three types of reports. For one thing, academic committees expect the literature review section of a thesis or dissertation to be longer than that of most journal articles.

Regardless of the purpose for which the final research report is intended, its basic components are the same (Bausell, 1986). Further, the elements of the research report (the Introduction, Literature Review, Methodology, Findings, Discussion, References, and Appendices) are required for writing most research proposals—whether you are applying to a funding source to secure a grant to enable you to conduct the research or whether you are writing a prospectus for a proposed thesis or dissertation. (Of course, if you are proposing research, you will not be able to fully develop the Results and Discussion section. The bulk of the proposal will be the first three sections. However, it is possible to briefly address what findings you expect and any known limitations of the study.) An outline of the major elements in research reporting is as follows:

Components of a Research Report

1. Introduction
   a. Description of Problem
   b. Statement of research question or hypothesis
   c. Significance of problem and rationale for studying it

2. Literature Review
   a. Theoretical and historical perspectives
   b. Identified gaps in literature
   c. Reiteration of purpose of study

3. Methodology
   a. Research design and data collection procedures
   b. Characteristics of subjects
   c. Sampling design
   d. Description of instrumentation
   e. Data analysis procedures

4. Findings (Results)
   a. Factual information presented
   b. Tables, charts
   c. Statistical and practical significance discussed

5. Discussion
   a. Brief summary of findings
   b. Explanation of unexpected findings
   c. Applications to practice
   d. Weaknesses or limitations of research
   e. Suggestions for future research

6. References

7. Appendices

Introduction

The purpose of the Introduction is to present the research question or problem and to place it within some context or frame of reference. This generally entails describing the problem and its extent. For instance, in an article entitled "To Parent or Relinquish: Consequences for Adolescent Mothers," the authors note that of the more than one million teen-age girls who become pregnant each year, about half give birth and 7 percent place the child for adoption (McLaughlin, Pearce, Manninen, and Winges, 1988). The authors discuss the assumptions held by some researchers and pregnancy counselors that mothers who relinquish their children suffer few negative psychological effects. The authors then summarize studies where these mothers were found to have negative psychological effects. The problem of psychological effects becomes important because of the apparent contradiction between what may be believed by some pregnancy counselors and the studies that found negative consequences. It is obvious that the problem introduced early in the article is worthy of further study. Introductions help the reader understand why the research is important and was conducted.

Sometimes the Introduction distinguishes the research being reported from similar research. Your research may be unlike other studies because you have approached the problem with a different theoretical perspective and have used innovative methods or found new ways to measure outcome variables. The Introduction gives you an opportunity to briefly present the unique features of your study. By the end of the Introduction the reader should be aware of the focus of your research, its significance, and why the study was needed.

The Introduction should also be viewed as an opportunity to awaken the reader's interest in your topic. Skillful writers are often able to do this by catching our interest with their first paragraph. Take, for instance, the first line of a recent article by Walter and Greif (1988): "Should we educate students for private practice?" This line alone is successful in posing an interesting problem to consider. Consequently, many social workers would want to read more of the article.

Consider a second example of a thought-provoking opening to an article (Johnson, 1988):

> For the past two decades, the hyperactive child has generated controversy. Debates have centered around whether a hyperactive syndrome exists[1]; whether its etiology is physiological or psychogenic[2]; and whether medication, diet, behavior modification, cognitive therapy, family systems therapy, or psychodynamic psychotherapy is the treatment of choice.[3] (P. 349)

If the problem of hyperactivity interests you, this paragraph should whet your appetite for the rest of Johnson's article. After reading this paragraph you probably want to know more about the controversy. Perhaps you want to discover whether the approach you would take is the one chosen by the author of the article. While examples of dry, uninteresting introductions could also be provided here, I suspect you have read enough of these and do not want to imitate them.

The easiest research reports to read are those that engage your interest. Williams and Hopps (1988) have noted, "Getting off to a good start truly is three-quarters of the battle" (p. 456). One way to do this is to present the problem early in the introduction instead of burying it toward the end. Material discussed in your Introduction makes more sense when the reader has a clear understanding of the problem prompting your investigation.

Review of the Literature

The literature review section of a report or journal article is where the notable and relevant theoretical explanations of the social problem or phenomenon of interest are summarized. You need not describe every study that has ever been conducted on your topic. Cite only those pertinent to the issues with which you are dealing (Kidder and Judd, 1986). For example, consider the following fictitious excerpt (note the use of superscripts):

> While little has been written in the literature of criminology about shoplifting, it is an area of interest to practitioners and social scientists because of the seemingly complex dynamics involved. Financial need does not appear to be a significant motivating factor. Almost all of the studies have shown that poverty is not a major explanation for shoplifting.[1] Shoplifters tend to come from all economic classes,[2] and the overwhelming majority of persons caught shoplifting do not intend to resell the item.[3,4] It has also been noted that in only a minority of cases is shoplifting associated with mental illness, and the majority of arrested shoplifters do not have any psychotic features.[5] Recent studies have shown that shoplifters are not apprehended differentially by race, sex, or age when control variables are employed.[6,7]

From this brief example we can learn that theories based upon economic deprivation or mental illness have not been found to explain shoplifting. Further, explanations involving a greater level of absent-mindedness among the elderly do not seem to be viable. Since these theories have been tested and then discarded, the way is open for a new theoretical explanation—perhaps that shoplifting is a help-seeking activity unconsciously motivated by high levels of stress.

This excerpt also demonstrates that quite a few studies can be succinctly summarized in a short amount of space. This is necessary when writing for journals as most do not want long manuscripts. Many times students provide too much irrelevant information in the literature review. It is, for example, usually inconsequential whether the studies were conducted in Idaho or Missouri, or whether very large or medium-sized survey samples were used. It is more important that the literature review show trends in the major findings of these studies. The location, methodology, sample size, and other facets of the earlier research take on more importance only when you describe your study as being different from or similar to that research. In this instance, you may want to go into more detail in describing the study you are departing from or replicating. Why is it important to replicate or depart from another study? There may be legitimate reasons. You may want to correct for problems the previous study had with internal validity. Otherwise, it is not important to go into great detail regarding the methodology and each finding in all of the prior studies mentioned in your review of the literature.

Another common mistake authors make is to cite lengthy passages of background material. This is done either because the writer does not know how to paraphrase or summarize or because these passages provide "proof" that the writer actually read the background material. About this, Leedy (1989) gives some good advice: "Review the literature; don't reproduce it" (p. 71).

After you have thoroughly reviewed the material available on your topic, this information must be organized in some fashion. Generally, the reviews can be organized in one of two schemes: by chronological order or by theoretical orientation. A chronological organization involves an overview of the problem—mention the classic or pioneering studies, then move on to more recent studies that are most like the research you have conducted.

The other approach, organizing by major theoretical orientation, is illustrated by the following example: In reviewing the literature on child sexual abuse, you have found a sizable number of articles written from a psychoanalytic perspective. Even though you may not subscribe to that set of theoretical explanations, you still owe it to your readers to acknowledge rival theories or explanations. This provides some of the controversy or interest that can make reading your article or report enjoyable. The rival theories, however, do not need to receive an equal amount of space or coverage.

Since new research is usually conducted on those topics about which there is not much literature, the review of the literature section helps to justify your research by pointing out gaps in the knowledge base. Unless you are replicating someone's study, you are likely to be conducting research in an area where not much is known. This gap in knowledge provides a major impetus for research.

After you have reviewed the relevant literature and noted the gaps in knowledge on a particular problem or topic, it is helpful to restate the purpose of your study. The reader may not be as familiar with the problem area as you are, and restating your hypothesis or research question will assist the reader in assimilating the potpourri of literature to which he or she has just been exposed.

The Method

The Method section of the report describes in detail how the study was done. In this section, the reader learns the procedures for and things you did when collecting the data. Typically, the following are described:

1. The research design. (Was it a single system design with multiple baselines, a survey research project, or some other design?)
2. Data collection procedures. (Did you use mailed questionnaires or personally interview the respondents? How was the informed consent obtained?)
3. The subjects. (How were they selected? What were their characteristics?)
4. The instrumentation. (What is known about the instrument's reliability and validity? How has the instrument been used?)
5. The statistical tests and measures to be used to analyze the data.

Following is a hypothetical example of a Method section.

METHOD

Subjects

The subjects were 350 first-offender shoplifters referred by the Municipal Court to the Downtown Mental Health Center during the calendar year 1990 for post-sentencing assessment. Their average age was 29 years. Seventy-five percent of the subjects were under the age of 45; 10 percent were 60 years of age or older. Eighty-six percent of the shoplifters were Caucasian. Slightly more than half (53%) were male; 57 percent were employed. Forty percent of all shoplifters were married. Divorced, separated and widowed persons made up 20 percent of the sample.

Procedure

Upon referral from the Court and contact with the Downtown Mental Health Center for a scheduled psychosocial assessment, each subject was asked to complete the Symptom Checklist 90-Revised (Derogatis, 1983). This instrument is a 90-item self-report of psychological functioning with nine symptom scales and three global indices. The reliability and validity of the SCL-90-R are excellent and well-documented. Test-retest and internal consistency coefficients have been reported to range from .77 to .90 on the nine dimensions. The SCL-90-R has been used in a broad variety of clinical and medical contexts and has received positive independent evaluations (Edwards, 1978; Dies and MacKenzie, 1983).

After completing the SCL-90-R, each subject met with one of the Mental Health Center's social workers for a psychosocial assessment. These assessments were later typed and after any personally identifying information had been removed, were presented to a panel of three mental health program directors from an adjoining county. This panel independently read the assessments and reviewed the scores from the SCL-90-Revised in order to check for appropriateness and agreement with the initial recommendations made to the Municipal Court. The panel rated each assessment using a scoring scheme where 10 indicated complete agreement with the assessment and recommendations and 0 indicated their complete lack of agreement concerning the reports made to the Court. The panel's ratings were summed to produce an overall rating. Each assessment could then receive a rating ranging between 0 and 30. Pearson Correlations were used to determine the association between the two dependent variables: overall assessment ratings and the SCL-90-R scores. A t-test was used to test for differences in the dependent variables when the first-time offenders were grouped by whether or not they received mental health counseling within the year following their arrest.

Enough information should be provided in the Method section to permit replication by any other interested researcher. In this section, operational definitions are reported along with procedures that were followed in collecting the data. Setting or location of the study can be important to mention, as well as the specifics of the data collection. For instance, Behling (1984) suggests that in field interviews, using white interviewers in a black community may lead to a distortion of the gathered information. In other words, rather than just stating that four interviewers were used, the researcher ought to specify the sex, age, and race of the interviewers.

The Results

This section of the report or article contains what you actually discovered from conducting your research. The Results section summarizes the data. It does not present the raw data; it reports aggregate or average scores. Up to this point, you have not revealed your findings. Now it is time to exhibit your findings. Your task in this section is to present the results factually, without opinion. The facts must stand by themselves.

You can organize your findings in many ways. The most common practice is to present the major findings first. If you have used several hypotheses, report your findings relative to the first hypothesis, then move to the second hypothesis, and so on.

Many researchers and would-be authors often feel overwhelmed because there appears to be too much information for a single research report. This can happen when they have lots of hypotheses or as a result of doing data analysis to the point that their shelves sag from the weight of computer printouts. Thinking that findings are all equally important contributes to a feeling of drowning in data. It might be helpful to realize that you do not have to present any more data than is needed to test your hypotheses (Mullins, 1977). Becker (1986) notes, "We know we cannot describe everything. In fact, one aim of science and scholarship is exactly to reduce what has to be described to manageable proportions" (p. 133).

I find it helpful to get a blank sheet of paper and write down what I would report if I were limited to one major point. I then ask myself, "What is the second most important finding coming from this study?" This process continues until all of the important points have been identified. Once the important findings have been noted, I begin thinking about how I will present them. Tables and charts are helpful in that they visually break up the narrative while providing precise information that makes pretty dry reading if it is incorporated into the text.

Most research reports contain tables as a way of summarizing data or reducing verbiage. You should develop at least one or two tables for your research report, particularly if you have gone beyond univariate analysis. However, having too many tables is almost as bad as not having enough. Because of space limitations and the expense required to reproduce tables, you will seldom see journal articles with more than four or five. When too many tables are employed, it is hard for a reader or reviewer to keep all of the main points in mind; the information tends to run together.

In the Results section you will also report the outcomes of the statistical tests you have conducted. For example, if your studies found that BSW social workers received higher quality assurance ratings than MSW social workers, it will be important to determine if the difference in ratings is statistically significant. Do not allow your readers to conclude that a difference of three points, for example, makes BSW social workers superior to MSW social workers if a t-test or other appropriate statistical test reveals no statistically significant difference in their scores. Report the average scores, the results of statistical tests, and the associated probability. (Refer to chapter 9 if you need to see examples of tables or ways to express statistical information.) Further elaboration and explanation of the data are usually presented in the Discussion section.

The Discussion

The Discussion section often begins with a brief summary of your findings. It is not necessary to go into a lot of detail—this information was just exhibited in the Results. Just address the major findings or the highlights of your study. Once that is done, you can begin to expound on the findings. Perhaps you were surprised to find that the BSWs in your study performed better than the MSW employees; here is the place to elaborate the reasons for your surprise. You can reveal any unexpected findings—as well as what didn't go as planned.

Most importantly, the Discussion section should interpret the findings for the reader and address the relevance of these findings for practice. What do the findings mean or suggest to you? Are you recommending that social service agencies hire BSWs rather than persons with other undergraduate degrees? Does additional training seem to be indicated for the type of employee covered in your study? Do social work educators need to re-examine and possibly revise the curricula at their institutions? What implications does your study have for practice or policy? Discuss findings that have practical significance—even if there was no statistical significance. As Reid (1988) has indicated, our findings do not always "prove," "establish," or make a point so strongly that there can be no other interpretation. Usually, Discussion sections contain what he calls "appropriately qualified language"—phrases that indicate that the findings "provide evidence for," "suggest the possibility that," or "raise questions about."

The part of the Discussion section that many researchers do not like to write is the description of what did not go according to the research design. Sometimes secretaries forget to administer questionnaires. Clients drop out of studies or forget to bring needed documentation. Questionnaires may not be mailed on time. These glitches are normal in applied social science research. Social workers don't have the same degree of control that laboratory scientists have. So, admit any major departures from planned research procedures. The problems you encountered in collecting your data may well explain why you got the results that you did. For instance, someone forgetting to mail reminder postcards could have caused you to have a lower response rate for one group than for another. A change in agency policies during the middle of your study could have changed staff morale or increased the proportion of employees who felt "burned out"—which in turn could have affected the quality of their work. Also, recognize biases that may have crept into your study or that you discovered too late to do anything about.

Your study may have significant limitations. While you had hoped for a representative sampling of social workers from all educational backgrounds, and you heard from 75 percent of all the BSWs, perhaps only 8 percent of the MSWs responded. Eight percent certainly would not represent the majority of the MSW sample. Your subjects may not be representative because the sample was not random, or the study may not be generalizable because other agencies do not organize their services in the same way. You cannot survey adults in one locality (e.g., Moorhead, Minnesota) and generalize those findings to adults in another completely different location (e.g., the Everglades) unless you sample from both locations. In this section you can discuss the extent to which it is possible to generalize your research.

Many authors conclude their research reports and journal articles by indicating areas for future research. As a result of their experiences, they may have suggestions for other researchers about procedures, instruments, the operationalization of variables, sampling techniques, and so on. This is done for altruistic reasons—a researcher is not planning on further work in that area and wishes others to benefit from what has been learned in the process of conducting the present research.

References, Appendices, and Abstracts

Whenever other written documents have been cited in your research reporting, they need to be listed in the **Reference** section at the end of the report or manuscript. References are usually listed alphabetically by authors' names, and there are various styles or ways in which the titles can appear. The reference style that you use is likely to be more important to academic committees and journals than it will be to funding sources. Some journals have their own style. When preparing your Reference section, look for examples or ask a person in authority which style you should use. (This is discussed a little more in the next section.)

The **Appendix** is where you place a copy of instruments, written instructions given to subjects, or important materials that may have been used during the course of your study. Research reports (especially those prepared for academic committees) are not complete without a copy of your instrument. However, most journals do not require or expect you to submit a manuscript with an appendix. Journals seldom have the space to publish instruments used in research reports.

Abstracts are brief summaries of reports or manuscripts. Generally, they average 100 to 150 words, (although some journals may want a 25 to 50 word abstract). Abstracts are prepared to help readers decide whether they want to read a journal article, to help those who are attending national or regional conferences decide which presentations they will go to, and to help those who are categorizing research know which subject headings to use. Abstracts are almost always difficult to write because of the need to compress a voluminous report into one paragraph or less. When you write an abstract, limit yourself to two or three sentences to introduce the study and two or three sentences to present your major finding. If you get stumped, look at several abstracts in a recent issue of *Social Work Research and Abstracts* for ideas on how to be succinct.

Writing for Professional Journals

You must remember a few additional things if you decide to prepare your research report for submission to a professional journal. First of all, journals vary considerably in the way they want manuscripts structured. Some journals use a combined Results and Discussion section. Some want a separate Conclusion and others don't. When you prepare a manuscript, have a specific journal in mind. Become familiar with that journal. Are its articles written for the practitioner or for the scholar? Journals have different audiences. Journals that want articles for the practitioner may expect case examples, vignettes, or suggestions for working with a particular type of client. Other journals expect sophisticated analytical procedures. Some journals want a very detailed literature review, while others don't. You will have more success placing articles in a journal when you become well acquainted with it (e.g., know the style, format, and type of article that the journal tends to publish).

Journals are relatively specialized. Practically all journals carry a statement informing readers and prospective authors of the type of content with which they are concerned. By reading such statements, prospective authors determine if their manuscripts would be appropriate for the journals. For instance, this statement is found in the *Journal of Independent Social Work:*

> This journal is for the full or part-time self-employed social worker. It addresses the needs and interests of professional social workers who provide clinical and proprietary services outside of traditional social agency auspices. Contributors to the *Journal* include social workers and members of other disciplines who are concerned about private and proprietary practice and innovative means of social service delivery.

When writing for a journal, keep in mind that the entire manuscript (including references) should not exceed sixteen or seventeen double-spaced pages. Since it is not unusual for research reports and theses to contain a hundred or more pages, probably the biggest chore before you will be trying to find a way to condense the literature review to two or three typed pages.

Journals want original manuscripts that are clearly written, of timely interest, appropriate to the journal, of the right length, and in the correct style. Journal reviewers look for an adequate literature review, reasonable research design, and the correct use of statistical techniques. But beyond those considerations, reviewers must decide whether or not your manuscript makes a "contribution" to the knowledge base. Reviewers may decide that your manuscript makes no contribution because of severe limitations in its generalizability, or because a more thorough literature review would have revealed the existence of studies similar to the one being reported. A manuscript might even be judged "interesting" but not relevant to social work practice.

You will probably increase your chances of publication if you find a journal that, in the last six years or so, has published similar (or somewhat related) articles to the one you are preparing. While this is no guarantee that the journal will publish your article, at least it indicates that the reviewers have had an interest in your topic. Study the articles that have recently appeared in the journal. Observe the reference style, the use of tables, the length of the literature review, and the general level at which the article is written.

When you have narrowed down your choice of journals to one or two, obtain their "Information for Authors." You can write, for instance, to the publications office of the National Association of Social Work (NASW), and they will send you a brochure covering the NASW journals (*Social Work, Social Work Research & Abstracts, Health and Social Work, and Social Work in Education*). Other journals print instructions for authors once or twice a year within an issue of their journal.

In recent years there has been a movement toward the use of the reference style of the American Psychological Association (APA). This reference style is a good one to learn even if you don't use it to write journal manuscripts. The APA style is widely accepted and convenient to use. A professional appearance, the correct reference style, a catchy title, and a thought-provoking introduction will undoubtedly improve the odds of your manuscript getting a favorable response from reviewers.

After you revise and polish your manuscript to the point where you think it is finished, set it aside. After several days, reread it. Make necessary revisions, and prepare a clean copy. Share that with two or three persons whose opinions you respect. Find someone who can give you constructive criticism without battering your ego. If you know that you are weak in the grammar department, seek a reviewer who knows that area.

One thing that you should *not* do is send your manuscript to more than one journal at a time. Most journals will not review your manuscript if it is being reviewed by another journal. If your manuscript is rejected by the first journal you choose, do not be discouraged. A rejection does not necessarily mean that your manuscript is poorly conceptualized or written. It could be that the journal just accepted a similar article on the same topic last week. Or, it may mean that the journal is planning special issues, and your manuscript does not fit their needs. You may have submitted your article to an inappropriate journal. Sometimes, reviewers may not completely understand your approach. Reviews are conducted "blind"—that is, you will not know who read your manuscript and will have no way of knowing whether the reviewer knew as much about your topic or your methodology as you do. So, even good articles can be rejected. If your first effort is rejected, dust off your pride and try to objectively read your manuscript again. Revise it if necessary, and submit it to the second journal of your choice.

Journal reviewers usually make one of four decisions: they accept, accept on condition, reject, or reject but encourage resubmission. Most journals send the reviewers' comments when revisions are needed and when a manuscript has been rejected. I have run into only one journal that did not send back the reviewers' comments when a manuscript was rejected. Generally, but not always, when the requested revisions have been made, your article will be accepted.

Even if your manuscript is rejected twice, it still may have a chance at publication. You may want to get Mendelsohn's (1987) *Author's Guide to Social Work Journals* for suggestions of additional journals that might be interested in your manuscript. This guide also gives the acceptance rate of over sixty journals. Some journals accept proportionately a much larger percentage of manuscripts than others.

If your manuscript has been rejected three times, should you continue trying to get it published? This is the point at which I become frustrated and tired of working with one manuscript and I quit. However, if you feel that yours is basically a good manuscript, and some of the reviewers have encouraged revision, then you should try it again.

Getting a manuscript published is like most other things in life that require practice. The more you practice, the better you will become at this activity. Carlton (1988) says that it is like learning to ride a bicycle. The way to learn is by getting back up and trying again! Along the way, there are some very helpful resources available to you in learning how to write more professionally. I recommend Strunk and White's (1979) *The Elements of Style,* Mullins' (1977) *A Guide to Writing and Publishing in the Social and Behavioral Sciences,* and Becker's (1986) *Writing for Social Scientists: How to Start and Finish Your Thesis, Book, or Article.* And, of course, there are many other books that librarians can recommend to assist you with your writing.

Reading and Critiquing Research Manuscripts

Students have a tendency to believe that any research that manages to appear in print is "good" research. I wish that this were so. Unfortunately, some pretty shoddy research can be found in journals without too much difficulty. As I stated in the beginning of this book, one reason you are required to enroll in a research methods course is to help you recognize poor or inadequate research. Flawed research (if unrecognized) could lead you to conclusions that are not warranted and could be dangerous to your clients.

Using the major content areas of research reports, we can construct a set of criteria to use in evaluating research reports, journal articles, or manuscripts. (These criteria can also be used to double-check your manuscripts.) I'm indebted to Garfield (1984) for his observations and guidelines on this topic.

CRITERIA FOR EVALUATING RESEARCH REPORTS

1. Does the Introduction provide a clear notion of (a) the problem, (b) the purpose of the research, and (c) its significance?
2. Are the stated hypotheses reasonable? Do they appear to logically follow from the review of the literature?
3. Is the literature review (a) relevant to the study, (b) thorough, and (c) current?
4. Is a research design stated? Do the subjects appear to have been selected without overt bias? If there is a control group, does it seem to be an appropriate group for comparison? Is the number of subjects sufficient?
5. Is there a discussion of the reliability and validity of the instruments that are used?
6. Is there enough information on (a) the procedures, and (b) the in-

struments and the operational definitions of the variables to allow you to replicate this study?

7. Are statistical tests present when needed? If statistical tests are used, are they the appropriate tests?
8. Are the findings discussed in terms of their implications and practical significance? Are the conclusions supported by and do they logically follow from the data that have been presented? Is the author guilty of overgeneralizing? Has actual or potential bias been recognized?

When evaluating a research report, you should find yourself answering "yes" to most of the criteria questions. Strong research articles will elicit a greater number of affirmative responses. Weak articles will receive a larger number of negative responses. You can use these criteria not only to evaluate the research reports prepared by others, but also to check your own report or manuscript to insure that you have included all of the crucial elements.

This chapter has attempted to provide you with instruction in the key components in research report writing. Three points cannot be emphasized enough: (1) the importance of studying examples of other research reports and literature; (2) the importance of social workers publishing their research results, and (3) the need to have perseverance when first efforts are rejected by journal reviewers.

When you publish your research, you contribute to the knowledge base of social work and allow others to build upon your research. Knowledge is an incremental process; it moves forward in small steps rather than large leaps. Any movement toward the goal of advancing social work knowledge starts with understanding the research process. Knowledge tends to become obsolete with the passage of time, so it is necessary that social workers not only read research as a way of keeping up with new developments in the field but also engage in research and seek professional outlets for the dissemination of research efforts. Otherwise, as Williams and Hopps (1987) have noted, "the profession does not advance, clients cannot thrive, and practice does not improve" (p. 376).

QUESTIONS FOR CLASS DISCUSSION

1. Discuss the ways in which a research report is similar to and different from the customary term paper.
2. Discuss what it is about a "good" journal article that makes it interesting or fun to read and what it is about some journal articles that make them dull and uninteresting.

3. How is writing for professional audiences different from writing to relatives or friends?
4. Think about the various sections of the research report. Tell the class what you think would be the most difficult section to write and your reasons for this.

MINI-PROJECTS FOR EXPERIENCING RESEARCH FIRSTHAND

1. Select a term paper you have recently written. Prepare it as you would if you were going to submit it to a social work journal. If you do not have real data, use fictitious data for the Results section and for the purpose of preparing a table or two. If you are feeling especially brave, exchange this effort with a classmate for friendly criticism concerning your writing style and understanding of this chapter.
2. Go to the library and locate several dissertations on topics of interest to you. Select one and summarize the important points made under each of the major sections of the dissertation. Briefly discuss what you learned from this project.
3. Interview one or more faculty members about their experiences with professional writing. What have been their joys and frustrations? What advice do they have for you?
4. Find an evaluation report or some research reported in a journal article. Using the criteria suggested in this chapter, evaluate the research. What did you learn in the process?

RESOURCES AND REFERENCES

American Psychological Association. (1983). *Publication Manual of the American Psychological Association.* 3rd ed. Washington, DC.

Bausell, R. B. (1986). *A Practical Guide to Conducting Empirical Research.* New York: Harper & Row.

Beaver, M., Gottlieb, N., and Rosenblatt, A. (1983). Dilemmas in manuscript evaluations. *Social Work,* 28 (4), 326.

Becker, H. S. (1986). *Writing for Social Scientists: How to Start and Finish Your Thesis, Book, or Article.* Chicago, IL: University of Chicago Press.

Behling, J. H. (1984). *Guidelines for Preparing the Research Proposal.* New York: University Press of America.

Carlton, T. O. (1987). Who are our authors? *Health and Social Work,* 12 (Spring), 82–84.

Carlton, T. O. (1988). Publishing as a professional activity. *Health and Social Work,* 13 (Spring), 85–89.

Garfield, S. L. (1984). The evaluation of research: An editorial perspective. In

A. S. Bellack and M. Hersen (eds.), *Research Methods in Clinical Psychology*. New York: Pergamon Press.

Johnson, H. C. (1988). Drugs, dialogue, or diet: Diagnosing and treating the hyperactive child. *Social Work*, 33(4), 349–355.

Kidder, L. H. and Judd, C. M. (1986). *Research Methods in Social Relations*. New York: Holt, Rinehart and Winston.

Leedy, P. D. (1989). *Practical Research: Planning and Design*. New York: Macmillan.

McLaughlin, S. D., Pearce, S. E., Manninen, D. L., and Winges, L. D. (1988). To parent or relinquish: Consequences for adolescent mothers. *Social Work*, 33 (4), 320–324.

Mendelsohn, H. (1987). *An Author's Guide to Social Work Journals*. Silver Spring, MD: National Association of Social Workers.

Meyer, C. H. (1983). Responsibility in publishing. *Social Work*, 28 (1), 3.

Mullins, C. J. (1977). *A Guide to Writing and Publishing in the Social and Behavioral Sciences*. New York: Wiley.

Reid, W. J. (1988). Writing research reports. In R. M. Grinnell (Ed.), *Social Work Research and Evaluation*. Itasca, IL: Peacock.

Ross-Larson, B. (1982). *Edit Yourself: A Manual for Everyone Who Works with Words*. New York: Norton.

Strunk, W. and White, E. B. (1979). *The Elements of Style*. New York: Macmillan.

Walter, C. A. and Greif, G. L. (1988). To do or not to do: Social work education for private practice. *Journal of Independent Social Work*, 2(3), 17–24.

Williams, L. F. and Hopps, J. G. (1988). On the nature of professional communications: Publication for practitioners. *Social Work*, 33 (5), 453–459.

Williams, L. F. and Hopps, J. G. (1987). Publication as a practice goal: Enhancing opportunities for social workers. *Social Work*, 32 (5), 373–376.

Appendices

Appendix A

Attitudes about Research Courses

1. Check the following courses that you successfully completed in *high school*:

   Algebra I _____   Geometry _____

   Algebra II _____   Calculus _____

2. What is your age? _____

3. What is your gender? Male _____ Female _____

4. Consider for a moment the extent (if any) of your fear of research courses. Indicate your fear on the scale below:

No fear				Some fear				Lots of fear	
1	2	3	4	5	6	7	8	9	10

5. On the following scale, rate your perception of how useful you think research courses will be to you.

Not very useful				Some use				Very useful	
1	2	3	4	5	6	7	8	9	10

6. On the following scale, rate your interest in taking research courses.

No interest				Some interest				Lots of interest	
1	2	3	4	5	6	7	8	9	10

In order to better understand your feelings about research, indicate whether the following statements are true or false.

7. T or F   I dread speaking before a large group of people more than taking a research course.

8. T or F   I would rather take a research course than ask a waitress to return an improperly cooked meal to the chef.

9. T or F My fear of snakes is greater than my fear of taking a research course.

10. T or F My fear of spiders is less than my fear of taking a research course.

11. T or F I would rather take a research course than ask a total stranger to do a favor for me.

12. T or F My fear of research is such that I would rather the university require an additional two courses of my choosing than take one research course.

13. T or F I dread going to the dentist more than taking a research course.

14. T or F I fear a statistics course more than a research methodology course.

15. T or F I have always "hated math."

The following symbols frequently appear in research studies that utilize statistical analyses. To the best of your ability, identify the statistical symbols. If unknown, write "unknown." (Example: the symbol + means addition)

16. F

17. df

18. t

19. r

20. X^2

21. $p < .05$

22. $\bar{X}$, M

23. SD, S

Appendix B

How to Use a Table
of Random Numbers

Assume that you have 500 clients and you need to select a random sample of 25 from that population. You have already made a list of these persons and accurately counted or numbered them from 1 to 500. In order to draw a random sample, you will need to get a random starting place on the Table of Random Numbers. Before you do this, you need to think about a way to encompass every numerical possibility that will occur within your population. If you choose a single digit number—for example, 9—as the starting place, any number larger than one digit (the numbers 10 through 99, and 100 through 500) would be excluded. There is no possibility of their being chosen. If you choose a two-digit number, you would still exclude the three digit numbers. Therefore, you have to look at the numbers in the Random Number Table in groups of three—numbers such as 009, 147, 935, and so on. This will allow the lowest possible number (001) and the highest possible number (500) in your population to have an equal chance of being chosen (as well as all the numbers in between).

Now you are ready to draw a sample from the Random Number Table. Since the values on the table are arranged in no particular order, it makes no difference where or how you start. You could, for instance, roll a pair of dice. The number of dots on one could direct you to a particular column and the value on the other would direct you to a particular row of random numbers. You can start from the top or bottom of the table and from the left or right side. You could also shuffle a deck of cards and select two cards—again letting the value of the first indicate a specific column and the value of the second, a particular row.

A third way to find a random starting place would be to shut your eyes and, holding a pencil or pen, let your hand come down somewhere on the page. Start from that point and take the next twenty-five three-digit numbers. Of course, if you select a number like 947 or 515, you will have to discard them as they fall outside of the range (1–500).

As you look at the Table of Random Numbers, you will notice that they are grouped in sets of six. It makes no difference if you ignore the first three digits and use the last three of each set or vice versa. When you have selected twenty-five three-digit numbers falling between 1 and 500, you have your random sample! For your convenience, six-digit random numbers have been provided, as well as two-digit numbers. All of the random numbers appearing in these tables were created using StatPac (Walonick Associates, Minneapolis, MN) a computer software program for IBM personal computers.

Table of Random Numbers

360062	190148	438921	828610	137813	597216	745136	848373	980702	292403
934762	289048	055252	239359	049231	215708	828323	995602	968653	358123
316630	308216	845177	333584	306213	537904	849376	571680	527394	587341
827749	459314	277743	328793	589905	452433	234203	534213	474746	301166
103359	918057	943330	745098	125601	036980	264454	594793	641501	882535
375215	397377	256691	478121	756814	210058	534319	441724	852186	016678
711032	882621	934206	136008	254288	288709	678536	919749	453691	818526
804845	256068	781681	476628	926897	721293	885133	841857	170057	958707
597462	768354	455724	262587	204958	059064	129034	774120	391834	283950
383424	363439	565399	148896	123675	712072	996343	282454	249228	733297
845446	785274	471471	718267	294703	952780	751216	614147	457324	357589
171037	236626	116308	872015	117031	393199	195654	417915	018433	885064
663704	963322	005562	992787	948421	510794	503441	139789	965668	766346
523120	499512	649587	503120	800718	621563	607424	665129	444721	989526
943685	339626	172547	475197	315309	814281	493565	095760	286835	187233
558632	445148	561021	599971	695121	839266	279515	263519	094626	630463
688812	481716	366194	887525	382441	049265	372731	024735	983979	595913
432063	938512	127163	196425	190817	044621	282333	700128	923578	279450
616425	385590	995664	296416	700414	148695	772517	274528	450435	312249
177081	382698	762128	096542	471251	085339	773561	531650	371110	232144
530653	007347	034621	130744	819405	044061	723251	190820	948230	420664
859438	714944	839905	399521	403420	389841	865691	925150	534086	261256
478363	028813	179916	334684	484782	273687	169375	159339	855149	501638
179879	858717	458259	662477	496169	146879	054723	012672	049258	883983
197394	745101	457920	776831	870531	729547	653602	451897	126884	288820
864168	863472	759723	713886	954710	314435	427718	136254	608664	820371
289783	139474	443702	674947	482657	948359	675381	826215	567342	320576
453771	612352	964705	584665	576308	021767	131857	121105	116437	586709
771929	432675	678846	540545	261755	722765	349004	558358	061999	470437
438957	456465	462582	436340	439747	995892	780771	086956	331691	334670
423067	313598	952164	288314	368104	215367	758617	797918	015908	268229
635581	071294	187198	997320	028534	678312	990718	802314	896228	742233
469967	251190	422673	372251	056526	859375	364695	542428	278938	354415
229743	588774	943979	332417	965270	655637	884089	696910	950841	324693

191392 506200 244620 456768 704170 114582 215714 082047 211036 557119
694263 645228 571122 404316 476840 552599 105398 446706 612208 069318
351932 442182 850948 841429 173236 187547 552477 131697 916519 029457
558148 431434 478713 007287 886565 575708 286567 724930 298812 943466
038521 199608 271446 416385 236335 462221 229815 538351 988086 718374
864765 228339 185429 574355 140673 021209 909292 244733 669420 291568
974542 569344 959914 700605 782962 169014 973246 671660 192281 661616
264162 109862 867096 687032 598209 665463 066929 722172 590366 238613
445488 309098 421077 946418 127374 286528 764465 273529 294707 920736
467002 286904 132511 993433 649861 827461 222143 556678 432181 456489
986860 978646 111117 024382 603227 377658 573793 128952 716583 775441
169511 226369 780706 930881 685925 294012 262731 544159 377025 570185
308173 625996 969762 979549 664350 012532 512684 588049 318207 564618
878811 783706 910275 112341 218124 652945 171602 527991 229607 815838
278763 297234 048362 308910 187519 185283 364950 433522 704987 059778
530363 171119 888942 167106 088337 519772 911971 607160 913710 779405
866869 688575 126713 737843 574003 216753 721812 813626 255670 771795
891861 442215 376581 850219 389477 925962 585869 161312 936721 760627
322786 491593 429552 836224 607442 327051 112775 664766 725967 795476
076249 431363 462194 445651 805690 228695 133676 011440 587539 484783
874146 718672 417301 913406 186209 028230 580430 488330 156319 472929
104513 534446 071772 923958 277696 438183 363891 736907 792323 033881
272359 342335 479491 752199 439043 135940 177676 489942 823149 389964
837251 449346 990749 232106 849040 246120 915151 046574 086474 951102
300239 526082 275425 864644 255618 586659 586779 634811 760206 651101
326919 522280 135116 633716 242288 394810 469045 913214 872541 623147
286540 344675 688627 747112 218430 889465 713441 164061 743321 129213
562576 417784 123878 615964 731064 206033 649060 029306 462497 898382
147167 122636 428552 479679 677090 334296 418436 971886 821828 209413
315649 417693 433447 275273 904126 206837 305433 749136 239819 340865
648650 778748 858718 907534 373539 203721 640184 172232 611261 695838
834730 325729 777355 126053 304084 159225 329256 882337 370627 413617
987275 175087 613310 441852 625687 662889 133838 518255 276538 821307
251799 323724 543163 013816 700677 155137 326035 491384 273298 032312
753162 993738 040435 680578 852692 539350 267744 294590 782261 034416
784092 496125 541474 182310 976291 621721 230184 471211 841234 930067
841844 938184 109491 957664 477333 847088 913504 515006 077653 126463
545078 063366 627602 995358 264044 544670 882557 476983 389775 456239
164724 120527 179080 309514 047799 061393 645651 769262 163020 459569
761433 081901 050561 360229 561105 175595 713613 669764 123888 087305
902684 551644 837068 171911 627997 674947 239108 661286 731266 497194
261632 555061 730594 275155 828748 240707 615985 267413 621999 374517
958988 356182 869666 864566 413596 101896 333437 354502 938975 863428
748569 455584 418153 160238 095463 330085 258035 676887 492603 251398
995430 641294 427426 455163 943985 384488 136526 964447 746515 708724
956215 830348 525163 609376 455178 737630 152265 501178 703582 295828
511139 546370 855892 789137 746091 842430 607468 087634 739539 400568
189068 404796 138075 639059 919469 252411 707994 210365 141856 495632
589571 313497 071962 517638 720857 612681 382192 322761 077542 828422
984835 822396 659712 589836 271442 033396 303404 613157 532634 037025
845293 981683 615881 219591 527250 452723 708748 830794 564915 434747

124531	129637	652386	578694	131967	450529	117483	486800	816065	227018
384639	949459	093621	295163	276654	473410	491026	594617	795927	569888
243543	695889	922952	881611	877041	352198	915765	396644	081382	975151
622302	483201	644443	967914	390779	151218	644301	899950	062328	025854
857471	031119	165942	167312	924395	321514	366357	392558	956718	249373
178286	684356	809681	131210	176870	448290	609916	973228	379069	791758
443008	158904	779758	189283	350316	979783	587586	374269	589338	968024
598940	868212	983014	378833	826406	891028	734779	456553	288100	592301
370939	841968	182186	454701	230046	045351	844519	428438	950725	112235
398881	185248	365169	472322	751988	275591	454914	904038	886313	776566
156138	853547	912549	723498	325563	964226	493813	063187	617240	290437
408062	150806	152468	739663	981826	202206	698117	590745	814507	112806
721228	112073	056712	264597	451561	147033	100817	535994	326176	614676
721190	399214	293671	353228	931598	325218	335996	935316	867382	373235
154787	240715	535107	689927	762804	321127	775267	792724	467721	155978
532643	369843	798877	608447	172582	429622	143483	417422	287601	057343
154144	691289	519238	863037	622625	197219	371853	899947	595789	309547
746845	478417	342906	350916	514353	088278	507124	685727	594705	656146
001035	537965	927346	685597	076802	730995	592412	870556	090309	634497
377141	615820	622926	964942	143322	550171	325874	362046	561667	626383
135918	415509	545895	146601	144155	929658	071321	203839	814732	952532
670012	611934	878476	206920	071128	566623	775407	723438	125868	362163
735642	074829	697719	112493	206493	228157	680488	816144	307254	101267
694556	165996	438329	225530	689537	928896	492600	869972	615567	786554
484205	333404	735725	462430	474932	391296	794264	192903	849922	147401
862537	675645	905221	283924	694956	264651	187131	111245	153893	168577
610323	954314	499918	203838	622421	964812	658753	258581	440881	827922
824517	677577	142000	853789	327631	005242	575257	611859	586983	997421
425936	475266	965271	630342	811155	290622	282301	529180	961431	071887
249194	821913	226211	214979	142871	323025	866573	239377	196238	124983
624517	718822	914510	807246	287277	222788	972259	101272	368951	145111
588724	622573	651468	149139	210402	561132	473894	713883	034079	333652
444542	120017	512157	242871	815654	472193	531818	303038	159597	463842

24	05	35	72	53	97	56	04	97	75	15	12	35	23	94	96	95	70	37	44
65	94	98	51	65	60	65	87	05	91	71	54	45	83	31	42	41	93	89	98
83	38	35	06	01	82	53	67	24	04	43	39	20	47	70	46	28	65	09	56
98	38	94	52	86	06	90	94	11	88	31	37	29	51	15	54	71	70	10	66
97	21	59	36	07	87	22	45	01	22	90	50	20	11	74	44	71	55	31	40
63	27	69	38	17	77	35	69	83	43	67	07	50	17	65	45	75	88	27	20
84	45	52	45	65	70	82	89	91	24	94	47	59	75	14	78	87	24	27	09
52	23	62	72	26	36	55	79	77	76	85	28	52	04	51	82	32	40	52	64
32	96	64	53	63	97	30	99	35	21	78	89	22	35	90	08	93	32	72	44
50	78	88	85	42	88	20	86	38	63	76	09	37	83	74	74	24	37	09	51
06	19	39	97	91	28	94	16	65	94	62	25	61	63	86	87	38	13	53	80
12	03	03	27	74	80	60	68	06	51	94	73	80	15	76	04	09	07	43	00
82	24	80	04	12	00	91	52	55	96	50	25	18	54	03	47	40	84	32	98
30	94	19	05	63	21	06	51	42	51	80	24	19	92	90	59	87	75	25	69
83	37	12	32	42	20	55	14	01	38	74	51	13	37	89	32	63	88	28	46
85	66	88	13	37	09	77	11	40	09	15	03	85	35	04	75	79	86	51	62
92	00	87	93	88	04	36	59	69	14	51	75	83	78	39	12	10	22	82	41
60	51	55	79	56	39	49	59	96	62	75	76	84	09	93	15	48	90	14	13

48	32	19	35	57	26	79	52	53	26	18	00	58	38	18	64	68	14	38	24
94	67	67	56	46	12	99	94	97	08	77	25	34	85	91	49	54	80	78	92
45	76	36	57	05	45	64	95	21	54	34	97	64	43	44	19	23	95	54	33
65	31	88	44	29	07	58	43	93	20	74	61	73	97	23	43	96	73	18	55
88	87	40	47	88	35	29	50	32	16	13	81	68	64	83	53	10	57	31	51
67	71	02	31	99	68	34	88	92	86	18	38	91	11	80	97	39	88	13	14
68	93	02	45	95	71	99	11	54	26	27	33	18	09	66	80	45	55	42	81
58	49	16	33	18	97	53	97	11	55	74	94	65	66	39	74	82	65	42	09
15	72	97	85	77	39	64	67	87	66	28	92	82	07	34	38	57	81	48	64
44	94	80	90	78	45	83	34	45	18	60	71	73	51	27	76	85	51	29	94
32	83	21	38	47	87	23	97	38	89	83	72	44	66	18	67	72	46	97	38
07	69	16	09	94	51	35	18	69	27	96	15	54	47	81	69	73	12	37	64
54	40	07	75	21	35	68	94	75	85	46	90	68	97	87	91	03	16	00	53
86	95	66	28	20	22	16	18	98	93	83	43	25	58	10	80	99	90	94	15
35	64	89	69	82	87	46	12	25	59	29	48	46	88	01	67	64	13	31	13
94	80	15	98	90	06	66	91	95	64	17	81	69	47	80	93	67	71	38	11
66	08	77	92	77	01	06	18	28	63	98	78	18	84	14	73	11	53	93	40
28	73	84	96	78	21	86	12	99	57	90	51	51	74	19	25	30	54	83	34
46	15	42	79	55	04	53	08	36	64	62	04	09	37	99	23	56	76	79	99
79	56	67	84	28	57	81	39	71	08	38	23	26	59	41	74	68	15	57	58
95	24	40	38	32	39	25	63	96	49	04	20	29	04	93	98	83	47	90	30
25	53	02	01	38	07	87	04	86	93	38	78	85	31	22	42	37	56	44	86
82	95	94	98	92	95	41	35	45	12	51	41	72	99	90	20	22	63	85	37
22	91	86	32	55	63	36	67	77	72	91	00	56	07	51	45	62	39	75	43
63	23	41	94	82	83	83	78	40	71	15	09	70	63	88	23	00	18	03	52
01	86	03	55	74	15	86	21	88	03	36	81	39	09	83	95	83	57	50	57
64	85	26	07	27	50	94	09	43	31	06	77	38	59	17	33	60	24	87	71
20	37	72	07	32	82	94	44	77	74	38	96	35	71	27	09	49	94	86	36
71	32	19	72	38	69	35	49	56	45	59	96	66	87	53	79	69	43	46	96
47	92	32	73	45	59	45	94	43	05	66	98	53	25	35	35	21	62	92	95
36	98	50	11	94	50	52	41	11	64	26	48	68	90	26	54	84	24	81	36
50	61	17	98	18	35	64	71	31	53	03	41	30	96	55	51	28	04	07	48
49	38	52	47	68	02	89	66	49	88	25	65	66	34	83	89	73	84	30	04
63	10	89	95	52	26	86	28	76	07	66	70	19	51	88	11	99	20	56	41
94	52	53	53	73	91	76	55	54	77	54	83	08	70	32	01	22	96	99	38
63	64	04	59	43	30	66	98	46	97	51	61	73	34	16	45	24	20	76	86
89	21	74	95	68	47	07	01	17	52	81	37	19	24	24	26	38	89	87	79
45	60	17	16	09	78	76	45	89	01	98	55	28	52	09	95	62	43	89	47
45	49	53	33	11	95	34	17	96	60	67	99	13	42	21	04	27	63	54	90

Appendix C

Drug Attitude Questionnaire

Part I. Please read each of the following items carefully and rate your agreement or disagreement by checking the appropriate blank to the right of the question.

	Strongly Agree	Agree	Undecided	Disagree	Strongly Disagree
1. Using marijuana or beer often leads to becoming addicted to more harmful drugs	___	___	___	___	___
2. Drugs are basically an "unnatural" way to enjoy life	___	___	___	___	___
3. I see nothing wrong with getting drunk occasionally	___	___	___	___	___
4. Too many of society's problems are blamed on kids who use alcohol or drugs regularly	___	___	___	___	___
5. Even if my best friend gave me some drugs, I probably wouldn't use them	___	___	___	___	___
6. If I become a parent, I don't intend to hassle my kids about their use of drugs or alcohol	___	___	___	___	___
7. Certain drugs like marijuana are all right to use because you can't become addicted	___	___	___	___	___
8. It is not difficult for me to turn down an opportunity to get high	___	___	___	___	___
9. Marijuana should not be legalized	___	___	___	___	___
10. It is not O.K. with me if my friends get high or drunk	___	___	___	___	___

	Strongly Agree	Agree	Undecided	Disagree	Strongly Disagree
11. I would rather occasionally use drugs or alcohol with my friends than to lose this set of friends	____	____	____	____	____
12. Someone who regularly uses drugs or alcohol may be considered a sick person	____	____	____	____	____
13. Most of my friends have experimented with drugs	____	____	____	____	____
14. Personally, use of alcohol is more acceptable than use of drugs	____	____	____	____	____
15. Any addict with willpower should be able to give up drugs on his/her own	____	____	____	____	____
16. Either drug addiction or alcoholism leads to family problems	____	____	____	____	____
17. Most Americans do not heavily rely on drugs	____	____	____	____	____
18. Some experience with drugs or alcohol is important for a teenager in today's society	____	____	____	____	____
19. Kids who use drugs are less popular than kids who do not	____	____	____	____	____
20. Drugs or alcohol provide a good way to "get away from it all"	____	____	____	____	____
21. I think the legal drinking age should be lowered	____	____	____	____	____
22. Teachers should place more emphasis on teaching American ideals and values	____	____	____	____	____
23. It is all right to get around the law if you don't actually break it	____	____	____	____	____

Index